Evolving E-markets:
building high value B2B exchanges with staying power

Evolving E-markets:
building high value B2B exchanges with staying power

This Guide has been compiled from the contributions of the authors indicated in each chapter, and the views expressed by such authors do not necessarily reflect the views of their respective firms.

This book is intended as a general Guide only. Its application to specific situations will depend upon the particular circumstances involved, and it should not be relied upon as a substitute for obtaining appropriate professional advice.

While all care has been taken in the preparation of this book, neither the publisher, the sponsor nor any of the authors accept responsibility for any errors it may contain or for any losses howsoever arising from or in reliance upon its contents.

© 2000 in respect of each chapter resides with the author of that chapter.

ALL RIGHTS RESERVED. No part of this publication may be reproduced, stored in a retrieval system, or transmitted by any means, electronic, mechanical, photocopying, recording, or otherwise, without the prior written permission of the publisher and the copyright holder, application for which should be addressed to the publisher.

About the Publisher

This Guide is published by ISI Publications Limited.
All enquiries should be directed to ISI Publications at the following addresses:

9/F, Carfield Commercial Building
75–77 Wyndham Street
Central, Hong Kong

Tel: (852) 2877 3417
Fax: (852) 2877 0942/0914

The Zurich Centre
90 Pitts Bay Road
PO HM 1788 HM HX,
Pembroke, HM 08, Bermuda

Tel: (1 441) 292 5666
Fax: (1 441) 292 5665

25 Mount Ephraim Road
Royal Tunbridge Wells
Kent, TN1 1EN, UK

Tel: (44) 1892 548881
Fax: (44) 1892 515892

Managing Editor: W. William A. Woods
Publisher: Sarah Barham
Editorial team: Ian Hallsworth and Carol Bonnett

E-mail: info@isipublications.com
Website: www.isipublications.com

ISBN: 962-7762-62-8

Table of Contents

Foreword 1
Mary Coleman, CEO, RightWorks Corporation

Chapter 1 — Key Considerations When Setting Up B2B Exchanges 3
Arthur B. Sculley and W. William A. Woods

What is a B2B Exchange? 4
Why B2B Exchanges are the Killer Application 5
    1.   *Global reach* 5
    2.   *Dynamic pricing* 5
    3.   *More efficient distribution channels — 'B2O'* 7
    4.   *Revolutionizing supply chain management* 7
    5.   *Logistics, fulfillment and settlement* 8
The Seven Secrets for Success for B2B Exchanges 8
    Secret #1: Stay Focused — Specialize in a Vertical 8
    Secret #2: Play to Win — The Need to Dominate 9
    Secret #3: Maintain Commercial Neutrality 10
    Secret #4: Ensure Transparency and Integrity 11
    Secret #5: Add Value by Building a Virtual Community 14
    Secret #6: Make the Right Strategic Partnerships 14
    Secret #7: Operate as a Virtual Corporation 16
A Global Revolution? 18

Chapter 2 — Building a Winning Digital Marketplace with ICG's *Gameover Scorecard* 19
Todd Hewlin, Managing Director, Internet Capital Group

Introduction 20
Why Does 'Gameover' Matter? 21
The Paradoxical Role of Network Effects 21
How Network Effects Enable Winning Digital Marketplaces 22
The Bottom Line? 23
The *Gameover Scorecard* for Digital Marketplaces 23
In Summary 32
    Case Study 1: A Revolution in the Beef Industry 33
    Case Study 2: The Promise of e-Procurement Made Real 34

Chapter 3 — Building Brand and Community 37
Arthur B. Sculley and W. William A. Woods

Branding 37
Building Your Community 38
  1. *The six Cs of on-line services* 39
  2. *Establishing a trading community* 40
  3. *Enhancing B2B exchange community services* 41
  4. *Building a membership database* 43
  5. *Becoming the 'Bloomberg' terminal in your vertical* 43
  6. *Documents center* 44
  7. *Logistics and systems integration* 44
  8. *Sophisticated financial services* 45
  9. *Sophisticated securities such as derivatives* 45
  10. *The upcoming convergence of B2B exchanges and traditional stock exchanges* 46
  11. *Accessing content* 46
  12. *User group feedback* 47

EXCHANGE FUNDAMENTALS 49

Chapter 4 — Supply Chain Management 51
Chris Renner, Founder, INC2inc Technologies and Jeff Schutt, CSC Consulting

What is Supply Chain Management? 52
Supply Chain Management and B2B Exchanges 55
Supply Chain Execution 56

Supply Chain Planning 60
Product Life-cycle Management 65
Supply Chain Systems and Integration 67
Summary: Adding Value with Supply Chain Management 69

Chapter 5 — Logistics 73
Christopher C. Cusick and Mark W. Pluta, Logistics.com

What is Logistics? 74
Classification of Logistics Providers 75
Frequently Asked Questions 77
    1. *Why can't I just link to someone like UPS or FedEx?* 77
    2. *What if I have customers overseas?* 77
    3. *What if I need someone to warehouse my goods?* 78
    4. *Can I give my customer immediate quotes?* 78
    5. *Will my customer be able to use a preferred transport provider?* 79
    6. *What kind of data do I need from the customer and supplier to ship the goods?* 79
    7. *How do I know my customer will be getting the best value?* 79
    8. *How frequent or reliable are my shipping patterns?* 80
    9. *Do I need to hire dedicated operations staff to supplement my logistics service?* 80
Questions to Ask Your Transportation Marketplace 80
    1. *How much transportation has been procured through your marketplace? How long have you been in business?* 80
    2. *How many transport providers do you have relationships with?* 80
    3. *What modes do you handle?* 80
    4. *How much logistics domain expertise do you really have?* 81
    5. *Can your transportation marketplace handle international shipments? Are you global?* 81
    6. *What is your pricing structure?* 81

Chapter 6 — Business-to-Business Market Models 83
Blair LaCorte, Senior VP of Strategy and Electronic Commerce, VerticalNet

Market Formats 84
Information Transactions 85
Product Transactions 87
Linkage between Off-line and On-line Markets 88
Information Markets 88
Product Markets 89

Market Tools 91
Examples 92
Conclusion 93

Chapter 7 — Catalog Content Management 95
Trey Simonton, EVP, Business Development, ec-Content

Content Management as a Foundation 96
Varying Models for Managing Content 97
The Importance of Quality Catalog Content 97
    1.   A uniform structure for catalog information 98
    2.   Content normalization 98
    3.   Personalization of catalog information 98
Understanding the Costs of Content Management 99
Getting Your Head Around Supplier Issues 100
    1.   The importance of supplier relationships 100
    2.   Establishing contract pricing 101
    3.   Suppliers can be reluctant to commit 101
    4.   Enabling suppliers to participate 101
Establishing a Content Management Strategy 102
The Build vs. Buy Decision 102
    1.   Building an internal content management team 102
    2.   Buying or outsourcing content from a third-party content service provider 103
Complete Content Management Strategy 104
Conclusion 105

Chapter 8 — Selecting the Right Trading Platform 107
Ramesh Patil, CTO, RightWorks Corporation

What is a Trading Platform? 108
What are the Characteristics that Define Successful Exchanges? 109
    1.   Ease of use 110
    2.   Business adaptation 110
    3.   Full transaction life-cycle 111
    4.   Full procurement support 112
    5.   Global availability and reliability 116
    6.   Participant self-service 116
    7.   Fast evolution 117
    8.   Commerce intelligence 117
    9.   Content 118

Qualities to Look for in Your Trading Platform 118
    1. Multi-organization capability 119
    2. Configurability 122
    3. Security 123
    4. Open interoperability 123
    5. Adaptability 124
    6. Scalability 125
    7. Globalization 126
Summary 126

Chapter 9 — Taking a Successful Exchange Public 133
Christopher E. Vroom, Managing Director, eCommerce Equity Research, CSFB

Assessing Market Opportunity: B2B is Real, It's Big, and It's Happening Now! 134
    1. Sizing the potential 134
    2. We see B2B exchanges creating better than $1 trillion in stock market value 135
    3. Value creation rests upon the economic benefits conferred by network participation 136
    4. Monetizing liquidity 139
    5. B2B solutions fundamentally alter information flows between channel partners 139
    6. Articulating the model 139
The Road to IPO: The Why, When, and How of Going Public 141
    1. Selecting underwriters 141
    2. Due diligence 142
    3. The roadshow 143
The IPO is Just One Step in a Long Journey 146

Chapter 10 — Entrepreneurs vs. Industry Consortia 147
Arthur B. Sculley and W. William A. Woods

Entrepreneurial Markets 147
Industry Consortia 148
Upcoming Convergence 150
Anti-trust Issues 150
Pro-competitive Structural Features 150
    1. Trading system design 150
    2. Ownership structures 151
Monopsony Power 152
Conclusion 153

Chapter 11 — What's Next: e-Marketplaces Set the Stage for New Business Networks 155
Bruce Temkin, Director, B2B Research and Advisory, Forrester Research, Inc.

Corporate America Embarks on an e-Business Voyage 155
The Net Creates a New Environment 158
Firms Confront the New Business Realities 158
e-Marketplaces Grow Up 159
    1.   *Operate hands-free* 159
    2.   *Integrate participants* 161
    3.   *Weave-in transaction services* 162
    4.   *Configure trading rules* 163
e-Business Networks: The Future Market Context 164
    Principle 1: Links are free 165
    Principle 2: Information diffuses instantly 166
    Principle 3: Assets live on-network 167
The Implication — Focus or Die 167
A Quick Summary 168

Chapter 12 — Financial Services for B2B Exchanges 169
Content provided during a series of interviews with
Steve Ellis, Executive Vice President, Internet Banking, Wells Fargo Bank

Why is it Important for B2B Exchanges to Include Financial Services? 169
What Types of Financial Services are Relevant for Exchanges? 170
    1.   *Credit cards* 170
    2.   *Purchasing-cards (P-cards)* 171
    3.   *Escrow* 171
    4.   *Letters of credit and documentary collections* 171
    5.   *Factoring* 171
    6.   *Automated clearinghouse* 171
    7.   *Wires* 172
What Types of Companies Offer Financial Services to Exchanges? 172
    1.   *Electronic transaction payment providers* 172
    2.   *Electronic procurement software companies* 173
    3.   *ERP vendors* 173
So, Where is it all Going? 173
Financial Services for Next-generation B2B Exchanges 174
User Authentication — a Necessity for Credit Management On-line 174
Summary 175

EXCHANGE PROFILES ... 177

Profile *i*:	Arbinet-thexchange	179
Profile *ii*:	ChemConnect, Inc.	185
Profile *iii*:	Commerx, Inc.	189
Profile *iv*:	ec-Content, Inc.	193
Profile *v*:	Farms.com, Ltd.	197
Profile *vi*:	HoustonStreet Exchange	201
Profile *vii*:	INC2inc	205
Profile *viii*:	Instill Corporation	207
Profile *ix*:	Logistics.com, Inc.	211
Profile *x*:	Neoforma.com, Inc.	215
Profile *xi*:	SciQuest.com, Inc.	221

Contacts ... 227

Foreword

Mary Coleman, CEO, RightWorks Corporation

In this age of the Internet, our lives have changed — both personally and professionally — in profound ways. The way we communicate, how we process information, how we operate day-to-day, is fundamentally different. We live in a digital world — and what was once foreign to us is now routine. Without thinking much about it, we e-mail, check for breaking news, monitor the performance of our stock portfolios, and manage our business affairs from our Web browsers.

Nowhere has this change been more dramatic than in the area of business-to-business (B2B) e-commerce. Aberdeen Group estimates that the current volume of B2B trade outpaces consumer on-line spending by a factor of 10 to 1. Aberdeen Group and other analysts believe that what we are seeing now is just the beginning of a B2B e-commerce revolution that will shape the future of how businesses buy, sell, collaborate, and interact with one another.

As Bruce Temkin of Forrester Research explains in his chapter, 'What's Next?', the future market context of global trade lies in what Forrester calls eBusiness Networks, '…[r]esilient structures of interdependent players co-operating in real time over the Net.' The Internet continues to be 'front and center' as the New Economy unfolds, and the emergence of eBusiness Networks will give rise to the need for a whole new class of technology applications that enable companies to do business in new ways.

Today's e-marketplaces — on-line entities that enable multiple buyers and multiple sellers to exchange goods, services, and information in real time — are certainly the forbears of the next generation of applications that will 'power' the eBusiness Network environment. These e-marketplaces have demonstrated how the Internet enables companies to be more dynamic, agile, and efficient in satisfying demand. Clearly, a key to success in tomorrow's market context is to understand the principles of how to operate a successful e-marketplace today — whether private, independent, or as a consortium.

Who should care about B2B e-commerce? And how do you prepare yourself for the future? While you may or may not 'own' an e-marketplace, you are, or will be, a participant in one of them, if not more, as a buyer, seller, or even intermediary. You probably already 'deal' with other companies electronically as a buyer or supplier and are already putting e-business initiatives into effect that are designed to streamline your supply chain management, automate your purchasing processes internally and externally, and ultimately provide end-to-end e-business solutions that encapsulate your business rules and processes. In fact, the e-business initiatives you are grappling with today will have a decided impact on your 'readiness' for tomorrow.

So how do companies succeed today and position themselves for success in the future? The companies that will win are those that understand what it will take to do 'it' right. By 'it' we mean how you should think about e-marketplaces and your role in them — theoretically, in terms of business plans, funding, and incubation strategies, and practically, in terms of the goods and services offered, as well as the platform that these goods and services run on. And as we all know, in Internet time those who get 'it' and get 'it' quickly have an almost insurmountable advantage over their competitors.

RightWorks is proud to be the sponsor of this publication, *Evolving E-Markets*, the goal of which is to provide e-business managers worldwide with information and insights that will enable companies to meet and successfully compete in the next wave of B2B e-commerce. It focuses on both the business and technology fundamentals that must be addressed by e-marketplaces, but which are equally relevant to anyone who is grappling with how to leverage the Internet for automating purchase processes, streamlining supply chain management, or fully encapsulating business workflows and processes in end-to-end e-business solutions.

This book covers a wide range of e-business topics — how to get started, how to structure your business model, how to select the right technology platform, how to measure your success — and features: William Woods and Arthur Sculley, co-authors of *B2B Exchanges*; Todd Hewlin from Internet Capital Group; Steve Ellis from Wells Fargo Bank; Bruce Temkin from Forrester Research; and many more.

It is my sincere hope that *Evolving E-Markets* provides you with the context and criteria you need to make informed decisions in the new eBusiness Network economy. Whether you are just embarking on your e-marketplace initiatives, or consider yourself a seasoned veteran in the e-business world, I believe you will benefit from the information you will find in this book — it is based on the valuable experience and lessons learned by those who have forged ahead in the B2B e-commerce frontier.

Chapter 1:
Key Considerations When Setting Up B2B Exchanges

Arthur B. Sculley and W. William A. Woods

The New Economy has sparked a revolution in the way that businesses buy and sell products from each other as a result of the acceptance of the Internet by corporations. These 'Business-to-Business' (or B2B) transactions are increasingly being done over Internet-based Net markets, or B2B exchanges.

B2B exchanges resemble stock exchanges in many ways, including the way they are set up and organized and the trading methods they employ — but they are trading physical commodities such as paper, car parts, and shipping capacity, or financial services such as insurance and credit derivatives, rather than stocks and bonds. Based on our combined experience of developing stock exchanges, we have been studying these emerging B2B exchanges and realized that they all share the same fundamental design issues that stock exchanges have grappled with over the last 300 years!

In our best-selling book entitled *'B2B Exchanges: The Killer Application in the Business-to-Business Internet Revolution'* (ISI Publications), we try to analyze the nature of this revolution in B2B transactions. We make the claim that 'the Internet changes everything in B2B' and that most corporations will have to re-invent themselves over the next five years to remain competitive in the New Economy. Customers are becoming far more demanding, as the Internet has created a once-in-a-lifetime shift of power from the seller to the buyer. B2B exchanges, which are developing at Internet speed, are catalysts for this change. In an attempt to keep up with the pace of change, this new book brings together contributions from several of the leading B2B practitioners and seeks to document the evolution of E-markets over the last year.

The market for B2B e-commerce is already much larger than that for business-to-customer (B2C) transactions and it is predicted to grow much more rapidly. In our book we predicted that on-exchange transactions will exceed $600bn in value (30% of the total) by 2004 in the US alone: if B2B exchanges can capture revenues representing just 0.5% of this turnover, they will collectively generate $3bn in revenue per annum by 2004 — and that excludes the rest of the world! Since publication of our book, the Gartner Group has predicted that global B2B e-commerce will reach $7.29tn by 2004 and that 37% of this will be facilitated by B2B exchanges.

What is a B2B Exchange?

According to *The New Shorter Oxford English Dictionary*, an exchange is '... a building, office, institution, etc., used for the transaction of business or for monetary exchange'. The important point, which differentiates an exchange from other B2B e-commerce companies, is that an exchange involves multiple buyers and sellers, it centralizes and matches buy and sell orders, and it provides post-trade information (ie, it is a 'many-to-many' trading venue).

On the Internet, every website that enables buyers and sellers to come together and find each other is really a 'virtual exchange building'. Hence our effort to understand the phenomenon of formal B2B exchanges as they are developing on the Internet and to describe the anatomy of a model B2B exchange.

The unique feature of 'exchanges' is that they bring multiple buyers and sellers together (in a 'virtual' sense) in one central market space and enable those players to buy and sell from each other at a price which is determined dynamically in accordance with the rules of the exchange. Increasingly, *dynamic price-setting mechanisms* are being used by many exchanges for B2B transactions, because the Internet's ability to interconnect companies very cheaply means that an Internet exchange can bring together bids and offers from all over the world.

A B2B exchange can be contrasted with the procurement processes of one company, say General Motors, which sets up a website with an auction mechanism for suppliers to bid on contracts with GM. This is *not* a B2B exchange — although it *is* a B2B e-commerce site — because there is only one buyer. Similarly, a business that offers goods or services for sale to other businesses over the Internet is not an exchange, even if it provides a price-setting mechanism that is normally associated with an exchange, such as an auction — because there is only one seller.

It is interesting to note that GM, Ford, and Daimler Chrysler have announced an agreement to set up an on-line e-market called Covisint where they, and other automotive manufacturers, can buy parts from multiple suppliers — this is a true B2B exchange, as we have defined it. Four years ago there were no B2B exchanges outside of the securities markets. Today there are over 1,000 such exchanges operating on the Internet. These exchanges have a different market model from the companies that are specialized in what is commonly called 'business-to-consumer' transactions (B2C), or that enable consumers to sell goods or services to each other — a 'consumer-to-consumer' model, or 'C2C'.

For obvious reasons, media attention has tended to focus on those aspects of electronic commerce that involve consumers. The amount of publicity that Amazon.com has received in this respect is probably an historic record! But individual customers are not yet necessarily the best prepared and the best equipped to interact electronically. By contrast, businesses are used to interacting through networks, as they were already doing, in many cases, around Electronic Data Interchange (EDI) networks.

Why B2B Exchanges are the Killer Application

1. Global reach

The cost of accessing the Internet is falling daily, and the cost of sending information by e-mail or over the Web is a fraction of standard telephone, fax, and mail costs. This means that sellers can reach out to buyers all over the world and buyers can access sellers from all over the world. In the physical world, businesses and individual consumers will often pay a higher price or buy an inferior product simply because that is the only service available in their physical location. Now B2B exchanges are able to bring fragmented buyers and sellers together on the 'virtual' trading floor of the centralized market space.

B2B exchanges create a community of those buyers and sellers in a structured and organized fashion. After viewing the offers posted on the exchange, communications between potential buyers and sellers are specifically targeted to the interested parties. The on-line exchange thus generates great sales leads to pre-qualified buyers. Unlike e-mail on the Internet generally, communications through a central exchange can be organized, encrypted, authenticated, time-stamped, tracked, and verified.

The low cost of getting connected, irrespective of geographical distance, enables fragmented buyers and sellers to find each other through a B2B exchange without incurring real-world search and travel expenses or high commissions for using intermediaries. In addition, by aggregating multiple sellers in one place, an exchange creates a one-stop shopping experience for the buyers. Even when a supplier of parts puts up its own on-line store front to sell directly to the manufacturer, it will find that a B2B exchange is more attractive to many buyers. This is because a neutral, third-party exchange can post the store fronts of multiple suppliers in one place — thus facilitating the manufacturer's search for the best product at the best price.

2. Dynamic pricing

In the industrial world, most prices are set by a one-on-one negotiation or by the seller, who generally has the greater economic power and can publish a catalog with non-negotiable prices. An alternative method is to bring all the potential buy and sell orders together and let those competing offers set the highest price or the price which maximizes the amount sold. This is the approach adopted by most stock exchanges with their central market matching systems for securities. It is also the price discovery mechanism adopted by eBay to run its on-line auctions for consumers.

Increasingly, dynamic price-setting mechanisms are being used by many B2B exchanges for business-to-business transactions, because the Internet's ability to interconnect companies very cheaply means that an Internet exchange can bring together bids and offers from all over the world. Initially this may be as simple as on-line catalogs, which can have the price updated more regularly. The next level is automated 'request for proposal' mechanisms that enable buyers to obtain quotes from multiple suppliers. More sophisticated still is the use of real auctions to provide a dynamic forum in which competing bids are brought together.

On-line auctions developed initially in the C2C space as a highly efficient way to facilitate person-to-person transactions (eg, the sale of antiques or memorabilia between individuals on eBay). Selling one-of-a-kind, previously-owned items in the pre-Internet, physical world was very difficult. Consumers trying to sell one-of-a-kind products were often constrained to a small, localized marketplace in which to locate potential buyers (eg, flea markets, garage sales, local classifieds, etc). Now, companies like eBay have enabled consumers to offer their personal items for sale on a global basis through on-line auctions.

Seller-driven Auctions
In this approach the seller drives the auction. The seller lists the item to sell, and multiple buyers submit upward price bids for the designated item or service. This format is utilized by eBay and tends to lead to an increase in the price bid as time extends and the close of the auction approaches. The system works well for sellers, who can get the highest price for their goods while using the Internet to maximize their reach to a large number of potential buyers. This facilitates efficient market pricing. The system works especially well for items that are unique and differentiated, but are relatively simple to describe and understand. The system is less favorable to buyers, because there is no negotiation between the buyer and the seller — just a competition between all the buyers.

Buyer-driven Change
What most distinguishes the New Economy and the new form of commerce from the previous ones is the once-in-a-lifetime shift of power from producers to customers. The buyer is now in control of everything. Customers are aware that they can demand the best quality, the best service, and the lowest prices; they also want everything customized and they want it immediately. They are far more demanding than in traditional commerce, because they can now access suppliers from all over the world. In the world of B2B procurements, this process has seen the emergence of 'buyer-driven' or reverse auctions.

In a buyer-driven auction, the standard eBay-style auction format is inverted, with buyers specifying the items they want and multiple sellers competing for the buyer's business in an auction format. In this type of auction, the price tends to fall over time as you approach the close of the auction and the suppliers seek to undercut their competitors. This approach clearly favors the buyers, especially if there are multiple sellers able to offer items that come close to meeting the buyers' requirements.

In B2B markets, a B2B exchange can often empower and advance the interests of the buyer. For example, one form of B2B exchange that is developing is an infomediary who represents business buyers and aggregates their information with that of other buyers and uses the combined market power to negotiate with, and seek competitive bids from, suppliers on their behalf. Shop2gether (www.shop2gether.com) is just such a B2B exchange with a specific focus on aggregating the purchase orders of educational institutions.

Multi-attribute Matching Systems
There are a number of software development companies that are very well positioned in this B2B space. Prominent names are Ariba, CommerceOne, i2 Technologies, Moai, Oracle, OptiMark Technologies, and RightWorks. These companies are helping emerging B2B exchanges to set up and develop. Interestingly, these companies have taken over from the 'ERP' experts like Baan, SAP, Peoplesoft, and others as the most important software houses in B2B. These companies are essentially 'infrastructure' providers to B2B exchanges. OptiMark Technologies is particularly interesting on the trading system side, because it has a number of patented matching algorithms that enable a trader to maximize the potential of executing a trade in a periodic auction by allowing the trader to indicate a range of preferences over a series of parameters — rather than just price and volume.

In the manufacturing process, for example, quality, time of delivery, and after sales service can be just as important as, and sometimes more important than, the price. Similarly, a manufacturer may wish to link a particular purchase, or the amount of that product to be purchased, to another purchase — for example, where both products are needed but in different quantities in order to manufacture the end product. More sophisticated trading applications are now being developed that allow a buyer to build up a 'profile' which indicates its preferences over these multiple attributes and to link orders for different products into one 'combination' order.

3. More efficient distribution channels — 'B2O'

Once a manufacturer goes on-line, it can reach out and touch the end consumers of its products, without the need for retail distribution channels. Those distribution channels were developed to enable the manufacturer to achieve the maximum distribution of its products in a pre-Internet environment. The distribution channels also helped the manufacturer to manage inventory levels of completed products, and to store that inventory, in return for a percentage of the sales price. Now a manufacturer can get orders from consumers directly over the Internet and then move to a build-to-order (B2O) program — just as Dell Computers has for PCs, a B2O business model can dramatically reduce manufacturing time, inventory levels, and distribution costs.

4. Revolutionizing supply chain management

However, the manufacturer still has to source all the raw materials and parts which go into producing the finished product. It is this 'supply chain management' process that is the B2B environment where B2B exchanges will flourish. B2B exchanges have the capability to tie together the manufacturer with its suppliers (tier 1) and its suppliers' suppliers (tiers 2 and 3). This can lead to greater efficiencies in the design of products and significant reductions in manufacturing time. In this way, the benefits of B2B exchanges will extend well beyond the function of bringing buyers and sellers together and will result in major process improvements as well.

5. Logistics, fulfillment, and settlement

A critical component of any e-market that seeks to expand its community of participants and facilitate automated and anonymous trading is an efficient clearing and settlement system.

Delivery of physical goods will always require the use of logistics companies like UPS and transportation services. Bulk trades of chemicals or car parts require a sophisticated fulfillment, tracking, and payments process. This is the next frontier for developing B2B exchanges and no doubt will be a critical issue for the readers of this book.

The Seven Secrets for Success for B2B Exchanges

The following paragraphs are excerpts of the key points from the seven chapters that comprise the heart of our book entitled *B2B Exchanges: The Killer Application in the Business-to-Business Internet Revolution*.

Secret #1:
Stay Focused — Specialize in a Vertical

The most important secret of success in the initial phases of developing a B2B exchange is to target a specific industry in which you have strong expertise, and then specialize in a vertical within that industry. Specialization enables you to dominate your chosen space quickly, which creates mind share and liquidity, and then helps you to scale up quickly. Specialization also enables you to tailor your business model to match the target market's distinct characteristics.

Once you have dominated your chosen vertical, you can start to widen the scope of your exchange into verticals within your chosen industry, but you can only achieve this luxury if you have proven liquidity and you have demonstrated the ability to dominate. The point here is that, in the exchange business, liquidity is king. Sellers will gravitate to the market that has the most buyers, and buyers like the market that has the best supply.

Vertical Specialization
Industry sectors can be divided into 'vertical' market spaces, which can be defined by geography, regulations, or product characteristics. These divisions act like fissures in the on-line world and can allow different B2B exchanges to service each of the separate verticals. The point here is that a laser-like focus on a specific vertical category can yield a tremendously profitable space for your unique B2B exchange.

Other important success factors in vertical specialization include:

- *Choosing a monster market* — it obviously makes more sense to focus on markets with high value/potential, where there is frequent trading, and where the most profits can be made.
- *Vertical knowledge* — this is critical for your exchange so as to build credibility within a vertical quickly, and to ensure that your exchange is tailored to suit that particular market.

MetalSite (www.metalsite.net) is a good example of an exchange with a specific focus from the outset. Situated as a trading hub for the steel industry, MetalSite started off by trading surplus or second-grade metals only — a unique specialization that allowed it to dominate that vertical. Then, having established a good name, some great publicity, and a proven track record in trading sub-standard steel, MetalSite was able to expand its product range and introduce primary-grade steel as a product.

The Rainforest Effect
In the ecosystem of a rainforest, there is intense competition to reach the sunlight at the top of the canopy of trees. In the same way, B2B exchanges must focus on a vertical, scale up quickly, and grow as fast as they can. Once you break through the canopy and achieve dominance, you can better afford to spread out and introduce new products, attack other verticals, and add extra services.

Secret #2:
Play to Win — The Need to Dominate
The previously discussed benefits of specialization mean that there will be only one major winner in each vertical sector. This means that a successful exchange must try to be one of the 'first to market' in its chosen vertical. Therefore, in true Internet fashion, the founders of a new B2B exchange must 'plant their flag, declare victory, and then run like hell'.

Viral Growth
For B2B exchanges, the site with the most or the best buyers will attract the most or best suppliers, which will generate transaction liquidity — and that, in turn, will attract more buyers. Once this 'virtuous circle' has been set in motion, it acts like a vortex that sucks more players into the exchange and becomes self-sustaining. This virtuous vortex also helps to repel potential competitors, because players who join one successful exchange will be reluctant to move to another exchange.

Liquidity, Liquidity, Liquidity
Achieving dominance means having the greatest liquidity — that is, having the most trades done on your exchange. At the same time, building volume of trades is more important than numbers of members at the start. This means you should target key players who are likely to trade the most and get them to join early. In addition, if there are any intermediaries that can 'make a market', they are like gold dust at the start.

Critical Mass
Liquidity is enhanced if you can build a critical mass of users as quickly as possible. In order to achieve sign-up, most exchanges will have to waive the standard subscription fees in the early stages. Waiving fees at the start can put a lot of pressure on your exchange's finances. However, market share is worth more than profits in the early stages of the launch of a B2B exchange.

Domination vs. Anti-dilution
Winning as a B2B exchange is about dominating your vertical; it is not about coming in second or third place while trying to avoid dilution of your existing market share. Therefore, for those exchanges that are running in second or third place, there is no point in trying to compete against each other; they must merge and seek overall domination.

Branding
Building a strong brand name is very helpful in achieving domination. Therefore, it is important to get the name right at the start. Use caution, however, in selecting a name that is too product-specific. While this may initially help to build brand recognition in your chosen vertical, it could later become constraining as you expand into other complementary verticals and outgrow the name.

Customer Care and Support
Always bear in mind that branding is only one factor in determining success or failure — providing the best customer care and support is much more important in building brand recognition and trust among users. In fact, sometimes it is justified to spend up to 80% of your resources on obtaining new members and keeping existing members happy.

Prepare for the Long Haul
Finally, achieving domination won't happen overnight. Indeed, if your exchange represents a major paradigm shift for the industry, then be prepared for a long haul in getting 'buy-in' and widespread usage.

Secret #3:
Maintain Commercial Neutrality
Because an exchange provides a centralized market space for multiple competing members, and both buyers and sellers, it must stay neutral in order to be credible and build trust. This need for neutrality must permeate the whole exchange: the way in which it is designed, the way it operates, and the way it secures users' confidential information. The exchange's trading rules must not favor any single participant.

This means that the exchange must be perceived as a neutral third party by all other parties, as well as actually act as a neutral body; and it must be designed to benefit all the players in the industry it serves. This may not be easy, because as the exchange starts to succeed and grow, key strategic partners or specific user groups will seek to control you.

Proportional Representation

As a successful B2B exchange develops and starts to dominate a particular industry, it will become increasingly more important for that exchange to represent all users of that market space. One way to achieve this is to partition the ownership between constituencies — sellers, intermediaries, and the general public. In this way, you can be sure that everyone is properly represented in ownership and on the board of the company.

Moreover, the only fair form of corporate governance is a 'one share, one vote' system. In such a system, a particular shareholder's influence is directly proportional to the amount of capital that they have provided.

Flexibility to 'Morph' the Business Plan

B2B exchanges must be incredibly light on their feet, be able to innovate quickly and turn on a dime. This means that business plans must be fluid and rewritten every few months if your plan is to stay ahead. This kind of flexibility is only possible in a highly entrepreneurial company that is not closely controlled by Industrial Age structures.

Maintain Confidentiality of Users' Data

Successful B2B exchanges will build up an extremely valuable database of information about their chosen vertical market space. Over time, this data will become a major component of the exchange's value proposition. However, determining who has access to the data is a significant issue for each exchange.

It may be necessary to have an independent auditor review the systems and business practices of the exchange on a regular basis in order to provide potential members with an independent confirmation that their data will be kept secure.

The Advisory Board and User Committees

Your B2B exchange must ensure that all of its user groups are represented in the decision-making process. The easiest way to achieve this is to institute an advisory board and to set up committees comprising the different user groups. The advisory board should provide a forum for the key players in the industry to have adequate input on policy without them having to have a controlling interest or to control the board of directors. A compliance function within the exchange should report directly to the advisory board.

Secret #4:
Ensure Transparency and Integrity

Because an exchange provides a centralized market space for multiple competing members, it must be an open and fair market in order to be credible and gain the users' trust. A fair market is one that is transparent and built on integrity.

Some members may resist this if they believe that they can profit more from inefficiencies in the market (eg, a lack of pricing transparency). Successful exchanges will set and enforce market rules that do not favor any one user or group of users.

Need to be a Self-regulatory Organization
The exchange can only ensure that it is open and fair if it is prepared to regulate the users of the exchange's centralized market facility. The form of regulation most appropriate for an Internet-based exchange is self-regulation. A B2B exchange should be a self-regulatory organization (SRO); an SRO imposes regulations on its own members and then enforces those regulations.

Self-regulation is really enlightened self-interest, since it is always in the best interests of the exchange to maintain an open and fair marketplace.

Transparency
Transparency is a critical element of fairness and should be enforced by the exchange. At a minimum, all transactions made on the exchange should be reported to the exchange with full details on price and volumes. With fully automated execution, these details are immediately captured by the exchange's systems; but with post and browse and some auction-based exchanges, the information must be given to the exchange by the parties to the trade.

The exchange should have rules and regulations that encourage transparency.

Pricing transparency creates a more efficient market, which often leads to lower prices. Full disclosure is the 'mantra' of a fair and open exchange.

Transparency also applies to the products traded through the exchange's systems. Sellers must disclose full information about the items that they are selling in order to enable the buyers to make a reasoned assessment of the true value of the products. The exchange should therefore enable sellers to put full product specifications and details on the website.

Integrity
The centralized pricing system is the most important function of an exchange, and the exchange must seek to ensure the integrity of that pricing mechanism. The key elements of a fair system are:

- equal access;
- the order with best price has highest priority;
- first in, first out (FIFO);
- effective procedures to ensure that each seller's products are posted correctly and that buyers' bids and orders are transmitted accurately; and
- trades are consistently executed in accordance with the published rules of the exchange.

Equal access means that every trading member has equal access to the exchange's trading system, irrespective of size or duration of membership. Price priority means that a new order which sets the best price (ie, the lowest ask or the highest bid price must take priority over other orders with a less attractive price).

The rules of a successful B2B exchange will require members to honor the integrity of the exchange's pricing mechanism. This means that members must agree not to do anything that will hinder or disrupt the fair and orderly functioning of the market.

Finally, members should be under a general obligation not to mislead or deceive customers in advertising goods or services through the exchange or completing transactions through the exchange's systems.

The Exchange's Gatekeeper Role
In order to maintain credibility and trust, an exchange must regulate access to its centralized market space. In implementing this concept, the exchange must decide what standards and qualifications it will impose for joining the exchange and for continued membership. In all cases, the firm and the relevant employees of the firm should be fit and proper persons without any record of dishonest or fraudulent trading activities.

Standardization
One of the value propositions of an exchange as opposed to an unregulated telephone market lies in the standardization of the product, the legal environment, the trading and settlement terms, and the documentation.

A successful B2B exchange will draw up rules itself (or encourage members to adopt existing industry standards) that regulate the quality of the products offered on the exchange, the lot sizes in which they are offered, the way in which they are priced, the acceptable pricing increments (called the tick size), and the standard terms for trading and settlement.

Complaints and Dispute Resolution
The members of the exchange, as members of a community, should be required to honor the just and equitable principles of conduct set out in the exchange's rules and commonly practiced in the market space where they are conducting business. This should include a requirement to honor the trading obligations to one another that arise from trading on the exchange. Successful B2B exchanges will provide a mechanism, which may be formal or informal, for a prompt and orderly resolution of complaints and disputes between trading members.

Systems Integrity
The exchange must ensure that all of its systems are robust so as to avoid systemic failures. As users become dependent on the exchange for pricing, trading, and data, it becomes more and more essential to provide fully redundant, highly secure systems. In the B2C space, the bad publicity

experienced by eBay following several well-publicized outages of its core systems demonstrates graphically the dangers of system failures for a B2B exchange.

Security of data on the exchange's systems must be high (eg, through the use of serious levels of encryption) to build up the trust of members. Members must be satisfied that their confidential data are secure within the exchange and that there can be no unauthorized use of that information.

B2B exchanges must adopt sound self-regulatory practices to avoid calls for government legislation to regulate and license their activities as national markets once they become dominant in their industry.

Secret #5:
Add Value by Building a Virtual Community

Although the primary function of an exchange is to provide a centralized pricing mechanism and market space, successful B2B exchanges will grow beyond this and develop into fully-fledged exchange communities. This means that they will provide the services that allow people in the same vertical to network effectively and to access all the business information they require in one place. Successful B2B exchanges will become powerful virtual communities.

Enhancing B2B Exchange Community Services
The elements of a B2B exchange community are similar to those which have worked in the B2C and C2C space — after all, businesses are run and managed by individuals — but the focus is on supporting those individuals when they make business decisions, rather than on their personal spending or lifestyles. The ways in which a B2B exchange can develop the community around the central core trading functions are addressed more fully in the chapter entitled Building Brand and Community.

Secret #6:
Make the Right Strategic Partnerships

The universality and ease of use of the Internet means that you no longer have to bring people into one physical trading floor to create liquidity. However, it is only possible for a new B2B exchange to challenge an entrenched Industrial Age market if the new entrant can build liquidity at much lower cost. Increasingly cheap computing power and telecommunications are the weapons that allow Internet-based trading networks to challenge traditional trading mechanisms. But the successful exchange must be able to build that liquidity quickly and expand to meet the demand in 'Internet time'. By far the easiest way of achieving this, as proven by the successful B2C applications, is to work with strategic partners from the very beginning.

Potential Partners
The potential partners for a B2B exchange include deep pocket investors, buyers in the chosen market space, sellers, existing broker intermediaries, new infomediaries, content providers, IT vendors,

and trading systems software developers. However, it is critical for the exchange to remain commercially neutral. This means that no one user group (eg, buyers, sellers, or existing brokers) should be able to control the market.

Customize the Market
As part of the laser-like focus and specialization that is required to dominate a particular vertical, a successful B2B exchange must tailor its applications to the specific needs of its chosen market space. The best way to achieve this is to work closely with the potentially big users of the exchange and literally 'get inside their heads'.

Vertical Knowledge
Some B2B exchanges are being developed by experienced vertical industry professionals who have seen that, with Internet technologies now being adopted by business, there is an enormous opportunity for them to start up a B2B exchange. These professionals typically have deep knowledge of their particular industry and strong relationships with the main buyers and sellers in that vertical space. Others are being formed by consortium of existing industry players. In both cases, their vertical knowledge is critical in order to build credibility for the exchange within that vertical quickly and to ensure that the exchange is tailored to suit that particular market.

Where a B2B exchange does not have the necessary level of vertical knowledge on day one, it must move quickly to secure such expertise. The vertical knowledge of an exchange and the early sign-up of key industry players are major barriers to entry for potential competitors and ensure that the laws of increasing return apply to that B2B exchange.

Outsource the Technology
We strongly advise the builders of B2B exchanges to outsource the technology development in the early stages. It is critical for a successful B2B exchange to focus on its core competency — the specific industry expertise that will enable it to create the best business solution possible for that market space — and let the outside technology experts build the systems.

Indeed, one of the great opportunities spawned by the growth of B2B exchanges lies in the provision of technology, marketing, connectivity, content, and consulting services to these new exchange companies.

New Age Thinking
In the Industrial Age, a common approach to project development by companies has been to start by engaging a large firm of outside consultants. The methodology behind this approach is largely based on the belief that it is wrong to take key senior executives away from their existing jobs in order to develop a new project, and that an outside firm of consultants can approach all interested parties (including potential competitors) and come up with an independent view. This approach is not ideally suited to the development of a B2B exchange, because B2B exchanges need to:

- emerge and launch in 'Internet time';

- have entrepreneurial leadership and be very flexible;
- be designed as neutral third-party applications, rather than as units within an existing industry player; and
- have very sound vertical knowledge and hands-on industry expertise.

Infomediaries
One of the most obvious areas for an emerging B2B exchange to seek strategic partners is in the development of community services. Since the core competency of an exchange is the centralized trading facility, it is unlikely that the exchange will initially have either the resources or the experience to develop many of the potential add-on services that a full community requires.

Sources of reliable historical market data are key potential partners. The value of a trading facility is greatly enhanced by the availability of market data, such as historical prices, volumes, and analytical research services. Whilst this content will develop on the exchange as it grows, it may be necessary in the early stages to buy in the data from the existing traditional market space.

Secret #7:
Operate as a Virtual Corporation

In the New Economy, the winners will be flexible corporate structures which can 'morph' their business plans and innovate in real time. The B2B space is evolving rapidly, and only those companies that are light on their feet will be able to survive. B2B exchange companies must be able to move quickly, to innovate, and to scale-up fast.

Since B2B exchanges are a new species of B2B application, the founders of these companies have the opportunity to start with a clean sheet and adopt the best practices of Internet start-ups. Invariably, this means that B2B exchanges should be 'virtual corporations'.

Anatomy of a Virtual Corporation
There are eight key guidelines for virtual corporations, as follows:

- concentrate on core competencies;
- outsource the rest;
- remain flexible at all times;
- keep staffing levels low;
- plan to operate on a 24 x 7 basis;
- choose professional advisors who specialize in Internet start-ups;
- build partnerships with key corporate leaders; and
- develop strong funding support.

In e-commerce, you must be able to operate around the clock, unlike bricks-and-mortar businesses which operate on a 9 to 5 basis.

An important early first step in launching a B2B exchange is obtaining first-class legal and accounting advice on the design of the market, the rules and regulations of the exchange, and the legal documents for transactions made on the exchange. Choose a top firm of accountants as auditors, but pressure them to accept low fees for their audit services in the early years. And don't worry about them; they will do very well for fees if and when you go public. Some service providers and consultants may accept equity in lieu of fees in the start-up phase.

Outsource, Outsource, Outsource
In order to be able to concentrate on the core competency of quickly building a customized trading facility, it is critical that the exchange's staff are not distracted by the need to add other services to the exchange. Outsource everything else, including:

- the technology build;
- the addition of content and community services; and
- the provision of logistics and document processing.

Think Private, Act Public
Smart Internet entrepreneurs establish their businesses as limited liability, private companies, but act as if they are publicly-listed companies from day one. Acting like a publicly-listed company means that you should prepare to go public from day one.

This approach includes:

- hiring the best lawyers and accountants with experience in taking an Internet company public;
- forming 'tier 1' relationships;
- having annual audits on your financial statements from the end of the first year;
- having a proper board of directors with an audit committee and a compensation committee; and
- setting up a strong, independent advisory board.

Customer Care
Exchanges have multiple types of customers and they all demand a very high level of attention. Successful exchanges must focus on marketing to potential customers, since new trading members are particularly essential in the early stages in order to build liquidity on the exchange.

In addition to the usual marketing efforts to secure new members, an exchange must have a thorough customer care and user support program. This must include regular training sessions, a 24-hour, seven-days-a-week help desk, and trading desk facilitators to encourage new listings and trades.

Jurisdiction Shopping

As an Internet-based application, B2B exchanges must be prepared to position themselves as global players from day one. Where revenues are likely to be generated from all over the world, it makes sense to start off by incorporating a holding company in a leading neutral jurisdiction like Bermuda.

Funding Options for B2B Exchanges

As with all Internet and e-commerce start-ups, the initial capital will probably come from the three 'Fs' — 'Family, friends, and fools'! After that, the first and second financing rounds are critical. You must try to choose financial partners who have deep pockets so that you can tap those partners for the serious money quickly when you later need to scale up.

When seeking venture capital, always remember that a VC investor looks for:

- a monster market — avoid markets with few buyers or dominated by a few sellers (eg, the market for semiconductors — Intel and IBM);
- management experience, including a high level of specific vertical knowledge;
- speed to market;
- scalability; and
- a business model which works, with revenues and a clear path to profitability.

A Global Revolution?

Until now, most revenues and thus the greatest economic impact of e-commerce has been in the US where the e-commerce and information technology industries together account for a third of real economic growth over the past three years. According to a study released by Andersen Consulting (www.ac.com), Europe is now rapidly eroding the US lead. Andersen's predict that by 2002, European e-commerce revenues are expected to equal 55% of the US total. By 2003, the on-line population of the European Union is expected to match that of the US.

The Asian economies are also embracing the New Economy with both arms. Our book, **B2B Exchanges**, was at the top of the *South China Morning Post's* best-seller list in Hong Kong for several weeks, and is being sold in the Chinese language in mainland China. And the number of B2B exchanges emerging in Asia is now accelerating rapidly as the concept spreads.

All around the world, corporate spending on integrating the Internet into everything a company does is accelerating, now that the need to spend the IT budget on Y2K fixes is over.

William Woods is the CEO of the Bermuda Stock Exchange. Arthur Sculley is a partner in Sculley Brothers LLC. Together they have co-authored the best-selling book B2B Exchanges: The Killer Application in the Business-to-Business Internet Revolution *(ISI Publications). William can be reached at* william@b2bexchanges.com *and Arthur at* arthur@b2bexchanges.com.

Chapter 2:

Building a Winning Digital Marketplace with ICG's *Gameover Scorecard*

Todd Hewlin, Managing Director, Internet Capital Group

Since early 1996, Internet Capital Group (ICG) has been a leader in building businesses that enable the Internet transformation of industries that we now call B2B. ICG's current network of 77 companies delivers technologies, business services, and digital marketplaces used by customers globally to reduce costs, expand revenues, and reinvent their businesses around the Internet. ICG has grown to become the world's largest holding company of B2B businesses with a significant presence in North America, Europe, and Asia.

As ICG amassed deeper and deeper experience about what it takes to build a winning digital marketplace, we recognized the importance of institutionalizing our intellectual capital in order to best serve all the companies in the ICG network. This institutional knowledge is now encapsulated within ICG's *Gameover Scorecard for Digital Marketplaces*™.

The *Gameover Scorecard for Digital Marketplaces* represents an amalgamation of learning, experience, and expertise within the ICG network. It brings together tried, tested, and proven methodologies, best practices, and business principles for helping digital marketplaces establish a dominant position in their markets.

While the entire *Gameover Scorecard* is beyond the scope of this chapter, we have summarized the 20 most important attributes that separate the winners from the also-rans with respect to digital marketplaces. Whether your company is building a private or public trading exchange, joining a consortium, or simply deciding which marketplace you should partner with in your industry, the

Gameover Scorecard can help you assess the value of that marketplace and track its progress toward becoming the leader.

Introduction

While we are still in the early stages of B2B e-commerce, digital marketplaces promise to unlock previously untapped economic value in nearly every industry while also serving to fundamentally transform the way businesses interact, communicate, and conduct commerce.

Digital marketplaces help buyers find, pay for, and receive the products they need faster and cheaper than ever before. They help distributors broaden the base of products they can sell, reduce inventories, and improve back office operations. And they help suppliers reach new customers at lower selling costs, develop better products faster, and lower their input costs.

In fact, B2B e-commerce is transforming today's industries even faster than most experts had predicted — both in the US and across the globe. For example, look at how many click-and-mortar companies have joined with dot.coms to create on-line marketplaces to better enable and integrate their value chain. Or consider how the early pioneers of digital marketplaces have already moved into the second or third tier of extending their customer value proposition. We are even seeing earnings expectations and stock prices beginning to move back together instead of apart.

In an amazingly short time, the perceived ability of B2B to fundamentally transform global industries has moved from speculation to mass validation. For example, Alan Greenspan, Chairman of the Federal Reserve, frequently speaks of how technology is finally delivering on its promise of improving productivity at the national level. GE's CEO Jack Welch has talked about re-engineering what has become the most valuable company in the world by making the Internet pervasive to how each GE business unit runs.

In the first half of 2000, we saw literally hundreds of announcements involving the formation of new B2B exchanges. In the manufacturing sector, new digital marketplaces were announced for the airline, automobile, consumer electronics, rubber, steel, and consumer goods industries. Other digital marketplaces recently formed include those for the hotel/hospitality, construction, mining, travel services, foreign exchange, and bond trading industries. We have even seen new digital marketplaces formed for the buying and selling of cattle, chickens, turkeys, fish, and seafood.

Ultimately, digital marketplaces promise to fundamentally transform industries and our global economy. They are already reducing both process and product costs. They are delivering higher revenues at a reduced cost of sales. They are integrating supply chain transactions in unprecedented ways. And they are enabling businesses to outsource many non-core business activities to increase flexibility and reduce management complexity. In fact, once all of these outcomes of the B2B transformation are taken into account, many industries expect 15-30% reductions in the end-to-end costs of their supply chain. Over the coming years, this profound impact on industry economics may well reflect the greatest incremental change in corporate productivity ever.

Why Does 'Gameover' Matter?

To be successful in this Internet-enabled economy, those seeking to build digital marketplaces must make achieving 'Gameover Position' in their industry their sole mantra. Why? Because competition between digital marketplaces in any given industry is a winner-takes-most battle. By winner-takes-most, we mean that once the leading digital marketplace gets to critical mass, the second- and third-tier players are relegated to niche positions with much less attractive value propositions and economic models. Once this competitive lockout occurs, the game is essentially over.

What does it take to achieve Gameover Position? Simply put, a digital marketplace puts itself in Gameover Position when it solves one or more critical industry pain points in such a unique and compelling way that it becomes the *de facto* standard for enabling B2B commerce in that industry — positioning it to achieve a virtually untouchable competitive position in its market.

We are too early in the B2B e-commerce revolution for most digital marketplaces to claim Gameover Position yet. However, over the next two years, ICG believes that nearly every industry sector will have a single digital marketplace that has moved into Gameover Position.

Each of these winning digital marketplaces will be able to:

- define the standards for how information is shared and commerce is conducted;
- capture the lion's share of liquidity in the most attractive products and services;
- demonstrate the network economics that make it the most valuable company in its market by an order of magnitude; and
- play the role of consolidator, not consolidatee, in rationalizing its market.

The Paradoxical Role of Network Effects

The rule of network effects is one of the primary forces driving the Gameover outcome we just described. 'Network effects' refers to the reinforcing dynamics that bias the leading player in a market to grow and the other players to shrink as the market matures.

The impact of network effects has two contrasting points of view. On the one hand, the winning digital marketplace in each industry will become a very valuable company with a highly defensible competitive position. But on the other hand, there are going to be many more losers than winners in this treacherous battle to achieve Gameover Position.

How Network Effects Enable Winning Digital Marketplaces

The most important network effect for digital marketplaces is the linkage between buyer and supplier adoption. The more buyers that choose a specific digital marketplace as their buying platform, the more sellers feel they have to be part of that platform to both service their existing customers and grow their business by reaching new customers.

At the same time, every new supplier that joins a marketplace increases the value proposition of that marketplace for the buyers. While industrial buyers deeply value their existing supplier relationships, they need to frequently calibrate those relationships against the price, quality, and service offerings of others. Buyers also need access to liquid 'spot' markets where they can find new suppliers to meet their needs during periods of peak demand, or where they need to buy products or services for the first time. In both of these areas, the more suppliers that have adopted a digital marketplace, the more of each buyer's requirements will be fulfilled through that marketplace.

Buyer/seller network effects are not the only factors that impact the win or lose outcome of today's digital marketplaces. Another factor is who owns control over important industry and technology standards. In fact, for on-line commerce to be fully realized, standards are needed with respect to how information is described and exchanged, as well as how end-to-end business processes are conducted between buyers, distributors, and suppliers.

In highly concentrated industries, these standards may be agreed to through collaboration between the small numbers of large companies that control the majority of the commerce in that industry. In these industries, other smaller participants simply comply with the standards proposed by these large players. Examples include automotive OEMs, airlines, and some industrial commodities.

However, in more fragmented industries, digital marketplaces are in a race to get a critical mass of customers behind their data and business process standards. In these industries, the final standards will become clear as the winning digital marketplace emerges. In turn, control over these critical standards gives a digital marketplace its power. By shaping the evolution of these standards, digital marketplaces can continually distance themselves from their competitors.

Finally, the underlying economic model of digital marketplaces reinforces this winner-takes-most dynamic. Digital marketplaces incur significant up-front costs on technology to build their products, and on sales and marketing to win a critical mass of early customers. However, incremental customers and, in particular, incremental value-added services sold to existing customers represent almost pure margin. These high margins allow the first digital marketplace to reach critical mass to price its products and services very aggressively versus the second- and third-largest players, thereby reinforcing its ability to sustain its Gameover Position.

The Bottom Line?

The digital marketplace that gains these 'network effects' first in a market becomes the 'gorilla' (a term coined by Geoffrey Moore and Tom Kippola in *The Gorilla Game)*, controlling the standards and capturing the lion's share of customers, revenues, and margins in its industry. As soon as these reinforcing dynamics become clear, the capital markets respond with Darwinian clarity, rewarding the Gameover player handsomely and positioning the also-rans to be acquired, relegated to a niche position, or simply to go away.

Examples in previous waves of technology abound. Consider Microsoft's ability to define the standard in the spreadsheet market over Lotus. Or Oracle's dominance in the relational database market over Sybase, Informix, and Ingres. Or Siebel's leadership in the customer relationship management (CRM) market over Aurum (now part of Baan). In each case, the winner's market capitalization has at times been 10 times that of the next largest competitor.

The *Gameover Scorecard* for Digital Marketplaces

Given the paradoxical win/lose dynamics facing today's digital marketplaces, and our belief that nearly every industry sector will have a single digital marketplace in Gameover Position within two years, ICG developed its *Gameover Scorecard* to help B2B companies track which marketplaces have the potential to gain a leadership position in their respective industries.

Encompassing well over 100 characteristics and attributes, the entire *Gameover Scorecard* is both too detailed and too proprietary to present in this chapter. However, we have distilled the *Gameover Scorecard* down to the 20 most important attributes, organized into four clearly defined steps. These steps are:

1) Define your value added.
2) Build a winning strategy.
3) Assemble a killer team.
4) Assess your market traction.

This abridged *Gameover Scorecard* should serve as a guidebook for anyone seeking to build a winning digital marketplace or evaluating which marketplaces to partner with. Again, these attributes apply whether the marketplace will be developed by a consortia of leading bricks-and-mortar companies, an independent group of entrepreneurs, or a mix of both.

In the next section, we will explore the most important attributes in each of the four steps, provide examples of how to execute against those steps, and conclude with two case studies of digital marketplaces that ICG believes are closing in on Gameover Position in their markets.

Step 1: Define your value added

Sources of customer value	Potential in your market		
	1	2	3
1.1 Cut the administrative costs of buying and selling	Admin costs insignificant relative to value of goods traded	Admin costs over 30% of value of goods traded	Admin costs exceed value of goods for average purchase order
1.2 Help buyers find the suppliers and products they need	Few important buyers/suppliers; commodity products	Fragmented buyers and suppliers; 1000s of SKUs	Fragmented market with 1000s of buyers and suppliers; millions of SKUs
1.3 Help all buyers get the best prices	Similar prices paid by all buyers for similar products	Some buyers pay 10-30% more than others for similar products	Some buyers pay over 30% more than others for similar products
1.4 Reduce inventories and streamline the supply chain	Tightly coupled supply chain; limited inventory reduction potential	Excess inventories prevalent; some offline solutions in place	High demand volatility; little current supply chain integration
1.5 Drive collaboration between buyers and suppliers	Little potential to tailor / differentiate products	Unmet customer needs for tailored products	Individual customer needs vary widely; value in tailoring
1.6 Total economic value creation potential within 3-5 years	Under $1 billion in economic value	$1 to $5 billion in economic value	Over $5 billion in economic value creation potential

The first step in the path to Gameover Position is to determine how you are going to create the most value for customers in your target market. In fact, being totally explicit about your target customers and value proposition is critical as it both influences the likelihood that you can establish Gameover Position and the future value of your company if you get there. As such, Step 1 of the *Gameover Scorecard* is all about your customers' ROI.

Simply put, winning digital marketplaces will be the ones that unlock the greatest value and deliver the highest ROI to their buyers, suppliers, and distributors. While this is certainly a fundamental precept for most savvy business managers, it is nevertheless an important theme to reiterate given the 'build it and they will come' attitude that many now-floundering dot.com businesses started with. In fact, ICG believes that delivering sizable, rapid, and measurable bottom-line impact for your customers must become your business's stated mission if you want to achieve Gameover Position.

Ultimately, the digital marketplace that wins the race to unlock the greatest economic value will secure lasting relationships with the best customers and capture most of the gross profits in its industry. Winning an 'unfair' share of the most aggressive customers in your industry is absolutely critical, as the decisions of these leaders tend to influence the choices of the next tier of customers. Although the exact means to deliver this compelling customer ROI vary by industry, the key ones are:

- cutting administration costs inherent in the order-to-payment cycle for the buyer and the sale-to-collection cycle for the supplier;
- helping fragmented buyers and suppliers find each other;
- aggregating the spending of small and mid-sized businesses to deliver them better prices;
- reducing inventories and manufacturing costs by streamlining the end-to-end supply chain; and
- enabling seamless collaboration in areas such as product development and project management.

A good example of a digital marketplace that figured out how to unlock unprecedented economic value is eMerge Interactive, the leading B2B value chain integrator serving the US beef production industry. While the US beef production market is huge — over $40bn annually — it is highly fragmented with over one million individual businesses producing over 25 million head of cattle each year. The inability to link decisions the producers make (what cows are fed, what they are vaccinated with, and how they are treated) with the quality and safety of the steaks, roasts, and hamburger patties delivered to consumers helps explain the growing number of vegetarians. Further, the wide range of business practices has resulted in a very inefficient supply chain. Industry experts estimate that more than 2.4 billion pounds of beef are wasted annually in the US alone.

eMerge not only recognized that there was a huge opportunity to build and deliver a digital marketplace for the buying and selling of cattle and beef; they were also able to clearly define a unique value proposition — namely, providing information transparency for all industry participants at the individual cow level to lower total supply chain costs, improve beef safety and quality, and enhance animal handling and welfare.

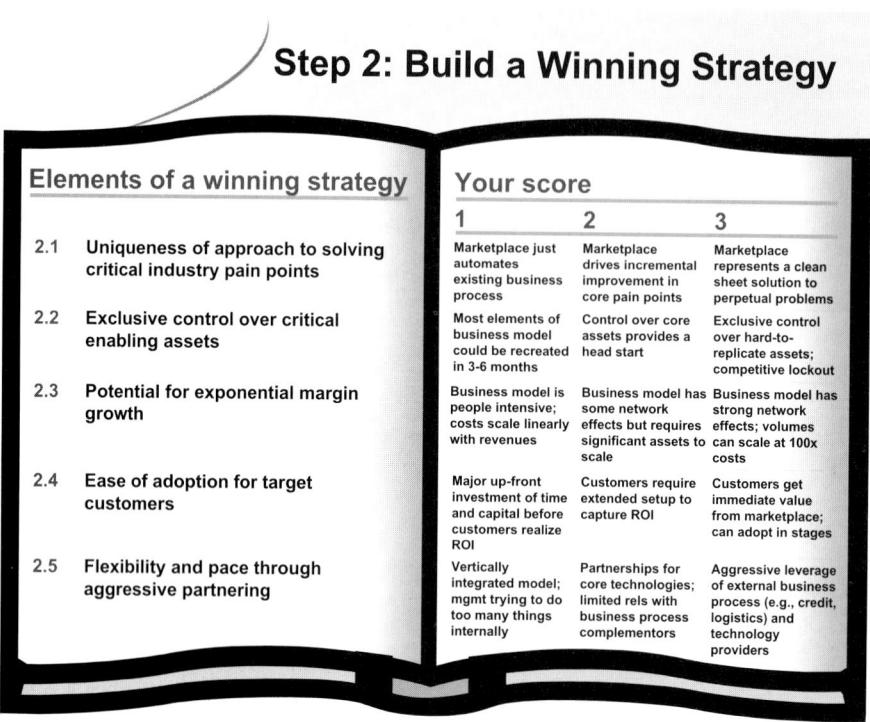

Step 2: Build a Winning Strategy

Elements of a winning strategy	Your score 1	2	3
2.1 Uniqueness of approach to solving critical industry pain points	Marketplace just automates existing business process	Marketplace drives incremental improvement in core pain points	Marketplace represents a clean sheet solution to perpetual problems
2.2 Exclusive control over critical enabling assets	Most elements of business model could be recreated in 3-6 months	Control over core assets provides a head start	Exclusive control over hard-to-replicate assets; competitive lockout
2.3 Potential for exponential margin growth	Business model is people intensive; costs scale linearly with revenues	Business model has some network effects but requires significant assets to scale	Business model has strong network effects; volumes can scale at 100x costs
2.4 Ease of adoption for target customers	Major up-front investment of time and capital before customers realize ROI	Customers require extended setup to capture ROI	Customers get immediate value from marketplace; can adopt in stages
2.5 Flexibility and pace through aggressive partnering	Vertically integrated model; mgmt trying to do too many things internally	Partnerships for core technologies; limited rels with business process complementors	Aggressive leverage of external business process (e.g., credit, logistics) and technology providers

Step 2 en route to Gameover Position involves executing a business strategy that can simultaneously deliver the customer ROI you have identified and establish deep, sustainable competitive advantages that position your digital marketplace to capture a substantial portion of the value you create.

The first element of a winning strategy is to clearly identify the pain points that must be solved for your industry to realize the value of B2B. For example:

- In distributor-centric industries such as industrial MRO or auto repair shops, the pain points tend to be around the inability of buyers to easily find which local distributor has the item they need in stock out of the millions of possible SKUs.
- In commodity industries such as energy and chemicals, the pain point is finding the supplier that can deliver the commodity reliably at the lowest total delivered cost.
- In global supply chains such as apparel or electronics, the pain point may be sourcing and co-ordinating manufacturing from a fragmented set of contractors 12 time zones away.

The second key strategy element is obtaining exclusive control over the critical enabling asset required to solve these pain points — for example, a proprietary commerce-ready catalog in industries with extreme product complexity; a best-in-class software application; or a combination of on-line and off-line assets, or an exclusive commitment for dominant industry volume. Without exclusive control over these critical enabling assets, even digital marketplaces that have identified and solved their industry's pain point have few barriers to entry and little hope of the attractive margins that produce Gameover players.

For example, eMerge created a standardized, centralized system for identifying and tracking the buying and selling of cattle all the way across the supply chain, regardless of where the cattle originates from or where in the country the processed beef ultimately ends up. Similar to the concept of a unique patient record in healthcare, eMerge can track what a cow has been fed, what vaccinations it has received, whether it has ever been sick, how many times it has changed hands, and whether it ever came into contact with other cows that were sick. To create this unique record, eMerge uses a unique cow-tagging technology that provides the equivalent of a bar code for cattle. When combined with a Web-based universal on-line database, eMerge provides supply chain visibility that has never before existed in the beef industry.

Leveraging the network effects for potential exponential growth is another important winning element. The current value of a digital marketplace is the discounted value of its future cash flows from transaction, advertising, subscription, and value-added services fees. For some business models that are people-intensive, the costs of growing the marketplace increase linearly with revenues producing a much less attractive cash flow picture than other business models where revenues can scale very quickly with little incremental cost.

It is also important to make it easy for your target customers to adopt the technologies required to use your digital marketplace. For example, many winning marketplaces are providing customers a migration path for their existing business processes by offering both private and public marketplaces based on the same platform. The private marketplace option enables a buyer to keep their existing supply relationships 'closed' while leveraging the integration benefits of the standard platform. Over time, these same buyers will tend to use the public marketplace in parallel to meet their spot needs and to calibrate their existing suppliers.

Finally, partnering is a critical element in your ability to implement a winning business strategy. This is particularly important in the first one-to-two years of existence when your internal efforts need to remain focused on developing core capabilities and competencies. For example, ICG operates its $9bn business with under 200 employees. In fact, ICG's internal mantra is that every employee's job function must directly influence the company's core value proposition of building the best businesses in B2B. Activities that are not central to this goal are outsourced to best-in-class vendors. Ultimately, this enables ICG to remain nimble, lean, and flexible enough to react quickly to market shifts.

The same rule applies to creating a winning marketplace strategy — focus your efforts on the core activities where you can truly differentiate yourself from your competitors and partner with others to gain access to complementary products and services.

ICG Commerce is a good example of a digital marketplace that is well on its way to creating a winning position with the help of strategic partnerships. ICG Commerce was co-founded by ICG and entrepreneur Rick Berry, who built PSI, a procurement consulting firm that was already helping companies like Schering-Plough save $100mn a year on purchases. ICG had decided to build a new type of company, called a total procurement services provider, that was part strategic sourcing consultancy, part software firm, and part digital marketplace. It would use Internet technology and world-class procurement approaches to help large and mid-sized corporations save money on their purchases of a very broad range of goods and services. The core of the offering would be the delivery of optimal pricing from a preferred supplier base through the aggregation of volume. Together, ICG, Berry, and his PSI team set out to build this new type of company.

ICG acquired a majority stake in PSI and re-launched it as ICG Commerce. ICG Commerce immediately partnered aggressively for enabling technologies (eg, RightWorks and CommerceQuest); consulting and systems integration (eg, Breakaway Solutions); and access to leading supplier networks (eg, e-Chemicals). This partnering approach positioned ICG Commerce to deliver value for its customers much sooner than it would have if it had tried to build these parts of its business in-house. The results are outstanding, with growth from 30 to 400 employees in just six months; the rapid creation of a global footprint across North America, Europe, and Asia; and an expected 100-plus customers at the end of its first full year of operations.

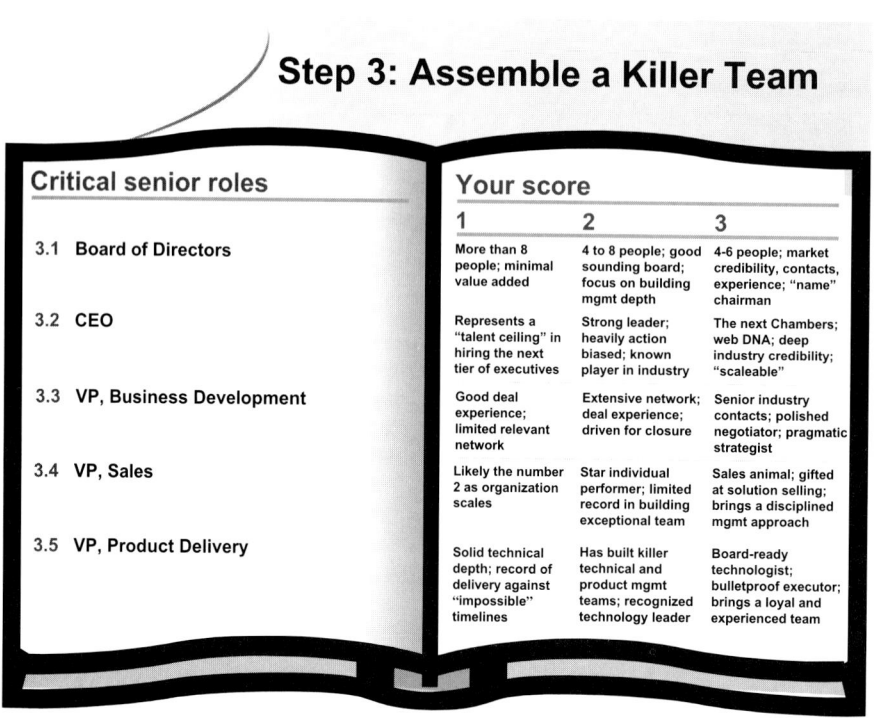

Step 3: Assemble a Killer Team

Critical senior roles	Your score		
	1	2	3
3.1 Board of Directors	More than 8 people; minimal value added	4 to 8 people; good sounding board; focus on building mgmt depth	4-6 people; market credibility, contacts, experience; "name" chairman
3.2 CEO	Represents a "talent ceiling" in hiring the next tier of executives	Strong leader; heavily action biased; known player in industry	The next Chambers; web DNA; deep industry credibility; "scaleable"
3.3 VP, Business Development	Good deal experience; limited relevant network	Extensive network; deal experience; driven for closure	Senior industry contacts; polished negotiator; pragmatic strategist
3.4 VP, Sales	Likely the number 2 as organization scales	Star individual performer; limited record in building exceptional team	Sales animal; gifted at solution selling; brings a disciplined mgmt approach
3.5 VP, Product Delivery	Solid technical depth; record of delivery against "impossible" timelines	Has built killer technical and product mgmt teams; recognized technology leader	Board-ready technologist; bulletproof executor; brings a loyal and experienced team

The quality of the executive management team and business advisors you attract into your business will determine your success or failure in executing your gameover business strategy. While there are many important team members, ICG considers the most critical roles to be the board of directors, CEO, and executives responsible for business development, sales, and product development.

One important general attribute to look for when recruiting business executives and board members is their inherent ability to scale as the job grows. In other words, it is important to attract and hire people who are fully capable of running the organization as it grows to 10 times, or 100 times, in customer base and business volume. You need to look for both past experience in organizations much larger than what you have currently built, as well as intrinsic qualities of leadership, aggressiveness, and business maturity.

To attract such stellar employees, you must understand and effectively articulate the first two steps in the *Gameover Scorecard* — defining your value added and creating a winning strategy. In fact, the more compelling your vision of transforming the way businesses operate in your industry, the easier it is to recruit outstanding people.

Resist the traditional wisdom that great businesses require thousands of people. This bias for 'throwing more people at it' forces you to accept 'average' performers. Digital marketplaces are incredibly high-leverage businesses that can deliver enormous impact with relatively few people, so you can afford to be very aggressive in only hiring the best. Every industry has latent entrepreneurs that view the B2B transformation as their opportunity to leave their mark on their sector. Seek these people out to form the core of your team.

Start right from the top by recruiting a world-class board of directors. To get the most value from your board, keep it small and fill it with seasoned, experienced business people who can provide sharp focus and expert guidance along the way. ICG believes the ideal number of board member seats is between four and six, with eight being the maximum before vibrant discussion and active involvement wanes. A great board adds its own level of credibility to your business and should be proactive about securing key partnerships and landing critical reference customers.

Perhaps the toughest role to fill, your CEO must be a strong leader; one who is heavily action-biased and a 'known player' in the industry. More that that, to drive your marketplace into Gameover Position, the CEO needs to posses a unique combination of qualities — vision, pragmatism, drive, energy, charisma, and more — that can propel him or her to become one of the recognized innovators in your industry.

Below the CEO, the three most critical positions are the VPs of Business Development, Sales, and Product Delivery. The VP of Business Development must not only have expertise in building strategic alliances to get you access to complementary products and capabilities; he or she must also work with the VP of Sales to ensure appropriate channel partners are in place to reach your target customers quickly. Examples of these partners include systems integrators, industry-focused software companies, and leading off-line distributors and intermediaries.

The VP of Sales must be the quintessential 'sales animal', able to communicate your value proposition in your customers' terms. Digital marketplaces are not a simple sell; they are more akin to selling major enterprise software or large systems integration contracts with multiple layers of decision-makers and the need for a solution selling approach. Look for past experience with this type of selling, as well as a knowledge of working through channels to reach more customers more quickly.

Finally, the VP of Product Delivery must have two key skills. First, he or she must be the senior executive charged with constantly bridging the gap between the customers' evolving requirements and your organization's ability to deliver on time and on budget. This person must balance being the voice of reason in not over-committing, while also out-pacing your competitors in adding new functionality, products, and value-added services. In parallel, the VP of Product Delivery must build an elite team of in-house technical talent and individuals that work with your go-to-market partners. A past track record of attracting and retaining outstanding technical talent is a good indicator of whether you have selected the right person for this role.

Step 4: Assess Your Market Traction

Elements of market traction		Your score		
		1	2	3
4.1	Share of "best" customer commitments	Clear gap versus competitors in wins with most important customers	Market share of "best" customers evenly divided with closest competitor	Market share leader in commitments from the key reference customers in the industry
4.2	Leadership in current net revenues and growth rate	Net revenues lagging market leader; competitor is emerging industry standard	Clear lead in net revenues today; net revenue growth rate similar to closest competitor	Net revenue leader today; net revenues growing at 3x the rate of closest competitor
4.3	Third-party perception of market leadership	Viewed as "second tier" by analysts and industry leaders	Consistently described as one of top 3 players by analysts and industry leaders	Consistently viewed as category leader by analysts; always on customer short-lists
4.4	Access to public acquisition currency	IPO more than 12 months away	IPO likely within 12 months; no other player public in your market	Already public; market cap at least 3x any public competitors

So you have clearly defined and articulated your customer value added and ROI proposition for your marketplace. You have built a winning business strategy that, once executed, has enabled you to create real business value for your customers while also allowing you to rapidly grow sustainable margins, not just revenues, for yourself. And you have assembled an exceptional team of business executives that have delivered in the face of tough competition. But are you on track to capturing Gameover position in your winner-takes-most market?

Each stage of building a digital marketplace requires you to be intellectually honest with yourself and your management team about your true competitive position. In a world where you need to attract scarce talent and capital, there can be a strong tendency to start 'believing your PowerPoint' instead of listening to what your customers and those who influence your potential customers are saying. Resist this temptation within your senior team by agreeing up front on the objective measures you will use to track your progress toward Gameover Position.

While there are a number of crucial business metrics and milestones for assessing market traction, this early in the game the four most important ones are:

- your market share of the customer volume commitments;
- the pace at which your net revenue is growing;
- your perceived market leadership as judged by industry and financial analysts; and
- access to public acquisition currency to drive and consolidate your market.

First and foremost, you must be able to accurately assess who is getting the lion's share of the best customers in your market. And by 'best' customers, we don't necessarily mean the biggest customers. We mean the customers that are the most aggressive in assessing their options and that will serve as a proxy for other industry leaders. In addition to helping you drive the next wave of customers and revenues, best customers propel product innovation — pushing you to develop or enhance features and capabilities for them faster than your competitors. This pressure ensures that you are always in the lead when it comes to product innovation.

In terms of assessing the pace at which your revenues are growing, ICG believes that gross transaction revenues is not a particularly useful metric. What really matters is net revenues — that is, the revenue that 'sticks' to your digital marketplace, not the gross value of the products and services bought and sold. This is the best measure of your value added as perceived by the people that matter — your customers. You should review net revenues in terms of absolute dollars versus plan; rate of change quarter-over-quarter; and versus the best data you can find on the net revenues of your competitors.

Ultimately, you are looking for evidence of network effects kicking in within your marketplace. This drives your marketplace to pull away from your competitors and put you in Gameover Positio

The next important metric for assessing market traction is to objectively look at how you are perceived in the industry. Are you consistently mentioned by industry and financial analysts as one of the top three players? Do you always make the short list when industry leaders are evaluating which digital marketplace to partner with? Have you attained measurable, recognized status as the category leader?

Hire the best PR people you can find. Read every analyst report you can get your hands on. Look at how and where you are mentioned in the business press and trade media. Who do these people say you compete with? How do they think you stack up? If you are not being mentioned, or if you are being characterized differently than your desired positioning, take responsibility for proactively changing that perception.

In today's highly competitive Internet marketplace, mergers and acquisitions (M&A) have become an essential tool that B2B companies can use to significantly accelerate traction in their markets. In fact, M&A is an excellent way to fill gaps in current services or offerings or, more importantly, to acquire the necessary assets and competitive lock-out to move into Gameover Position.

However, even in these times of more sane stock market valuations, your ability to leverage M&A aggressively requires access to a public stock currency. Ultimately, in the race to Gameover, those companies with the ability to quickly acquire the assets they need using their own stock have a distinct advantage. This puts a significant premium on both being the first marketplace in your sector to go public and on continually extending the gap between your market valuation and that of your closest competitor. In short, your market cap determines whether you will be the consolidator or the consolidatee in your industry.

In Summary

Digital marketplaces promise to unlock economic value in new and unprecedented ways while also fundamentally transforming the way businesses interact, communicate, and conduct commerce. At the same time, competition between digital marketplaces in any given industry is a winner-takes-most battle — meaning that once the leading digital marketplace gets to critical mass, the second- and third-tier players will be relegated to niche positions with much less attractive value propositions and economic prospects. Once this competitive lockout occurs, the game is essentially over.

A digital marketplace puts itself in Gameover Position when it addresses the most critical industry pain points through exclusive control over critical assets en route to becoming the *de facto* standard for B2B commerce in its industry. As a result, a winning digital marketplace will be able to define the standards for how information is shared and commerce is conducted. It will be able to capture the lion's share of liquidity and be first to critical mass. It will demonstrate exponential economics that make it the most valuable company in its space by an order of magnitude. And it will use its public stock currency to consolidate its market.

With years of experience and expertise focused on what it takes to build a winning digital marketplace, ICG's *Gameover Scorecard for Digital Marketplaces* represents the accumulation of industry-tried, tested, and proven methodologies, best practices, and business principles for helping digital marketplaces establish a dominant position in their markets.

Whether your company is a pure dot.com or a click-and-mortar hybrid, whether you are building a digital marketplace or deciding which ones to partner with, ICG's *Gameover Scorecard* can help you create more shareholder value more quickly in B2B.

Case Study 1: A Revolution in the Beef Industry

eMerge Interactive (www.emergeinteractive.com) is the leading B2B value chain integrator serving the US beef-production industry. The company's strategy is to revolutionize the beef production process and unlock previously unrealized value in the nation's beef supply system via eMerge's efficient e-marketplace, powerful information-management standards, and value-enhancing technologies.

Overall, the US beef industry represents a $95bn annual market, with the production side alone currently valued at $40bn. However, the cattle and beef production industry is highly fragmented and widely dispersed, encompassing over one million individual businesses nationwide. This fragmentation forces cattle producers, feedlots, and packers to operate in information vacuums. As a result, the cattle production chain is plagued by excessive animal transportation and handling, additional transaction costs, reduced beef quality, and product safety concerns. In total, industry experts have identified over $2bn in annual waste that stems directly from these supply chain inefficiencies.

eMerge recognized a huge opportunity to deliver information technology and tools that could help all the participants in the cattle industry lower supply chain costs, improve beef safety and quality, and even enhance animal handling and welfare.

Today, eMerge powers the world's most widely used on-line cattle-sales service; in addition, it has as developed state-of-the-art enterprise and supply chain management systems, and exclusive on-line content and analysis tools. Using these tools, eMerge clients are able to eliminate inefficiencies in the beef production supply chain, improve cattle health and genetics management, and even implement electronic source and process verification for their processed beef inventory.

eMerge focused its initial efforts on the US's 700 feedlots, which lie at the core of the beef production chain. The company also targeted the 250,000 beef producers that stand to extract the most value from a B2B-enabled supply chain. Because they were working from within the middle of the production chain, eMerge was able to penetrate the information vacuums in each segment (the producers, feedlots, and packers), and electronically integrate the overall marketplace. Ultimately, this eliminated unnecessary intermediaries, reduced animal stress and handling, and improved the overall quality of beef.

Further, with eMerge's ability to verify what each head of cattle has been fed and vaccinated with, the end customer is able to rely on claims that the beef they are buying as 'organic', 'hormone-free', or 'kosher' really is. Similarly, producers that deliver these differentiated classes of beef will see the results of their labor in higher prices. Consumers have already shown a willingness to pay substantially more for beef that more closely matches their tastes. For example, in many markets, consumers pay 50% to 80% more per pound for certified organic beef than for regular beef. This 'decommoditization' of the beef industry, and the ability to raise the total revenues of the industry, may well be the single greatest outcome of eMerge's end-to-end value chain solution.

The take-up of eMerge by the leading beef industry players has been exceptionally quick. eMerge's on-line exchange currently brings together thousands of cattle buyers and sellers through the CattleinfoNet portal. Its products and services are already being used by more than 50% of the nation's top 200 feedyards, which control 65% of the US beef cattle market, and its CattleinfoNet already hosts the industry's largest on-line inventory of cattle while serving as a source of proprietary information for beef-business professionals.

Case Study 2: The Promise of e-Procurement Made Real

ICG Commerce (www.icgcommerce.com) began in 1992, when Rick Berry, a Harvard MBA, started a procurement consulting firm called PSI. An aggressive entrepreneur, Berry quickly proved that he could improve a company's bottom line, and when he and his team of expert consultants helped Schering-Plough save $100mn a year on purchases, other corporations began to take notice.

Separately, ICG had formed an internal team in the fall of 1999 to identify the next wave of e-procurement businesses that would build on top of the heavy software infrastructure investments being made by major corporations. In a nutshell, ICG saw corporations with a lot of the 'I' in ROI but little of the 'R' to show for their e-procurement efforts. After talking to a range of early adopter customers, ICG identified a new space that was one part strategic sourcing consultancy, one part software firm, and one part digital marketplace. This hybrid, ICG believed, would be able to deliver a simple, compelling value proposition: the ability to efficiently buy core categories of goods and services on customers' behalf at lower costs than they could obtain internally. When they met in late 1999, the meeting of the minds between ICG's Bob Pollan and Rick Berry was immediate.

ICG acquired a majority stake in PSI and re-launched it as ICG Commerce with the goal of applying Internet and information technology to Barry's purchasing procurement expertise so that large and mid-sized corporations could more quickly capitalize on the benefits of e-procurement. ICG Commerce began to develop partnerships with top vertical exchanges across all industries, including those in ICG's network. Today, ICG Commerce serves a horizontal market and acts as a connector for other vertically-focused ICG partner companies.

ICG Commerce has grown to include a staff of over 100 strategic sourcing professionals with expertise in over 70 categories, supply chain professionals with expertise across all major industries, technology professionals that specialize in connectivity with leading enterprise software and ERP systems, and dedicated customer care/account management professionals who work closely with organizations to get the most possible from e-procurement.

With ICG Commerce, customers are able to realize significant unit-cost savings through strategic sourcing while also aggregating purchases for even greater volume price savings — all of which results in tremendous reductions in both transaction-processing costs and the direct costs of the products themselves.

ICG Commerce's unique and comprehensive delivery of e-procurement is fundamentally revolutionizing the way purchasing is done on-line, and is shifting the manner in which buyers and sellers interact. ICG Commerce's unique value proposition addresses the totality of its customers' purchasing needs, from assessment and strategic sourcing to transaction processing and analysis for continuous improvement.

Because ICG Commerce provides Web applications as part of its service and employs low-cost, any-to-any connectivity, buyers and suppliers can more quickly and easily integrate their operations and legacy systems. Implementation is faster too, since ICG Commerce purchasing teams and suppliers sit down at the table right away. On the front end, customers can sign on to ICG Commerce's on-line purchasing applications and begin buying from catalogs immediately. They pay a low transaction fee for the service and technology, and in return receive personal service and face-to-face, telephone or on-line support from category-specific purchasing professionals.

ICG Commerce built into its business model a win-win scenario for suppliers. ICG Commerce understands the important role suppliers play in the on-line procurement equation, something that ICG Commerce competitors ignored. ICG Commerce differentiated itself by offering a new channel for suppliers — bringing them the winning combination of greater business volume, reduced sales and transaction costs, and accelerated payment.

ICG Commerce also serves as a company's virtual buying team, configuring its services to work with clients in whatever manner makes the most sense. Some choose to maintain their own purchasing departments; others simply outsource that function to ICG Commerce. Either way, ICG Commerce is leveraging the Internet to put more purchasing power and expertise on a company's doorstep. One significant benefit is automated purchase aggregation, where similar purchases from several companies are combined into high-leverage deals, providing the best volume pricing to all participants. Through ICG Commerce's service, any organization can buy like a Fortune 500 company, and therefore leverage cost savings advantages across their entire range of corporate purchases.

Todd Hewlin is a Managing Director at Internet Capital Group. He focuses on helping ICG's partner companies implement business strategies that drive both rapid growth and sustainable competitive advantage. The Gameover Scorecard for Digital Marketplaces that he developed has been adopted as a strategic framework by many ICG companies. Todd is also responsible for the ongoing evolution of ICG's strategy as a member of its senior executive team. He has been featured in numerous publications, including Fortune, Information Week, *and* The Economist, *and speaks frequently at leading industry events.*

Prior to joining ICG, Todd was a partner with McKinsey & Company, a global management consultancy. During his six years at McKinsey, he led technology-intensive strategy projects for leading organizations worldwide. Todd's clients included leading technology companies, an Internet bank, a global satellite telephony start-up, and a range of traditional players who were wrestling with the impact of the Internet. These clients spanned McKinsey's San Francisco, Silicon Valley, New York, Toronto, London, Amsterdam, Sydney, and Seoul offices. Todd also co-led McKinsey's global Electronic Commerce practice.

Earlier in his career, Todd founded an IT consulting firm that created workflow applications for large corporate clients. One of his early applications to automate the reuse of telecom switching equipment produced over $25mn in annual hard-dollar savings for a $1mn total installed cost.

Chapter 3:
Building Brand and Community

Arthur B. Sculley and W. William A. Woods

Branding

Building a strong brand name is very helpful in achieving domination by making sure that your name stands out in the crowd. The NYSE's brand is powerful in the securities industry in the US and abroad, and Nasdaq struggles to compete with the pull of the 'Big Board'. In the paper industry, PaperExchange has already established a strong brand, as has e-Chemicals in the chemicals business in the US.

One element of branding is the choice of name. In many cases this will be driven by what Internet domain names are still available, so make sure you check what is available first. It helps if the name is short, memorable and, above all else, pronounceable! Moai (pronounced 'Mow Eye') is a good example of a strange-sounding name that works. Their website explains that the company is named after the giant stone statues found on Easter Island and that they chose the name because the statues 'instil in us a deep sense of wonder ...they remind us to think big and wild — to dare to do the impossible'.

One danger in choosing a name, though, is being too product-specific at the start. Initially, this may help in building brand recognition within your chosen vertical, but it can later become constraining as you expand the exchange into other complementary verticals and outgrow the name. For example, PaperExchange is very product-specific. The alternative is to choose a more general catchy name, such as Tradeout.com.

The Catastrophe Risk Exchange has established a strong brand name for 'Catex' in the insurance industry. Initially, their focus was on trading large-value property catastrophe risk contracts (known as 'cat' contracts in the business). However, the name 'Catex' could now be seen as a hindrance as it requires the exchange to constantly explain that they are NOT limited to just catastrophic risk products. CEO Frank Fortunato is quoted in an *Insurance Networking* article as saying that 'a common misconception is that Catex focuses solely on catastrophe exposures …., but Catex actually facilitates various risks, including environmental liability, marine, aviation, auto insurance, and others; less than 50% of transactions involve catastrophe exposures'. On the other hand, the name 'Catex' is now widely recognized in the industry and a change would require a significant re-branding. Clearly, it helps if you can get an all encompassing name at the start.

The same problem has been highlighted in the B2C world where companies such as eToys and Software.net have found that the name may not suit the company as it grows. In the case of Software.net, the company expanded from just software into game cartridges and some hardware products, so it decided to change its name to 'Beyond.com'. On the other hand, a generic name like 'Amazon.com' can continue to work even when the company has expanded from book selling to on-line auctions, music sales, and others.

One option is to make up a name. The industry consortium for the auto industry has abandoned the 'autoexchange'-type descriptive brand for the made-up name 'Covisint' (pronounced KO-vis-int). Apparently, the name is a combination of 'connectivity, collaboration and communication', 'visibility and vision' and 'integration and international' — go figure! Compare this with 'RightWorks', also a made-up name, but one which conveys a clear message about the company's objective of getting disparate systems to work together.

Finally, a good brand must be able to work all over the world, since your B2B exchange may well be a global business.

Always bear in mind that the correct name is not the only factor in determining success or failure; providing the best customer care and support is much more important in building brand recognition and trust among users.

Building Your Community

As discussed briefly in Chapter 1 of this book, the primary function of an exchange is to provide a centralized pricing mechanism and market space. However, successful B2B exchanges will grow beyond this and develop into fully-fledged exchange communities. This means that they will provide the services that allow people in the same vertical to network effectively and to access all the business information they require in one place.

In their groundbreaking book entitled *Net Gain: Expanding markets through virtual communities*, John Hagel III and Arthur G. Armstrong made the following observation:

> *The rise of virtual communities in on-line networks has set in motion an unprecedented shift in power from vendors of goods and services to the customers who buy them. Vendors who understand this transfer of power and choose to capitalize on it by organizing virtual communities will be richly rewarded with both peerless customer loyalty and impressive economic returns. But the race to establish the virtual community belongs to the swift: those who move quickly and aggressively will gain —and likely hold — the advantage.*

In 1997, when they wrote those words, the main impact of the Internet and virtual communities had been in the B2C and C2C space. Most businesses were not embracing the Internet and the first B2B exchanges were just being set up. Accordingly, their insights were mainly made in the context of on-line, consumer-oriented communities. However, their insights about setting up virtual communities apply equally to B2B applications.

Successful B2B exchanges will become powerful virtual communities.

1. *The six Cs of on-line services*

Steve Case, the CEO of America Online, is partly famous for identifying the six 'Cs' that make up a complete on-line service, namely:

- content;
- context;
- community;
- communications;
- connectivity; and
- commerce.

B2B exchanges must build all of these in order to create a valuable trading community:

- *commerce* — the centralized market space;
- *content* — trading data, pricing, product information, industry-specific news, etc;
- *context* — specialization in a vertical;
- *community* — added-value services that attract and hold new users;
- *communications* — the ability for members to meet each other and communicate with each other on-line; and
- *connectivity* — use of open, Web-based applications so that members can use the Internet to connect to the exchange.

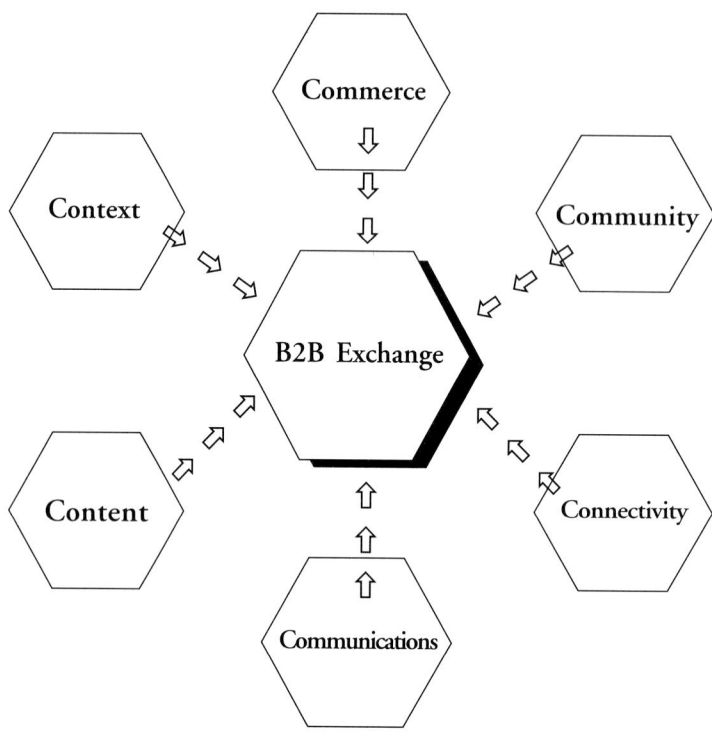

It is critical that a B2B exchange does not try to build its own network, but rather ensures that all its systems are on the Internet and that it offers its trading mechanism on the World Wide Web — since these are then open systems that are accessible by all.

2. Establishing a trading community

The first thing an exchange needs to establish is the appropriate trading mechanism. This may be as a catalog aggregator, a post-and-browse model, an auction mechanism, or a fully-electronic auto-matching system.

This centralized market space must be the exchange's core competency.

Next, the exchange needs to focus on signing up as many users as possible, as quickly as possible. Only then can the exchange add value by building a community. However, in all cases it is important for the exchange to expand on this core market space capability as quickly as possible.

The order of these stages is the direct reverse of the B2C and C2C community model where it is necessary to establish the community before the members are likely to transact between themselves.

With business-to-business exchange communities, the initial magnet is the commerce function; the community then develops around that.

In the process of signing up users, we have identified the need to smother potential users and signed-up members with customer care and support. Excellent customer care is critical in establishing the strength of your brand, creating user loyalty, and thus building a sense of community.

In *Net Gain*, Hagel and Armstrong identified three stages of entry in building a community and getting to a revenue-earning position. The first 'gate' which a virtual community must pass through is generating traffic (getting target community members to travel to your site). For a B2B exchange, this stage involves the establishment of the trading mechanism and the signing up of members to trade in the centralized market space.

The second 'gate' involves concentrating traffic (getting them to spend increasing time in the community). For B2B exchanges, this stage requires the addition of community services that engage the trading members and add value for them, such as:

- fostering relationships and networking between industry players; and
- aggregating trading data, organizing news feeds, and accumulating member-generated content.

The third stage identified by Hagel and Armstrong is locking in traffic (creating switching barriers that make it increasingly difficult for members to leave the exchange community once they have joined). For a B2B exchange, this third stage involves:

- expanding the exchange's functionality by providing access to third-party services, such as analytical research tools and historical data;
- tailoring the exchange community to individual members' needs by allowing them to customize their experience; and
- integrating member firms' back-office systems with the exchange, or providing back-office logistics within the exchange's website.

3. Enhancing B2B exchange community services

The elements of a B2B exchange community are similar to those which have worked in the B2C and C2C space — after all, businesses are run and managed by individuals — but the focus is on supporting those individuals when they make business decisions, rather than on their personal spending or lifestyles.

All communities need gathering places, and on-line these may be a mailing list, chat room, discussion forum, or conferencing facility.

The types of services that can be added include:

Industry Rolodex: The primary aim of the community service is to enable users in the same vertical space to network together. In the physical world, this normally occurs through specialist magazines, trade shows, and conferences. The B2B exchange can supplement, and even usurp, all of these physical mechanisms. Successful exchanges will add member communication services so that your exchange's address book becomes the 'Rolodex' for your vertical market sector.

News Feeds: Another aim of an exchange community is to give managers all the business information they require to do business in that specific vertical through one central resource and to help them process that information more efficiently. This is enhanced by the provision of customized news feeds that are industry-specific (eg, weather forecasts for commodity producers, shipping news for import and export markets). MetalSite provides news and columns from American Metal Market, Metal Center News, and New Steel.

Directory of Relevant Services and Resources: An organized directory of links to other resources on the network that will assist members of the exchange community, and a directory of buyers and sellers and intermediaries.

Scrolling Ticker: To display new bids and offers, postings, trade information and transaction prices, as well as news headlines in real-time. Any exchange worth its salt has a scrolling ticker.

Bulletin Board: In addition to any trading bulletin board, a general bulletin board for business networking is often a well-used feature and results in member-generated content.

Discussion Forums: Having empowered buyers through the centralized trading mechanism, it will also be important to allow them to communicate with each other, share experiences, and pass on knowledge gained from dealing with different suppliers. MetalSite provides discussion forums that are restricted to registered members only. Again, this creates member-generated content. These forums should be structured as threaded forums that are monitored by a customer care professional.

Industry Newsletters: The exchange should support its users with a customized monthly newsletter, including interesting articles from other publications, and by sending members' monthly e-mail messages to alert them to key new information.

Calendar of Industry Events: For example, PaperExchange has an industry calendar of events.

Job Search and Job Ads: PaperExchange enables users to post job listings and résumés, and PlasticsNet maintains a career center.

Classified Ads: This adds to the networking opportunity on the site. PlasticsNet has an active Classified Ads section for members.

Powerful Search Features: You should offer users a powerful search feature and classify goods and services in a logical way which enables traders to find what they are looking for quickly and easily.

4. Building a membership database

In order to improve the community and customize a user's experience, you will need to build and maintain a member database.

This starts with the system profile that each user is required to complete when they set themselves up as a member and a user of the system. However, the member database can extend over time to monitor the user's use of the exchange and so the profile can evolve.

One way to encourage use of the system is to reward members who trade frequently, by assigning them star ratings within the system. Members may also appreciate a system which allows suppliers' performance to be reviewed and rated by other members. In this way, other members can see which firms or traders are the 'stars' of your exchange and those members' achievements are acknowledged.

5. Becoming the 'Bloomberg' terminal in your vertical

In his autobiographical book *Bloomberg by Bloomberg*, Michael Bloomberg tells the fascinating story of how he set up Bloomberg Financial Services and quickly grew the company into the leading information vendor in the world. At least part of his success is due to his initial focus on the trading of bonds (fixed income securities). Within this vertical, Bloomberg had many years of experience, including being a partner and Head of Information Systems at Salomon Brothers, the large investment bank and bond dealer in New York. Bloomberg developed his terminals with all the historical data, real-time prices, news feeds, and yield curve analysis that the average bond dealer required in order to be able to trade effectively. Accordingly, bond-dealing rooms from New York to Hong Kong could be set up around the Bloomberg terminals as the primary information and dealing system. In much the same way, a B2B exchange should aim to make its website the centralized information source, ie, the equivalent of the 'Bloomberg' terminal, for that particular vertical.

This requires the exchange to ensure, first, that all the real-time pricing and trading data from its centralized market space are readily available for members. This can be achieved by having a scrolling ticker on the site and adding customized e-mail alerts (including wireless application protocol messages for mobile phone users) that advise members when new bids or prices are posted or trades have been made.

Second, the exchange must add streaming news services that are tailored to the needs of traders in that particular vertical. For example, Catex provides a news flash service that highlights any major insured catastrophes and provides a special weather tracking service. In future, it could add live news feed with the latest information and pictures of any insured disasters.

Third, the exchange should build up a database with historical pricing information and provide analytics and research. Analytics are the analytical services that traders require in order to be able to trade more efficiently. These may be specialized pricing models that allow the trader to construct theoretical prices (eg, a Black-Scholes pricing model for options or derivatives), or to test different trading strategies (eg, if he buys so much of product X, how much of product Y must he buy). Research is professional analysis of the market and market trends which can assist buyers and sellers to assess where the market is headed.

6. Documents center

One way of adding value and, at the same time, locking in members, is to standardize the contract terms, terminology, and documents used on the exchange in order to grow the market. This can be done by incorporating a 'documents extranet facility' on the website. In this documents facility, members can post documents for others to access, work on revisions to the contract documents, and download documents to their own computers. Sophisticated documents extranets should:

- allow a posting party to specify which other users can see and/or amend a document on the system;
- automatically alert those people that there is a document in the system for them;
- track revisions and changes;
- inform the posting party when other users access the documents; and
- provide a library with precedent documents and templates that can be used by members.

By providing precedent documents and helping members to draw up contractual documents on its website, the exchange can steer the industry toward more standardized forms and terms. At the same time, it can help to lock the members into your exchange whilst building barriers to entry for any potential competitors.

Additionally, for complex transactions, a secure communications service which facilitates collaboration (such as IntraLinks' DealSpace) will greatly assist the members in closing their trades.

7. Logistics and systems integration

In addition to the centralized market space, a B2B exchange can offer various centralized back-office and logistics systems or arrange to host the members' systems on its central hardware.

In the securities world, some smaller stock exchanges have purchased a fully-automated middle and back-office brokerage system that the exchange then operates on behalf of the broker members. This enables new trading members to get up and running quickly, since they do not have to buy their own systems, and ensures that they are committed to staying with the exchange.

For B2B exchanges that trade physical products, this can include the provision of invoicing, accounting, and purchase order generation services by the exchange (eg, ChemConnect.com). Enabling users to ship goods, track orders, and handle all of the logistics of delivery on-line, through the website, also helps to lock users into an exchange.

8. *Sophisticated financial services*

More sophisticated financial services can be added as the exchange develops, including:

- credit for buyers;
- credit analysis, credit enhancement, or credit insurance for sellers;
- payment processing;
- receivables management;
- insurance or warranties;
- shipping, warehousing, and inspection services;
- political risk insurance for international trades; and
- foreign currency services to minimize currency risk.

9. *Sophisticated securities such as derivatives*

Successful B2B exchanges can create indices and develop derivative products that help the members to hedge their physical positions or protect themselves from future price changes.

The first indices can be a historical weighted average of all transactions completed on the exchange for a specific product or a specific term, or in respect of a given region. Initially, the indices should be calculated for the most commonly traded product or combination of products within each category or region. Once an index has been developed, it can be traded in the form of an options or futures contract in which the value of the derivative contract is based on the level of the index at a specific future time.

For example, Catex may be able to create catastrophe risk indices based on the prices of given types of reinsurance deals made in their system and license those indices to insurance companies, investment banks, and/or derivatives exchanges for the trading of options or futures contracts. Those derivative contracts would enable the reinsuring companies to hedge their exposure on the underlying reinsurance contracts.

As the US deregulates electricity along the lines of the Scandinavian model, electricity may become one of the most actively traded commodities. In this vertical, Houstonstreet and Altra are vying for market dominance. Traders deal in electricity on a wholesale basis, buying it from power producers and selling to local utilities or to investors who take speculative positions. Each megawatt hour (MWH) produced gets traded many times before it is consumed. Electricity prices can swing from US$10 to US$1000 per MWH depending on the temperature, the time of day, and TV viewing habits — for example, as usage peaks during unusual heat waves or cold spells. In order to smooth out these huge price spikes, producers must manage the risk using derivatives with active participation from major financial market makers.

Houstonstreet is developing Forward Physical Electricity Contracts which enable power producers to hedge their exposure to sudden and dramatic shifts in the price of electricity based on such unforeseeable variables as weather changes or catastrophic events.

This would be a purely financial market for price hedging, risk management, and trade in forward and future power contracts. The trading time horizon is up to three or more years; contracts will be divided into weeks, blocks, seasons, and years.

10. The upcoming convergence of B2B exchanges and traditional stock exchanges

Many of these new markets are starting by providing Internet trading mechanisms for physical products such as plastics, chemicals, and metals. Others are already focused on trading financial products such as forward contracts or securitized products. For example, CreditTrade is trading credit derivatives, and Houstonstreet.com is trading forward contracts on electricity, oil, and gas. However, all of these markets are keen to introduce financial products that can enhance the suppliers' and buyers' use of their system by providing hedging, risk management, and speculative opportunities. In order to trade financial products, exchanges need a powerful electronic trading capability, a central counter-party for clearing and settlement, and a strong regulatory framework. These are the three key strengths of traditional securities exchanges and create the value proposition for B2B exchanges to link with traditional securities exchanges.

11. Accessing content

Since time to market is critical, a B2B exchange should not delay its launch until it has all of these community services fully developed; rather, it should launch the basic trading service and seek to 'buy-in' or add as many of them as possible, as quickly as possible.
Examples of third-party service providers are:

- networking, forums, scheduling, and other 'group-ware' services (eg, Realcommunities.com, Koz.com);
- customized news feeds (Bloomberg, Reuters, and industry-specific news sources);
- logistics and supply chain management (eg, i2 Technologies, freightwise.com, Skyway.com);
- escrow services (eg, i-escrow.com);
- credit analysis (eg, ecredit.com);
- document management (eg, IntraLinks.com); and
- personalized stock tickers (eg, Yahoo! Finance on PaperExchange.com).

In addition, member-generated content is critical to building a sense of ownership and involvement amongst users.

Member-generated content will come through the addition of bulletin boards, threaded discussion forums, and communication services.

12. *User group feedback*

User groups are a perfect way for different users to have input.

One user group that all B2B exchanges should have is a systems user group to ensure that management is always receiving feedback on the website and other IT systems of the exchange from the actual users of those systems. Another common user group is the trading and settlement committee, which should have representatives of the buyers, sellers, and intermediaries and approve the trading and settlement rules and regulations of the exchange.

A B2B exchange should hold regular meetings of these user groups to obtain feedback on the systems and the community functions of the exchange so that they can be customized and improved.

William Woods is the CEO of the Bermuda Stock Exchange. Arthur Sculley is a partner in Sculley Brothers LLC. Together they have co-authored the best-selling book B2B Exchanges: The Killer Application in the Business-to-Business Internet Revolution *(ISI Publications). William can be reached at william@b2bexchanges.com and Arthur at arthur@b2bexchanges.com.*

2

Business ◄——► Business

Aerospace • Agriculture • Auto • Chemicals • Electronics • Construction
Energy • Financial • Food & Beverage • Travel • Industrial Equipment
Transportation • Media • Printing • Real Estate • Food Service • Retail

Exchange Fundamentals

Chapter 4:
Supply Chain Management

Chris Renner, Founder, INC2inc Technologies and Jeff Schutt, CSC Consulting

B2B exchanges, in essence, are meant to bring greater efficiency to trading partners. Three primary models for exchanges have emerged: the catalog model, the auction model, and the bid/ask exchange model. Interestingly, all three models have focused initially and primarily on price discovery — bringing the best price to both the buyer and the seller at any given point in time. While price discovery remains the primary attractor to many exchange participants today, we believe that for many industries, the true power of an exchange lies in the ability to provide a more complete supply chain solution to exchange participants, addressing not only the buying, but the planning and fulfillment as well.

Depending on the industry, greater savings may result from streamlining the actual procurement process than from simply negotiating a better price. Helping participants decide what to buy, how much to buy, and when to buy may actually be more relevant than helping them with what price to pay. Within the food and beverage industry, INC2inc recognized this early on, and has focused more on the savings opportunity surrounding the 'cost of purchasing the materials' than on the 'cost of the materials purchased'. We believe that B2B exchanges that deal in physical goods, where product is moved between sellers and buyers, need to address these issues in order to maximize the potential efficiencies presented by supply chain management.

As we have witnessed the evolution of technology and systems architecture, we have seen mainframes give way to distributed applications, and those give way to enterprise applications. And now, enterprise applications may be giving way to industry applications. We believe that the successful, fully integrated exchange providing planning, procurement, and fulfillment may very well prove to be the next generation of the Enterprise Resource Planning (ERP) — becoming what we are calling an IRP, the **Industry Resource Planning** application. As these functions extend beyond the traditional four walls of the enterprise, the neutral industry exchange can engage participants *at the industry level* to centrally manage the communication and facilitation of goods and services.

What is Supply Chain Management?

Supply chains are the participants and linkages that move and process material from its original sources to the users of finished goods (see Figure 1: The Supply Chain). Since supply chains were first recognized in the early 1980s, it has been understood that these chains involved the flow of material down the chain, and the flow of information in both directions. Supply chain management is, of course, the collection of processes and systems necessary to make this chain work effectively: the planning, ordering, customer service, production management, transportation carrier scheduling, order fulfillment, and measurement of performance. Most organizations would consider the flow of their direct material and finished goods to define their supply chain, and would not consider indirect material — such as maintenance, repair, and operating (MRO) items — to be part of their 'supply chain'.

Figure 1: The Supply Chain

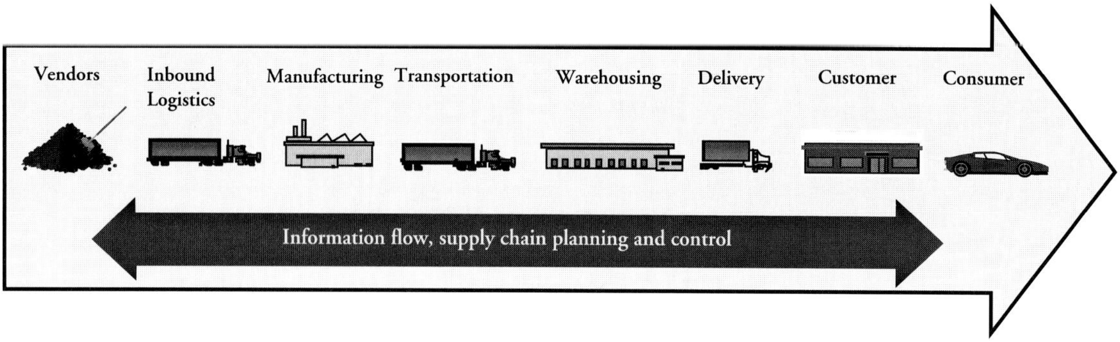

In the world of e-business it has become ever more apparent that a 'chain' is not a perfect metaphor, and that what are really being managed are 'supply nets' in which most participants are buying and selling to many other participants in a very complex way (see Figure 2: A Supply Net). This realization that a network is a better metaphor than a chain is important, because it helps us to see how B2B exchanges can assume central roles in managing the complex, inter-connected relationships of buyers and sellers. Exchanges can handle much of the bi-directional information flow, which has long been key to good supply chain management.

Figure 2: A Supply Net

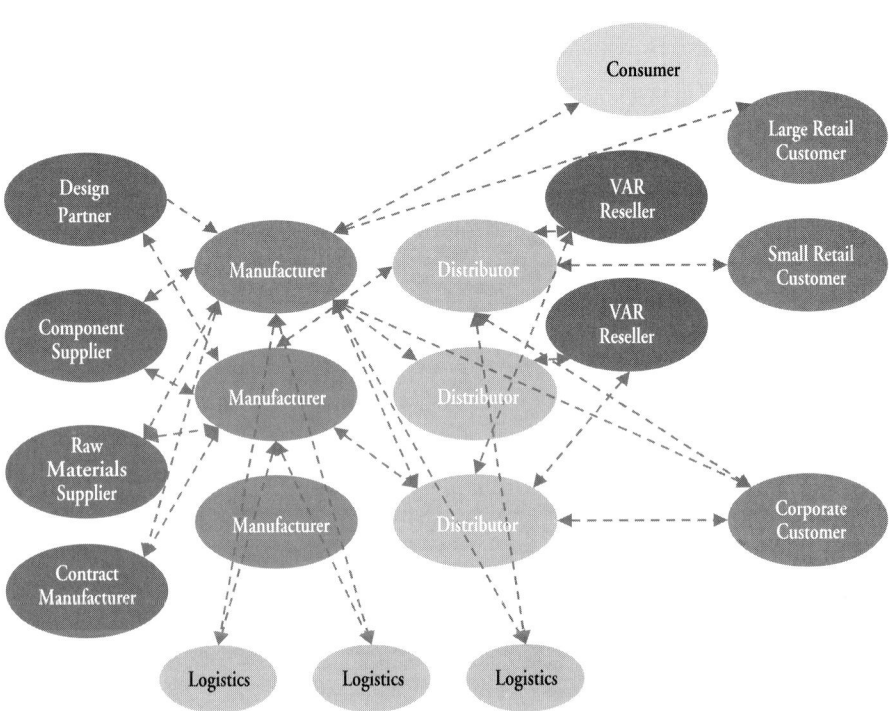

The fundamental economic objective of the supply chain is to provide goods at the end of the chain in the most efficient manner, so as to gain competitive advantage for that chain relative to *other competing chains* and to increase sales and profits for its participants. The broad acceptance of Electronic Data Interchange (EDI) among the largest players in a chain has validated the fact that a lot of information needs to be exchanged among the members of a supply chain. However, the high cost of implementation and maintenance has kept EDI beyond the reach of the vast majority of companies to date.

As the World Wide Web of the Internet has become commercially accepted over the last several years, it has been recognized as a superior method of communications relative to EDI for most purposes. Businesses have rushed to become e-businesses, not just so that they could sell from a website, but so that they could better manage their supply chains. And providers of supply chain management software have rushed to e-enable their systems so that they could support this new way of managing supply chains.

Indeed, as communication up and down the supply chain has become more the norm than the exception, the term 'collaborative commerce' has come into use to reflect the huge amount of planning and other types of communication that occurs via the Web. In this era, it is being recognized that the key virtues for supply chain optimization are:

- **Transparency.** Do your suppliers and customers make available all the data you need to be most efficient?

- **Synchronization of operations.** As data becomes available — for example, retailer point of sale information coming upstream to a manufacturer — operations can be synchronized so that all supply chain participants react to changes together, rather than relying on traditional cues, such as orders, which creates a 'bullwhip' effect in fluctuations (see Reference 1).

- **Velocity of material.** We have been operating with smaller and smaller inventories, meaning greater velocity of material, for years. With synchronized operations, we can reduce inventory further.

- **Flexibility.** In this world of e-business, supply chain relationships can change frequently, both in terms of partners and the business that is being conducted.

- **Community.** Being part of a larger group of market participants, seeing what others are doing, seeing the prices that are being offered, being able to conduct business when appropriate with companies who are not your traditional partners, all have value. Exchanges have been fundamental in creating these types of community virtues.

Supply Chain Management and B2B Exchanges

Not very long ago, some B2B exchange theorists felt that exchanges might replace traditional supply chains by simply providing more efficient price discovery. After all, if transaction costs could be lowered enough in exchanges, why not take advantage of exchanges' ability to find the best price each day for every item being bought and sold? Most B2B transactions could occur on a spot basis, with the buyer and seller having no particular expectation of ever doing business together again.

We believe, however, that the business factors that cause supply chains to be organized and sustained are strong, and unlikely to be completely negated by the dynamic pricing and sourcing aspects of exchanges. These factors include:

- The desire by many businesses to use annual contracts to lock in pricing and guarantees of volume for both buyers and sellers.

- The small number of realistic potential buyers and sellers in many industrial markets — organizations which really have the capability to supply or use the products.

- The unique material quality or capability specifications that are defined between only one buyer and one seller.

- The ability to operate more efficiently by planning continuing supply chain operations, rather than dealing with each transaction as a one-time, isolated business event.

- The continuing validity of the fundamental strategic sourcing premise: that it is usually more efficient to negotiate prices, manage material flow, and control quality with a small set of suppliers who are vitally interested in your business.

Depending on the industry, the value of a strong supply chain may actually represent greater efficiencies than what might be gained through dynamic sourcing. So the question becomes, where are the true savings within an industry, and to what extent can exchange-based supply chain management facilitate those savings?

We believe that exchanges may in fact be the best way to help supply chains achieve many of the virtues introduced above. Exchanges offer efficient ways to achieve higher material velocity and the synchronization that comes from collaboration, flexibility, and community. A B2B exchange does not need to exist principally for price discovery; it can actually help to conduct business more efficiently among participants who have *already found each other*. Indeed, a number of businesses that we have spoken to as potential Net marketplace participants have taken the attitude that they expect to continue to work with their current supply chain partners, but it would be nice to be able to see other players on an exchange and occasionally to check prices or availability with these business 'strangers'. For example, for the 18 months it has existed, INC2inc has focused on strengthening existing relationships rather than on the facilitation of new ones. The result has been early traction as well as an industry validation of our approach.

It can truly be said that supply chains need exchanges, and also that many types of exchanges can benefit by adding capabilities to support supply chains. Why do exchanges need to support supply chain management?

- Many of the supply chain management functions fall easily into the exchange space — for example, the sharing of a supply or a demand forecast between partners.
- These supply chain management functions represent an opportunity for exchanges to add value for their clients that the clients really want.
- Exchanges that provide these services will out-compete and ultimately displace exchanges that do not.

The best way to understand this logic is to examine the major types of supply chain management services that exchanges may offer: supply chain execution, supply chain planning, and product life-cycle management.

Supply Chain Execution

Supply chain execution functions are logistics-oriented business processes including order fulfillment, warehouse management, transportation management, shipment tracking and tracing, and collection of supply chain performance data. They represent the shorter-term, let's-get-the-job-done functions of supply chain management, rather than the longer-horizon planning functions described later.

Let's first consider a vertical industry exchange, as shown in Figure 3, perhaps addressing both the flow of direct material from suppliers to manufacturers and of finished product from manufacturers to distributors and retailers. The exchange designed to support this environment will typically provide for auctions and reverse auctions, seller catalogs, buyer requisitions (orders or releases against a blanket order), buyer management approval, and requisition acceptance by the seller. But many of the early exchanges did not address the actual delivery portion of the transaction — they left that critical step for the buyer and seller to handle elsewhere. In doing so they often forced the buyer and seller to come up with an ad hoc delivery arrangement that does not take advantage of the seller's negotiated transportation rates (which are typically based on guaranteed volume) — in effect, losing in freight costs what might have been gained in the basic exchange transaction.

As INC2inc has addressed the logistics component of the food manufacturing industry, we have identified a tremendous opportunity that deals with the consistent and costly LTL (less than truckload) deliveries that occur between trading partners. By inserting an exchange and centralizing much of the information that flows between these buyers and sellers, we now have visibility to product movement at an industry level that has never before been available. We can now provide a much greater level of efficiency surrounding the shipment of products between parties. Today, manufacturers of food products receive multiple LTL shipments from individual suppliers on a weekly basis — and often these shipments come from the same general area. By combining similar loads traveling to and from similar locations, trading partners can substantially decrease their shipping cost. Moreover, by aggregating the transportation procurement among multiple exchange participants, the exchange also has the ability to negotiate better freight rates for all members. This new opportunity for efficiency is a direct result of the exchange model.

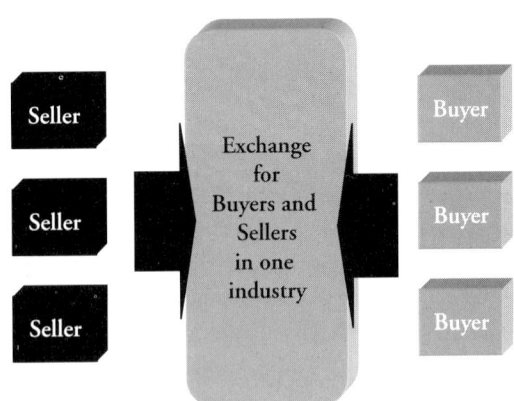

Figure 3: A Vertical Exchange in One Industry

More exchanges are now recognizing the value of offering a distribution solution in order to keep the total cost of doing business low, and to avoid opening the door to competitors. The functions that a distribution solution needs to address include:

- negotiation of rates with transportation suppliers;
- least cost modal and carrier selection;
- determination of ship date, document generation, and load tendering to the carrier;
- communication of an advance ship notice (ASN) and/or shipping notice to the buyer;
- integration of buyers' and sellers' contract carriers into the logistics solution;
- routing guide management;
- carrier optimization, including continuous moves and headhaul/backhaul matching;

- making shipment tracking information available to all participants in the order movement; and
- recording and reporting key logistics performance indicators, including:
  - shipment elapsed time;
  - total order cycle time;
  - completeness of order;
  - overages, shortages, and damage (OS&D);
  - additional charges;
  - on-time delivery; and
  - supporting freight payment and audit.

It should be noted that this list of distribution needs for exchanges tends to focus on transportation rather than warehousing. Warehousing is less commonly a part of an exchange solution, though it is a potential value-add function in certain situations.

How can an exchange meet these distribution needs? As illustrated in Figure 4, the four types of alternatives that should be considered are:

- **Third-party logistics providers.** '3PLs', as they are commonly known in logistics, are organizations that provide comprehensive sets of logistics functions on behalf of their customer, rather than the single function traditionally provided by a freight carrier or a public warehouse operator. Sometimes they own logistics resources of their own (asset-based 3PLs), and sometimes not. In the case of exchanges, perhaps they should be called 'fourth party', since a buyer, a seller, and the exchange are already involved. These organizations can typically meet all the logistics needs of the exchange's clients: transportation via multiple transportation modes and multiple carriers, warehousing, etc. Up until 20 years ago, there was very little available from third-party providers, but today they can manage just about any kind of logistics services. Part of the challenge for a new exchange, however, is getting an established logistics provider to take it seriously in terms of the time and investment necessary to set up a service relationship.

- **Logistics exchanges.** The right solution for a vertically oriented exchange may be a horizontal logistics or transportation exchange serving many different vertical industries that require logistics. A whole category of exchanges now exists to fill the needs of shippers, carriers, and vertical Net markets. Well-known ones include FreightWise, FreightMatrix, and the marketplace services of Logistics.com. They will post loads, conduct auctions, and tender loads to carriers under contract. These exchanges have the advantage of being part of the 'exchange culture', but many are still trying to get their operations established. As these exchanges grow we expect to see many types of services provided, including management of carriers and distribution centers, and provision of software to users.

- **Developing logistics execution capabilities of your own.** So far, few exchanges have chosen to use their precious resources of management time and capital to create their own distribution departments and manage a team of allied carriers themselves. And managing transportation efficiently requires a significant amount of volume. A mature capability also requires a transportation management system (TMS) for carrier management, load assignment, and performance tracking. These systems, which have grown up over the last 10 to 15 years, are today being evolved to better meet the specific needs of exchanges.

- **Application Service Providers (ASP).** Recently a new breed of supply chain execution solution has begun to emerge, perhaps best thought of as combining a TMS with a transportation exchange. These providers offer systems functionality, but the system is supported remotely. They are seeking bricks-and-mortar companies as customers, as well as exchanges. They offer a participant the ability to manage its transportation as a private market and to participate in a larger, user-defined community when it chooses. If a Net market feels that it is large enough to manage and negotiate relationships with carriers itself, but needs systems tools and other services, it can implement a TMS fairly quickly through an ASP and retain some ability to define its own business rules and processes.

Figure 4: Alternatives for Distribution Services

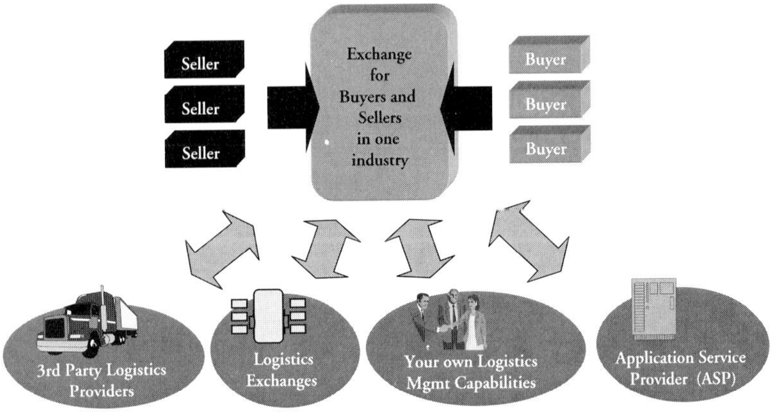

In addition to logistics fulfillment activity, an exchange needs to provide information from sellers to buyers about manufacturing status. The first principle of collaborative commerce introduced above is transparency, and a key example of transparency provided through an exchange is the communication of status information about manufacturing. In a make-to-order environment, an exchange can interact directly with manufacturing control and be told of the scheduled start date, scheduled completion date, and current work in progress associated with each customer's order. Supply chain-oriented exchanges have the security mechanisms in place to make manufacturing information of this type available to the appropriate customer, while keeping it hidden from inappropriate eyes. More sophisticated interaction between buyers and suppliers can also be facilitated by an exchange. For example, an exchange can transmit updated request dates from the buyer to the seller and also attempt to influence manufacturing priority.

In a make-to-stock environment, a manufacturer can make available inventory information as well as production schedules to partnering customers, thus providing additional insight into how much of a given item is likely to be available in the near future. And an exchange can transmit updated material requirements information from the manufacturer's systems to material suppliers as manufacturing schedules change, delivering information immediately to suppliers.

While we have not yet seen an example in practice, an exchange can also be used as a near real-time communications device for co-ordination between suppliers and manufacturers concerning just-in-time (JIT) material deliveries. For example, it is common in the food industry for packaging material to be delivered directly to filling lines on a JIT basis. An exchange that has had responsibility for managing the complete cycle of a material release can also support this last step, co-ordinating the exact time of the arrival of the material at the point of use.

Supply Chain Planning

While some amount of logistics execution support is appropriate for almost every exchange that deals in physical goods, supply chain planning functions are a little more specialized. Public exchanges that deal primarily in one-time spot transactions through auctions or reverse auctions are not typically going to provide a lot of opportunities for planning. Planning is appropriate where a buyer and seller expect to do a continuing stream of business with each other and need to plan how that business can occur efficiently. We see many examples of supply chain planning needs in private and quasi-private exchanges that deal with direct materials.

A private exchange — for example, a procurement portal for a retailer or a manufacturer — has enormous opportunities to plan supply chain activities between the sponsor of the exchange and his upstream and downstream supply chain partners. The private exchange can, in effect, function as an extension of the sponsor's internal supply chain planning.

A vertical quasi-private exchange typically has a moderate number of participants from one industry, both buyers and sellers, and many of them expect to do a continuous stream of business with each other. Certain types of exchange-supported planning are productive in this situation. They can:

- provide visibility of inventory and forecasts between pairs of buyers and sellers;
- provide a mechanism for collaboration between pairs of buyers and sellers on demand and supply, in order to resolve differences;

- identify the need for replenishment of inventory at buyer locations and then either alert the buyer or seller, or actually initiate a replenishment transaction. An exchange can be the driving agent in a pseudo-VMI (Vendor Managed Inventory) relationship, with the exchange itself taking on responsibility for inventory management at the buyer, rather than the traditional approach where the vendor controls inventory;
- provide a conduit for the transmission of available-to-promise and capable-to-promise queries and responses, and perhaps actually perform available-to-promise calculations and make the response for the seller;
- plan transportation usage at a high level (once down at the level of individual order fulfillment, this becomes supply chain execution, as discussed above);
- perform supply/demand co-ordination and sourcing, so that the market can work dynamically to find alternate sources of material when appropriate, split the sourcing of an item if supply is limited from the primary source and there is contractual flexibility to split the source, and optimize costs;
- provide industry-oriented statistics or event data to support demand planning (forecasting);
- report on material procurement by a supplier, so that a big customer a tier down the supply chain can see the full volume of procurement and perhaps use their own influence to obtain better pricing;
- combine projected need for a particular material across the exchange, so that if total demand is much greater than any one buyer's, the needs can be combined and a more favorable price negotiated with a supplier of that material (consortium buying); and
- provide structure and a communications channel for product design information and other product development/introduction/maintenance/discontinuance services — see the separate discussion below under product life-cycle management.

An exchange has to decide which of the above types of services it is interested in providing, and how to generate revenue from these generally value-added services. And, of course, for most of these services, each buyer/seller pair would need to agree that they wanted to take advantage of a particular service. Each buyer and each seller can be thought of as a thread in the cloth that is a many-to-many exchange, and each pair doing business must specify their own policies and needs. See Figure 5 overleaf.

Figure 5: Buyers and Sellers in an Exchange are the Threads in a Complex Cloth

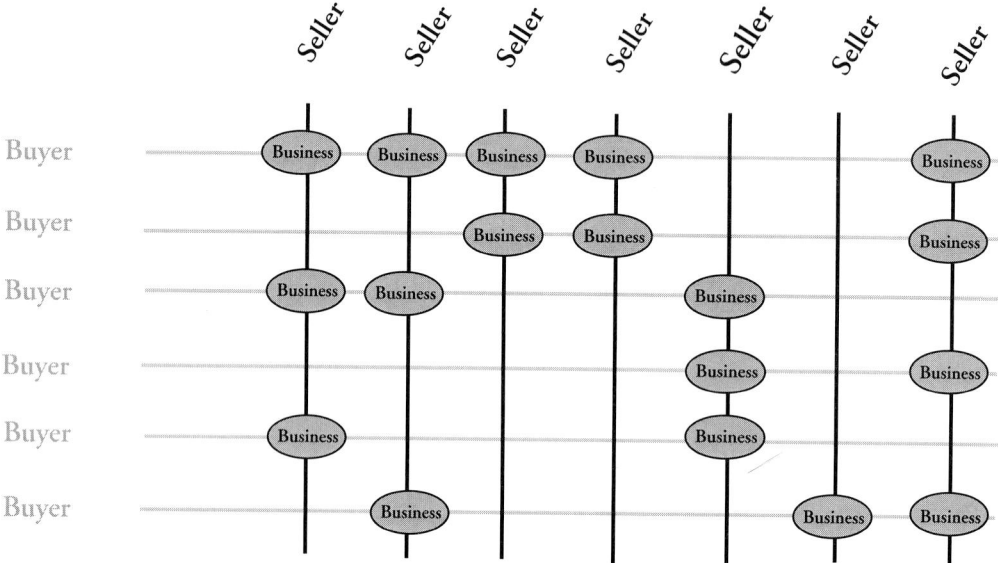

How can an exchange provide supply chain planning services? The essence of providing the service is making planning functions available to users through the exchange. As shown in Figure 6, these planning functions are ideally an extension of the commerce functions of the exchange. For example, the INC2inc exchange was created to provide ingredients and packaging between materials suppliers and food processors, and the fundamental function of the exchange is to transact commerce between these sellers and buyers. Many of the planning functions listed above are a natural extension of the commerce functions and should ideally work from the same transaction database. But as illustrated in the diagram, an exchange may choose to offer planning tools to its clients *essentially as an ASP provider would* — in other words, simply making software available without tying it to the commerce function on the exchange. In this role, the exchange reverses the position mentioned above (where it can be a consumer of TMS functions from another party functioning as the ASP), and becomes an ASP itself.

Figure 6: Supply Chain Planning Can be a Core Part of an Exchange or a Peripheral ASP Offering

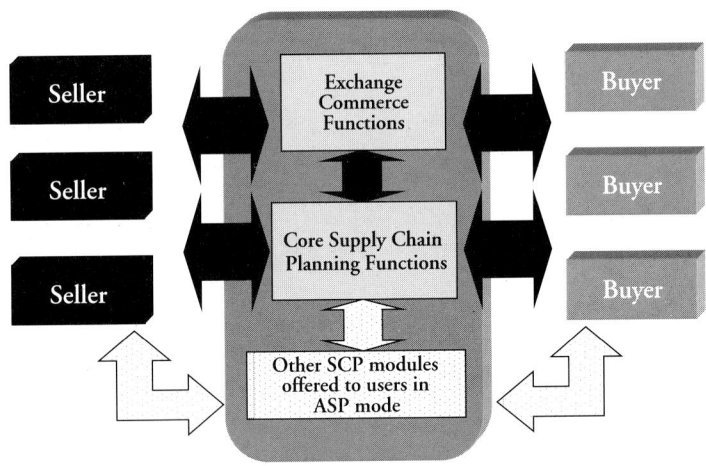

A private exchange focused on the needs of one supply chain participant can perform virtually any supply chain planning function for that participant. It can certainly perform all of the market-oriented services listed above, but from the perspective of that one participant. The sponsor can easily share its production schedules with its material suppliers and with its customers via its private market, allocate material sourcing among suppliers, allocate finished goods to customers and provide capable-to-promise responses to them, and so on. Consequently, the private exchange sponsor is much better positioned to use comprehensive supply/demand, cost-minimizing global optimization tools and production planning/scheduling tools than is a quasi-private or public market. It is really a matter of technical convenience as to how much of the internal planning function the sponsor moves from its legacy systems to its private market. It may be convenient to move much of the planning, so that it can, for example, use the private 'market' to communicate production schedules between its plants and its headquarters staff, or forecast data between field sales and central marketing.

Who supplies supply chain planning software? Supply chain planning has truly matured in the last 10 years and there are numerous sources of packaged systems, both from providers focusing on planning and, more recently, from ERP software providers. While numerous claims are currently made about planning software being ready for exchanges, the reality is that most planning software was designed for large inside-the-four-walls corporate supply chains, has been adapted over the last few years for e-business generally, and is only now being adapted for the new model of many-to-many exchange use. There are also some specialized software providers with a different starting point closer to exchange needs, such as Syncra, which focuses on collaborative planning, forecasting, and replenishment (CPFR) functions for e-business (see Reference 2).

To provide the simplest planning functions listed above — for example, visibility of inventory at a supplier or customer — it may be more cost-effective to develop the software as part of the exchange's basic capabilities rather than licensing it from a planning software partner. But given the constraints on most exchanges' resources, we believe most exchanges that need planning functions should work with software partners to provide these capabilities.

It should also be pointed out that the supply chain planning functions shown above generally require substantial amounts of data from the systems of users, too much for that data to be manually supplied to the exchange via a Web browser interface. Hence, planning is one of the key drivers forcing systems integration between the exchange and its users, as will be discussed below.

Can an exchange assume control of planning the complete supply chain, with several tiers of buyers and sellers? It is certainly conceivable, is technically possible, and definitely has some theoretical cost/service optimization advantages. But doing complete supply chain planning to any meaningful degree involves giving an exchange a great deal of power. This kind of positioning is definitely appropriate for a private exchange serving a channel master, but the situation is less clear when participants in a market consider sharing that power with a neutral exchange. An example of one capability and the limitations are shown in Figure 7. Given the production schedule of a finished goods manufacturer, a planning market can compute material requirements and set the production schedules of Tier 1 suppliers, and then determine the material requirements of Tier 2 suppliers. But as soon as a Tier 1 supplier has another customer for his manufacturing capacity who is not participating in the exchange, the ability to schedule production at Tier 1 or Tier 2 is lost, because the total requirement for product is not known.

Figure 7: Multi-tier Supply Chain Planning by an Exchange

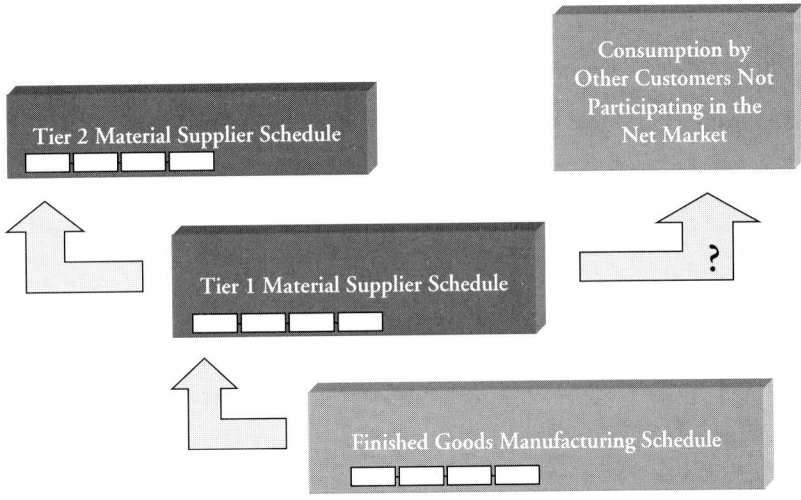

Product Life-cycle Management

One of the business functions that has, in recent years, moved from being an intra-company concern to an inter-company, supply chain management opportunity, is managing information associated with products. This functional area has given rise to corporate programs called Product Information Management (PIM), Product Data Management (PDM), and most recently in the Net-enabled world, Cross-enterprise Product Collaboration or Collaborative Product Commerce (CPC either way). The goal of CPC is to make it possible for all the players involved in creating or supporting a product, regardless of where they are located physically, organizationally, or in the supply chain, to interact knowledgeably and efficiently (see Reference 3).

CPC has sprung from the aerospace and automotive industries, where product engineering, production, and support have long been recognized as joint activities between a program manager and its contractors and customers, or between an original equipment manufacturer (OEM) and its suppliers. But the pressures to adopt product-collaborative techniques — rapid-fire product introductions, customer intimacy, rapid market changes, awareness of product life-cycle costs, new competitors, and globalization of product development and support — exist in many industries. While aerospace and automotive will likely stay in the lead on product collaboration, manufacturers in other industries are pursuing product collaboration programs as well — for example:

- high-tech electronics;
- medical devices;
- industrial durable goods; and
- consumer durable goods.

Can exchanges play in this game? They are already well on the way. MyAircraft.com, an exchange for aircraft manufacturers and operators, is developing the ability to search and access digital engineering and maintenance information, primarily to make engineering data provided by manufacturers available to aircraft operators. MyAircraft is also planning to provide operators with the capability to create custom revisions of the OEM-supplied information so that they can customize technical content for their own use (see Reference 4).

Silicon Valley Oil Company is an exchange created by Chevron to enable sales of lubricants and fuels to commercial and industrial customers. One of the ways that Chevron is providing leadership to this mid-tech industry is by making lubricant product information a fundamental part of the exchange. Their approach illustrates the point that an industry does not have to be high-tech to have product technical information be of great interest to participants throughout the supply chain, and that an electronic marketplace is perhaps the most efficient way to make data available to all of the interested parties (see Reference 5).

In addition to the downstream product information functions described above, exchanges have the potential to participate in the core design and manufacturing processes of product development programs:

- **Program management.** An exchange can be the primary mechanism for communicating program schedules and status.

- **Collaborative design.** With the adoption of standard formats for design information, a standard format accessed via the exchange can be used for many of the organizations participating in a joint design program, as well as within each organization.

- **Bid and proposal.** Exchanges may have begun with relatively simple auctions, but they can also provide support for complex bid and proposal processes.

- **Component supplier management.** Status reports, performance updates, quality assurance data: an exchange can be used to standardize and make more efficient the supplier management process in the context of a product program.

- **Material flow.** Material and sub-assembly releases for shipment, production schedule collaboration: these functions reach into the supply chain planning area discussed above.

For example, BuyPlastics.com is constructing a Net marketplace for the plastics industry that will feature collaborative design and product management as a core function, based on one of the leading existing product collaboration software suites. Their objective is to enable real-time design collaboration among customers, part designers, mold shops, part manufacturers, and plastic resin providers to help bring products to market more quickly (see Reference 6).

Within the food and beverage industry, INC2inc has also identified product life-cycle management as a natural long-term service offering to participants. As is the case with many manufacturing industries, a great deal of information gets exchanged between partners before any product is ever produced. Numerous iterations of recipes are central to the development process, and this cycle can naturally be streamlined through the introduction of a neutral party that co-ordinates this communication. Manufacturers in the food industry also deal with numerous regulatory issues that must be addressed at the plant level on a continual basis — for example, Material Safety Data Sheets (MSDS) documents, where INC2inc is already delivering value. By providing for the electronic delivery and presentation of these specific documents, INC2inc provides manufacturers with immediate access to important information relevant to all ingredients that are delivered from their suppliers.

Supply Chain Systems and Integration

Integration is a challenge in itself for the B2B exchange. Sophisticated systems must be integrated into the marketplace and operate as one, the marketplace must be integrated into a buyer or seller's legacy systems, and the marketplace may also have to integrate with other marketplaces in, or outside of, the exchange's direct industry.

For example, consider the supply chain planning functions. Supply chain planning tools can of course be used in a completely manual way. But users quickly tire of typing series of numbers (say, proposed production schedules), for perhaps hundreds of products, into a Web browser. The reality, then, is that planning functions must usually be integrated with systems on the buyers' and sellers' sides. The supply chain planning software providers continue to offer better integration tools, and in many cases offer pre-packaged integration with leading ERP systems. Most software providers are at least contemplating better data interfacing via Extensible Markup Language (XML – see Reference 7), but most are still in the early stages of that effort and appropriate XML data schemas are still being defined. So data interfacing between an exchange and users' systems, even for just the supply chain planning functions, remains an expensive obstacle to overcome today.

If an exchange is to be effective in streamlining the supply chain, several pieces of software are necessary to run each of the functional areas. Many of the marketplace software providers (Ariba, Commerce One) are forming alliances with functional experts, but these solutions are in the early planning stage and typically not production ready. Even when offered pre-configured integration complements, there is no guarantee that the chosen partner is the right choice for every function.

The marketplace, therefore, has the choice of waiting for delivery of an integrated package that meets the right needs, or assembling best-of-breed technologies. Given the pace with which technologies are changing in the Net market space, developing an architecture with plug-and-play capability is a necessity, not a nicety.

Integration between the marketplace and buyer/seller systems poses challenges for both the exchange and the customer. Two separate, yet related, sets of issues exist when companies look at integrating their supply chains into a marketplace. First, from the marketplace point of view: how does the marketplace need to architect itself to handle supply nets (and all inherent functionality) instead of one given supply chain? Second, from the exchange customer point of view: how does a company integrate its business processes and system with those of the marketplace, and to what extent?

A basic tenet of the exchange model is that a participant company can integrate with one marketplace, and thus be integrated with multiple companies on the other end of its trading activity — a buyer does not have to construct a connection for each if its 300 unique suppliers. Buyers and sellers are now using systems that extend 'outside their four walls', yet must maintain the integrity of their business rules. To successfully architect for this situation, the marketplace must incorporate the following design guidelines into its solution and, thus, its integration capability:

- The exchange must be client agnostic — ie, no specific business rules can exist in the marketplace functionality. The marketplace must be able to recognize a participant and, through integration, determine the appropriate rules to follow.

- The exchange must be able to enforce the business rules of the participating company.

- The exchange must provide real-time feedback of business rules pass/fail based on activity being performed in the marketplace. Users of a real-time, Web-based system do not want to learn after placing a transaction that it failed at point of entry into the seller's system. The integration architecture must provide a robust feedback mechanism to the user, as that user may be unaware of their trading partner's rules.

- Most importantly, the exchange must determine for what activities it will be the system of record. Can buyers perform planning activity outside the exchange and simply feed the results, or must it occur in the marketplace? Do transactions originate in legacy systems or the marketplace? Answers to these questions will drive business process design and the potential value a participant will derive from the exchange.

A participant must decide how to integrate with the exchange. Do they interact manually with the exchange via a Web browser, integrate at their firewall, or allow integration to occur behind their firewall? The answer should lie in how they plan to use the exchange's functionality. Basic transaction facilitation may not warrant full integration. Additional capabilities such as supply chain planning require extensive data sets and multiple iterations of activity. Elimination of re-keying on both accounts drives benefits in elimination of work effort and increased timeliness of information across a trading community. As a company adds trading partners, full integration also increases its ability to scale effectively. Without integration, companies will have huge administrative burdens and will likely lose any benefit to be gained from being an exchange member.

The largest challenge for marketplace users is in determining how to interact best with exchanges, while leveraging existing systems that most likely cost millions of dollars to implement. Can 'inside' purchasing modules be used and still generate benefit if integrated with the exchange? Most likely no, as the shared database of the exchange provides the benefit of accurate and timely pricing and product information to order from. Can forecasting, planning, and transportation be performed outside the marketplace? Potentially yes, as the output information can drive activity in the exchange and provide previously unavailable visibility to business partners. Thus, participants should look for exchanges that provide granular integration capability, so as to allow choices for the business process changes necessary to take advantage of any technology.

Summary: Adding Value with Supply Chain Management

B2B exchanges that deal with physical goods can substantially increase their value to their users by providing supply chain management capabilities. We have reviewed three types of supply chain management functions:

- **Supply chain execution.** Just about every physical goods exchange needs to provide at least basic capabilities to provide transportation services. Normally this should involve the exchange developing a relationship with a 3PL provider, or a horizontal transportation exchange — or an organization that is both. It makes little sense for most exchanges, particularly in their first couple of years as a start-up, to invest heavily to be self-sufficient in this area. But it is such a fundamental set of functions for buyer and seller convenience and cost avoidance that any exchange that fails to provide these capabilities will be at a competitive disadvantage.

- **Supply chain planning.** Planning is most appropriate where buyers and sellers expect to have an ongoing relationship, creating a supply chain (or supply net) with some longevity. At even the simplest supply chain planning level, such as inventory and forecast visibility and collaboration between buyer and seller, providing supply chain planning capabilities will add value. It will reduce the buyer inventory and the seller inventory necessary to provide a given level of in-stock performance. If automatic inventory replenishment is offered, it will improve inventory control and reduce transaction costs.

- **Product life-cycle management — everything to do with managing products.** While this set of functions has received little attention at most exchanges thus far, exchanges that support this area are being created in industries where there are complex product management issues. An exchange is a very natural environment for communicating and storing this type of information, and we believe product-oriented functions will have increasing influence on exchange business models and design.

Supply chain management services in an exchange tend to force issues around systems architecture and data interfacing. These functions in an exchange need to pass data to and from users' operations systems (such as ERP), and can compete for some business functions with user-installed ERP systems. It is important to architect an exchange so that users have a range of choices about how, and how deeply, they integrate their systems with the exchange.

Because of their substantial data needs, supply chain functions benefit more than most exchange services from the fundamental exchange advantage: 'You only have to build one interface to an exchange, versus building an interface to each individual supply chain partner'. As challenging as a full-spectrum interface is to the typical user's systems organization, the efficiency of working with one (or even a few) exchanges is far greater than doing it one supply chain partner at a time.

References

1. For example, see 'Information Distortion in a Supply Chain: The Bullwhip Effect', H.L. Lee, V. Padmanabhan and S. Whang, *Management Science*. Vol. 43, No. 4, 1997, pp. 546–558.
2. CPFR is defined by the Voluntary InterIndustry Commerce Standards association; see their site www.cpfr.org for the most comprehensive information on CPFR.
3. See 'Collaborative Product Commerce: Delivering Product Innovations at Internet Speed', Aberdeen Group, *Market Viewpoint*, Vol. 12, No. 9, 7 October 1999.
4. See the www.myaircraft.com site.
5. See the www.svoc.com site.
6. See the www.buyplastics.com site.
7. A good introduction to XML can be found at the www.oasis-open.org site.

The authors would also like to acknowledge the assistance and support of the following people and organizations:

Jeff Makohon — INC2inc Technologies
Chanda Ryan — CSC Consulting
Jim Roche — CSC Consulting

As Founder and Executive Vice President of INC2inc, Chris Renner was an early visionary identifying the Net market business model and applying it to the food industry. In 1998, he established the company's direction and now leads the company's strategic business and technology goals. His entrepreneurial experience uniquely applies a history of financial acumen with technology vision to all areas of business — including financial consulting, e-business strategy and execution, and the founding and acquisition of a successful start-up company.

Jeff Schutt, Ph.D., is a CSC partner with more than 20 years' experience helping companies create and refine their supply chains. Much of his focus has been on processes and systems for supply chain planning. He has recently worked with Net markets and other organizations that are engaging in collaborative supply chain management.

Chapter 5: Logistics

Christopher C. Cusick and Mark W. Pluta, Logistics.com

The concept of logistics was formalized in the military where the provisioning and delivery of resources (eg, munitions, troops, fuel, edibles) had life-and-death consequences. Over time, logistics techniques and practices were adopted by the commercial world to improve efficiencies and enable growth, evolving into a critical function that supported the entire business enterprise: from supplier procurement to final product delivery. Logistics has become the cornerstone of every bricks-and-mortar company and will continue to be so in the New Economy. Quite simply, the billions of dollars of goods purchased through your B2B exchange will ultimately need to be delivered from the suppliers to the buyers. (Of course, those B2B exchanges trading 'soft goods', such as electricity or financial instruments, have no need for a logistics provider.)

The awareness and recognition of the importance of logistics for a B2B exchange is growing rapidly. In fact, during the writing of this book, both *Fortune* and *Business Week*, in the issues for the last week of June 2000, published special articles concerning B2B logistics. Merrill Lynch, in their industry report entitled *The B2B Market Maker Book*, listed logistics as one of the top 10 questions that should be asked of B2B market makers. This highlights the value of logistics from an investor's point of view.

Most B2B exchanges would be well served by partnering with a logistics provider to outsource transportation services. By entering into an alliance with a logistics provider, a vertical market maker acquires instant leverage by:

- focusing on their value proposition — which lies in efficient information exchange between suppliers and consumers focused on a particular industry — to create the leading exchange; and

- providing world-class logistic services that contribute significantly to customer satisfaction and retention.

What is Logistics?

Logistics can be described as the process of managing the flow of product and information from seller to buyer in a typical supply chain. Very broad in definition, logistics providers tend to focus on various value-added facets of the business in addition to the fundamental need to transport goods from point A to point B. Some of these facets of particular importance to B2B exchanges include:

- *Transportation Procurement* — This involves working with transport providers to procure capacity for shipments. It also includes co-ordination of pick-up and delivery of shipments.
- *Aggregation* — Logistics providers which aggregate shipments can sometimes negotiate better rates with transport providers, minimize information flow, and provide value to both suppliers and buyers.
- *Tracking and Tracing* — Where is my shipment now? When will it get to where it is going?
- *Customs Brokerage* — Logistics providers providing customs brokerage services manage the process of bringing the goods through customs that involves calculation of both time and customs duties.
- *Consulting* — Logistics providers can assist clients by analyzing their process, costs, and business plans to reduce logistics costs and increase speed-to-market.

In addition to other supply chain activities (eg, order processing), logistics consultants often focus on the facets listed above as part of their recommendation.

From raw materials to the finished product, transport services and information technologies enable the flow of product through the supply chain as depicted below.

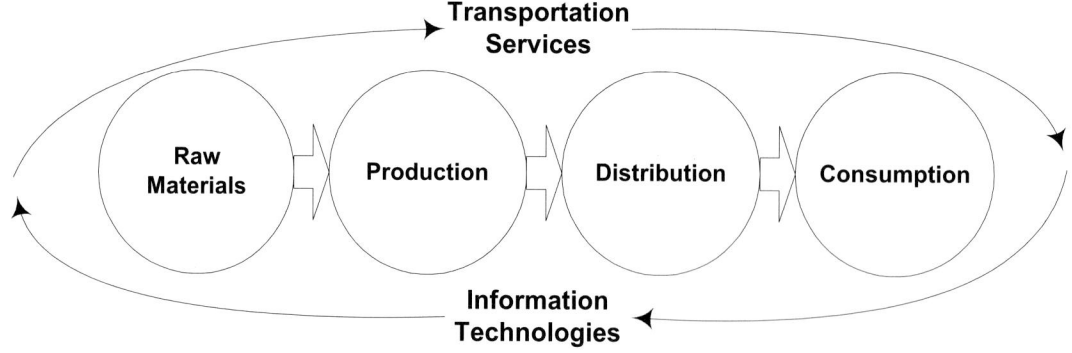

Classification of Logistics Providers

While traditional logistics companies specialize in various segments of the logistics value-chain, Web-based logistics providers, or transportation marketplaces, cater to the B2B exchange. However, without an understanding of the various types of logistics providers, it is difficult to see the benefits that Web-based providers have over traditional ones.

- *3PL (Third-party Logistics)* — Companies which do not have an in-house logistics group can outsource their operations to 3PLs. 3PLs, which can be small firms which customize their services to clients, or larger groups like FedEx Logistics and UPS Logistics, can co-ordinate design and management of product transportation, storage, distribution, and integrated logistics services. However, many of the established 3PLs in the industry are supported by transport providers, therefore potentially skewing their objectivity for assigning other transport providers on individual shipments. As you might expect, the larger players are often less flexible to the needs of B2B exchanges which may not yet command large volumes of transactions.

- *Carriers* — Large freight carriers, such as Schneider National and Yellow Freight, maintain large fleets of trucks. They can dedicate a transportation manager to arrange the collection and delivery of goods. While their fleets of trucks may seem boundless, establishing an alliance with a carrier not only binds you to their network but also limits your modes of transport. Furthermore, a nascent B2B exchange may not provide the liquidity necessary to negotiate discounted rates.

- *Freight Forwarders (FFs)* — FFs, such as Expeditors International or Nippon Express, provide consolidated freight routing and planning which includes door-to-door collection and delivery across multiple modes of transport. This typically includes value added services such as customs brokerage. Freight forwarders are most often involved in air and sea freight, and most are focused on international transactions.

- *Transportation Marketplaces* — New transportation marketplaces are forming to service B2B exchanges. They play a similar role to 3PLs, but most are not funded through transport providers and can therefore focus their resources on new solutions. Transportation marketplaces, such as Logistics.com and RightFreight.com, can provide a combination of transaction procurement, tracking and tracing capability, payment, and aggregation services to B2B exchanges.

Generally, transportation marketplaces provide the best opportunity for B2Bs to deliver logistics solutions to their customers. First, transportation marketplaces use the latest technology, such as XML, to ease information flow and increase automation. This offers B2B exchanges ease of integration and provides a seamless user experience to the consumer and supplier. Second, those transportation marketplaces are not backed by a particular transport provider and can offer neutrality across all carriers, thereby providing the best value. The same concepts that apply to your B2B exchange apply to the transportation marketplace.

The table below sets out some of the pros and cons of the various logistics providers.

	Pros	*Cons*
3PLs	• breadth of offerings • one-stop shopping	• bias towards assets • old technology • usually expensive
Carriers	• work directly with provider • simple relationship with one company	• might not have significant enough volume to negotiate discounts • problems with multiple modes • may require additional management
Freight forwarders	• handles customs work • has relationships with multiple transport providers	• might not have breadth of experience required • locked into one vendor and their transport provider relationships
Transportation marketplaces	• focused on serving B2B exchanges • neutrality between transport providers • easy integration with latest technologies (XML)	• new comers to an established industry • many to choose from, many will fail

Frequently Asked Questions

1. Why can't I just link to someone like UPS or FedEx?

Maybe you can. If your suppliers and consumers are in the US and are exchanging nothing but parcels, small package carriers like UPS, FedEx, and USPS can carry your low-cost goods and may offer the tracking features your customers expect. Even so, transportation marketplaces specific to this space, such as iShip.com and SmartShip.com, provide aggregation services across all the parcel carriers, offering a variety of rates and carriers, maybe a discount, with shipment tracking and drop-off locators.

Unfortunately, not many B2B exchanges can use the parcel carriers for the majority of their critical transactions. Generally speaking, exchanges focused on the Small Office Home Office (SOHO) and B2C markets only can get good coverage using their transportation services. For large shipments (ie, not parcels) and international customers, your exchange must partner with a transportation marketplace exchange to meet basic needs and achieve the greatest value.

2. What if I have customers overseas?

The issues get more complicated. Rates are often not instantly available, especially if your customers are looking for 'landed cost'. Landed cost means the total cost of the merchandise, including all expenses involved in bringing it to the purchaser. Internationally, this involves not just transportation costs from point to point, but various fees for documentation, port fees, etc. Even more significantly, it includes the cost of customs duty and import taxes.

Determining customs duties is a complex task, and in most parts of the world this is still processed on a shipment-by-shipment basis by licenced customs brokers working closely with the customs authorities in the importing country.

While FFs typically offer customs brokerage services, it can take days to receive a full quotation to determine a full landed cost for a given sale — and the process is not automated.

There are some B2B exchanges trying specifically to solve the landed cost problem. However, the process can be painful. Every product type offered must be manually classified ahead of time — in every country in the world where you may have clients! Further, the classifications have to be updated regularly, as rules and tax rates change frequently. The process can work, but it works best for exchanges with a limited number of products and a high volume of transactions. Examples of these companies are From2.com and MyCustoms.com.

Transportation marketplaces bring together a comprehensive solution by integrating both landed costs exchanges and traditional transport providers, such as FFs and carriers, to facilitate multi-border passage and provide door-to-door delivery.

3. What if I need someone to warehouse my goods?

If you pre-purchase the goods being sold and need to hold them in inventory, companies are being organized to warehouse your goods, pick up your orders, and ship them. 3PLs such as Menlo Logistics and UPS Logistics traditionally provide warehousing and other value-added services.

Transportation exchanges that have a full service offering are usually partnered with 3PLs and can integrate rapidly with a public warehousing option to meet any warehousing requirements.

4. Can I give my customer immediate quotes?

Virtually all bricks-and-mortar companies have their own individual contracts, with annual rate structures for shipping and related services. Since the negotiated rates are driven by volume over a particular lane or lanes, pricing varies significantly from customer to customer — for example, GM versus a local car dealership — and is renegotiated every year. For customers of your B2B exchange who may want shipping costs, there are ways to address the need for near 'real-time' quoting.

A few transportation exchanges such as freightquote.com have negotiated these types of contracts with a handful of transport providers; these negotiated rates are then instantly available. The initial response to these types of exchanges was very good, but has faded recently in recognition of quoting limitations (eg, North America trucking only), the lack of representation of established relationships, quality of service issues (eg, damaged or delayed goods), and price rigidity with limited capacity that could be optimized to reflect the minute-by-minute flux in pricing and availability in the global transportation marketplace.

Transportation exchanges that are carrier-neutral, such as GoCargo.com and Logistics.com, have the ability to maintain complex rate structures and the associated business privacy between customers and transport providers in a many-to-many fashion. It is important to note that carrier neutrality is a key criterion for widespread adoption. It is highly unlikely that transportation exchanges associated with a given carrier (eg, a subsidiary of, or funded by) will be allowed to store and access sensitive customer relationship data from a competing transportation provider. This enables 'quick quotes' via conditional lookup provided that the transportation exchange receives appropriate data describing the attributes of a shipment. For frequent shipments between certain customer/supplier locations, this type of quick quote provides a good level of confidence in pricing, but does not always account for day-to-day market conditions.

Transportation exchanges can also provide an estimated quote by deriving an on-the-fly rate structure from aggregated empirical data and landed cost calculators. This satisfies the shipping price input need for the decision point in the majority of B2B transactions. The final pricing can then be determined from select transport providers or by the spot market.

5. Will my customer be able to use a preferred transport provider?

Quality of service is a key decision factor for many shippers transporting valuable goods. First of all, look for a dedicated team of operations specialists in your logistics provider. Also, be wary of transportation marketplaces that can only provide lowest-price, open-ended auctions. This model may be very applicable for bulk commodity goods such as grain, but will rarely apply to large finished goods and many other types of shipments (eg, chemicals, perishables, semiconductors) where quality of service is significant for timely delivery of undamaged products. In the end, your customer usually has an established relationship with a particular transport provider. Make certain that the transportation marketplace does not short-circuit this relationship, but keeps these transport providers honest.

6. What kind of data do I need from the customer and supplier to ship the goods?

Here is a list of questions you need to ask yourself when determining the data requirements your logistics provider needs:

- What am I shipping? (product description/characteristics)
- What is the dollar value of my shipment? (product value)
- What am I shipping it in? (product packaging)
- What size am I shipping? (product dimensions)
- How much am I shipping? (product quantity)
- How heavy is my shipment? (product weight)
- Where am I shipping from? (product origin)
- Where am I shipping to? (product destination)
- When am I shipping it? (product ready date)
- When is the shipment due? (product due date)
- Are there special handling requirements? (hazardous materials)

7. How do I know my customer will be getting the best value?

Transportation marketplaces allow multiple transport providers to bid on an individual customer's business. Whether the business is an individual shipment (spot market) or a series of shipments (contractual basis), the idea is to drive the price down for the transportation service. Of course, value combines both price and quality of service. Look for transportation marketplaces that can take a transport provider's service level into consideration.

8. How frequent or reliable are my shipping patterns?

Predictable surges in product demand — for instance, at Christmas — can wreak havoc on a transport provider's network, impacting your delivery times. Even worse, unforeseen emergencies can cause tremendous demand and also impact delivery. Look for sophisticated tools that provide visibility into your carrier's network, reducing bottlenecks. Also, look for transportation marketplaces that provide complete procurement solutions to meet surge periods through the spot-market, or contractual solutions to negotiate mini-contracts for sustained periods of unusually high volume.

9. Do I need to hire dedicated operations staff to supplement my logistics service?

It is a good idea to retain a small staff of industry professionals to run the logistics center and/or interact with your preferred transportation exchange. This ensures that the needs of your exchange are properly represented and provides continuity with the virtual logistics team.

Questions to Ask Your Transportation Marketplace

1. How much transportation has been procured through your marketplace? How long have you been in business?

This is a crowded marketplace with an overabundance of offerings. Your relationship with your logistics provider is an expensive one to set up. An ephemeral Web company is not the alliance in which you want to invest. Ask your transportation marketplace how much transportation has actually been procured and managed through their systems. Some of the leaders in this space have done well over $1bn.

2. How many transport providers do you have relationships with?

To provide your customers and suppliers with the level of logistics service they are accustomed to, ask how many transport providers they have signed up. At the very least, ask how many of the transport providers your customers use are actually members of transportation marketplaces.

3. What modes do you handle?

Everyone wants to offer multi-modal capability, but few actually do. Most marketplaces specialize in a particular mode, say trucking, but have no capability to do ocean and air. Also ask what operational expertise the marketplace has to handle the different modes.

4. How much logistics domain expertise do you really have?

With shippers, third-party firms, and Web solution providers trying to take advantage of the fragmented transportation industry, be wary of exploiting interlopers with little logistics experience. Research the executive biographies of the officers of the firm in question. A perusal of the transportation marketplace's website can yield a wealth of information.

5. Can your transportation marketplace handle international shipments? Are you global?

The transportation marketplace must, at the very least, support air and/or ocean modes in order to handle international traffic. The logistics provider needs to have a presence or relationship in the target international market, so as to be able to provide logistics services between two foreign countries. Many exchanges say they have an international presence, but really only provide services in the US and Canada.

6. What is your pricing structure?

The predominant pricing structures for transportation marketplaces are either subscription or transactional. Subscription fees lend themselves well to track-and-trace and aggregations services, as well as landed cost calculations. Per transaction pricing models fit well with spot market exchanges. Some marketplaces have a flat-fee structure in place, while others take a percentage of the shipping cost.

The table overleaf lists most of the top transportation marketplaces identified by the type of service offered. *Land, ocean, and air* describe the mode of transport the marketplace provide and *international* shows whether or not they can ship internationally. *Manage shipper load consolidation, carrier selection, and tendering/booking* describe to what degree aggregation services are offered. *Tracking* shows whether track-and-trace services are available. The last two columns describe what type of transportation procurement is available; *spot* market for individual shipments or *contractual* for a series of shipments.

Christopher Cusick's background includes extensive experience in the areas of carrier management, 3PL implementation, systems integration, and daily traffic operations for multi-modal paper and retail accounts. In his current role, Chris is a business expert for Logistics.com's on-line products and manages the integration of carriers with the exchange. Prior to Logistics.com, Chris served in General Manager roles for J.B. Hunt Logistics, Inc. (Transplace.com) and Cardinal Logistics Management for paper and retail accounts. He holds a B.S. in Management from Rensselaer Polytechnic Institute in Troy, New York.

Name	Mode				Shipper functionality				Procurement	
	Land	Ocean	Air	International	Load consol-idation	Carrier selection	Tendering/ booking	Tracking	Spot	Contractual
BestTransport	X					X	X	X	X	
CapStan	X	X	X	X					X	
cargofinder	X	X	X	X					X	
cargosphere	X	X	X	X					X	
CarrierPoint.com	X			X		X	X		X	
Celarix	X	X	X	X		X	X	X	X	X
DAT	X								X	
Descartes	X	X	X	X				X		
efxit.com	X	X	X	X			X	X	X	
Elogex	X									
eTransport		X		X		X		X	X	X
FreightDesk.com	X	X	X					X		
FreightMatrix.com	X			X			X	X	X	X
freightquote.com	X		X					X	X	
freightWise	X						X		X	
G-Log	X	X	X	X				X		
GoCargo		X		X						
Logistics.com	X	X	X	X	X	X	X	X	X	X
LogTech Corporation		X	X					X		
Manugistics	X	X	X	X						
Nistevo	X				X			X	X	X
nPassage	X	X	X	X			X	X		
NTE	X						X	X	X	
RightFreight	X		X	X						
Shiplogix	X									
TransPlace.com	X	X	X	X		X	X	X	X	X
Transportalnet.com	X								X	
transportation.com	X								X	

Chapter 6:
Business-to-Business Market Models

Blair LaCorte, Senior VP of Strategy and Electronic Commerce, VerticalNet

Traditionally, markets have been defined as venues in which buyers and sellers transact goods and services. *Webster's* primary definition of a market is as follows: 'a meeting together of people for the purpose of trade by private purchase and sale and usually not by auction.' There are several interesting aspects of this definition. First, it implies that a sale is always consummated and, therefore, that a product transaction takes place. In turn, it excludes the type of transaction known as an auction. In fact, this definition does not encompass many of the venues, both off-line and on-line, that today would be considered marketplaces.

In reality, a market may not actually involve the sale and transfer of a product at all; it may merely imply an exchange of information. In addition, an auction, in which buyers or sellers bid on products or services, is just as much a market as any retail establishment, the archetypal marketplace in the minds of many people.

We begin this chapter on business-to-business market models by describing how very different market formats serve as a primary differentiator between marketplaces. One of the key distinctions that will be made is the difference between spot and open market purchasing and behind the firewall contract purchasing. Next, we will introduce the concept that markets can be segmented into the transaction of products and the transaction of information, with both providing a means for revenue generation. In turn, we will explore in detail the defining characteristics of different types of on-line markets in order to expose the reader to the broad array of buyer–seller markets that exist.

The success to date of such widely diverse markets underscores the concept that different players may ultimately be able to effectively engage very different markets using very distinct mechanisms. If we accept this assumption as true, it is feasible that multiple players, operating multiple marketplace models, will populate and thrive in the diverse on-line B2B landscape of the future.

Market Formats

The existence of a market implies that there is a 'selling' format in which buyer-seller interactions are facilitated. In essence, marketplaces can be described as falling under one of three primary selling formats: contract, spot, or open. E-procurement models are the predominant contract models emerging on the Web. E-procurement typically entails a buyer's legal agreement to purchase at a specified price (given a minimum level of volume) over a specified period of time. In general, these purchases are planned, multi-period buys. As is the case with futures purchasers, industrial goods buyers may pay more for the ability to lock in a specific price or for the added benefit of being able to reduce processing costs. However, this is usually counterbalanced by increased buyer purchasing power. Conversely, 'open markets' refers to less systematic purchases of both production and non-production materials. In an open market purchase, buyers are seeking new suppliers or are looking for a one-off purchase. Companies seeking capital equipment, new suppliers of components, or specialized, tailored products or solutions all conduct open market purchases. Finally, spot markets pertain to purchases of commodities, direct materials, or manufacturing components in liquid markets. Traditionally, spot markets were used to cover one-off product shortfalls in production cycles. However, as more liquid markets are created and as derivative products emerge in spot markets, an increasing number of manufacturers are looking to spot markets as a source of a portion of their production goods as well.

From a conceptual standpoint, behind the firewall contract buying is significantly different than spot or open buying. While contract buying is about creating efficiencies in existing relationships, open and spot purchasing are centered on finding the optimal provider or product in one-off, real-time events. Many of the emerging 'bricks and mortar' on-line markets are contract-based e-procurement solutions in that they link buyers and established sellers in 'private' networks. Among the leading B2B software suppliers that exist today — Rightworks, Ariba, and Commerce One — 'behind the firewall contract sales' describes most of the transactions taking place. The concept of taking advantage of transacting with well-known partners allows the individual parties to better manage inventory, authorize expenses, and achieve purchasing power.

In essence, behind the firewall contract purchasing represented one of the first dominant stages of B2B e-commerce. However, other models, which focus more on open and spot market purchases, are quickly gaining strength. While e-procurement is primarily about supply chain efficiency, spot and open markets are centered on marketing, pricing, and information efficiency. In open markets, buyers are able to quickly obtain information about a broad set of potential products, while sellers have the ability to reach new buyers and to communicate their company and product attributes with increased reach and cost efficiency. Conversely, in spot markets, buyers and sellers have access to price transparency and availability and can benefit from the efficiency of a real exchange. In general, as businesses become increasingly comfortable with and convinced of the value of making one-off open and spot purchases on-line, this type of marketplace should blossom.

Information Transactions

The primary reason a seller transacts information is to educate a purchaser. As part of their sales and marketing budgets, sellers facilitate multiple types of buyer education. For example, a seller may provide knowledgeable salespeople at an industry trade show, publish literature that describes the benefits and functions of a specific product, or simply create an educational layout for a print advertisement. A less obvious example of an information transaction is the concept of suppliers paying for information about potential customers in the form of leads or customer lists. Regardless of the mechanism employed, the end goal of seller-sponsored information is to influence a buyer's purchasing decision.

In general, sellers prefer buyers to source products based on the following sequence of events: select the vendor, select the product category, and finally, select the actual product. Figure 1 overleaf illustrates this possible buying sequence as well as a broader array of buyer sourcing patterns. What vendors fear most is that Internet marketplaces will alter the sourcing process that they have spent substantial sums of money creating. In particular, many sellers are afraid of losing the ability to influence the buyers' behavior prior to choosing a product. Stated differently, vendors fear that they will no longer be able to educate buyers prior to their deciding on which product they will purchase, forcing the vendors to compete on price. The low liquidity achieved in many 'pure-play' product-based e-commerce exchanges has been driven by the reality that sellers have little to gain by participating in such a market, as price becomes the dominant decision point in the buying process. This fear translates into enormous potential for companies that provide mechanisms for sellers to influence purchasing decisions via the Vendor Preferred Model, or other similar models where sellers have the opportunity to educate buyers as to the attributes of their company or product. Such models have the benefit of providing value to both buyers and sellers, thus creating an incentive for both to participate in the marketplace.

Figure 1

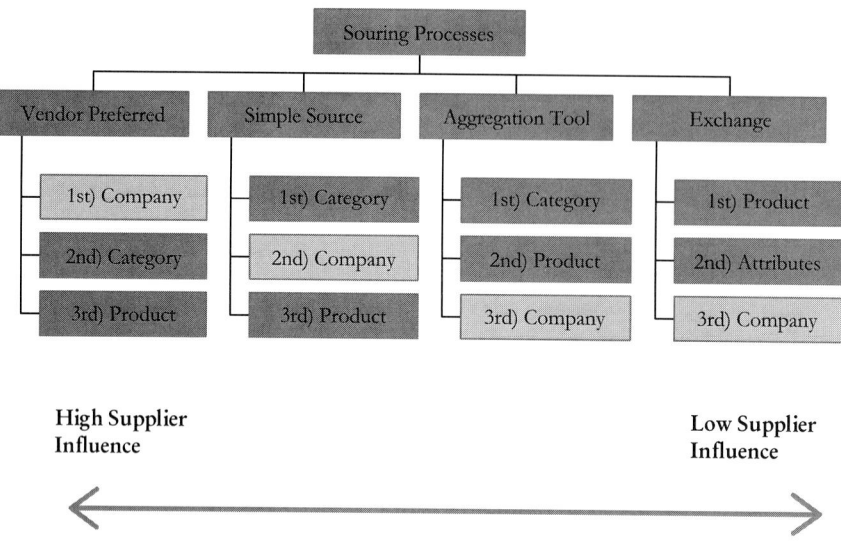

The importance of information transactions is underscored by the fact that most contemporary corporate websites do not have product transactional capabilities. Further evidence of the significance of 'mere' information is the emergence of the storefront, an on-line, structured directory of companies, products, and services. Through the use of storefronts, purchasers are able to educate on-line users about the company, its products, and its office locations, enabling purchasers to generate leads with companies of interest.

Information can also be transacted and paid for by the buyer. The most common examples of this are the subscription fees that potential purchasers pay for trade journals or indexes like the Thomas Register of American Manufacturers. Buyers sometimes go as far as purchasing premium content such as video demonstrations or proprietary information surrounding certain products. In specific circumstances, it is the buyer himself, and not the seller, who is willing to pay for his own education. Where information is lopsided but highly valuable, buyers will generally be willing to pay for it. The classic example is detailed information about stocks, such as analyst reports. Buyers feel that this information is critical to their purchase decision and therefore pay an on-line, or other, provider to receive this hopefully insightful information in a timely fashion.

An interesting dynamic in many of the buyer–seller transactions outlined above is that an intermediary often plays the role of bringing the buyer and seller together. In the trade show example, an intermediary usually hosts the event. Similarly, educational advertising is typically placed in trade magazines published by intermediaries. Going forward, it is important to remember that these forms of education are essential to a supplier's business and that intermediaries are often critical in facilitating such transactions, a pattern that is not likely to change with the growth of electronic commerce.

Product Transactions

Something as seemingly simple as a product transaction (including services offered as products) actually manifests itself in a variety of forms. Perhaps the simplest product transaction is the direct sale, in which a supplier sells product directly to an end user. However, probably the most familiar product transaction is the purchase and resale mechanism in which a company buys products and resells them directly to its customers. This transaction can take place at the manufacturer-distributor or distributor-retailer levels and is technically termed a 'merchant-of-record' (MoR) transaction, because the intermediary takes legal possession of the products during the sales process.

Yet another mechanism for transacting products is through an agent. Agents, who also act as intermediaries between parties, can be retained by either the buyer or the seller. An example of an agent representing a seller is an industrial representative who is paid a commission on all the products he sells. On the other hand, buyers may utilize a broker to act as an agent in purchasing a product that is either complex or difficult to source. Depending on the arrangement, the broker may charge either the buyer or seller a fee for his services. In general, though, most costs incurred by the seller will be passed on to the buyer in the form of higher prices.

The final mechanism for transacting products is listing fees. Simply put, these are fees that sellers pay to have their products prominently displayed in various media that are highly trafficked by targeted purchasers. An example would be the cost of posting an item in the classified section of a newspaper or a bulletin board listing on a website. As an aside, the value of listing fees is validated by the fact that newspaper classifieds are one of the most profitable sections of the newspaper. Figure 2 summarizes our discussion of information and product transactions and markets.

Figure 2

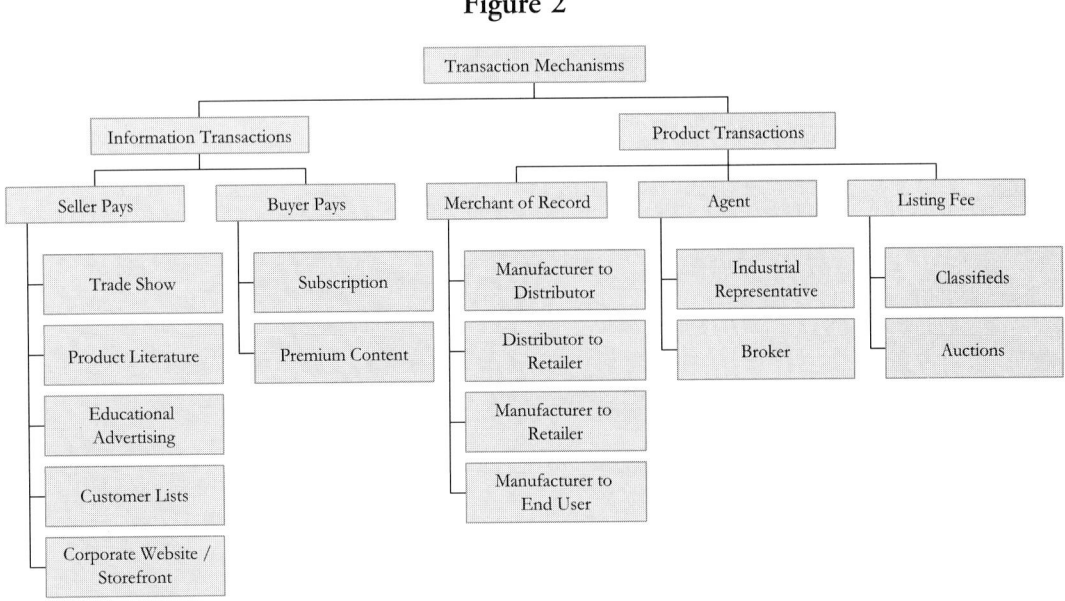

Linkage between Off-line and On-line Markets

Overall, on-line media do not change significantly the dynamics of between whom and how product and information transactions take place. In fact, once one examines and understands how information and product transactions take place in the off-line world, it is rather simple to draw parallels to the on-line world. Most Internet companies are focusing on closing product transactions over their system and extracting facilitation fees. What many companies overlook is the fact that suppliers have a budgeted amount of dollars that they can utilize to educate potential buyers. For example, if buyers frequent an Internet site, then suppliers will find value in being able to offer them an interactive, highly contextual sales pitch for their products. It is no coincidence that AOL sees the majority of sustainable value creation from its merger with Time-Warner as coming from the cross-sell of advertising dollars. Similarly, AOL is a perfect example of a company augmenting its subscription revenues with advertising sales. In general, given the importance of educating buyers, communication networks — including B2B industrial marketplaces — will always have the potential to derive revenues from the transaction of information (which may or may not lead to the consummation of a product transaction).

Information Markets

As we mentioned earlier, markets that center on the transfer of information are extremely prevalent in the business arena. In order to simplify matters, we can categorize information into two primary categories: buy-based, or structured information; and non-buy-based, or unstructured information. Structured information pertains to systematically displayed standardized information on suppliers and transactions, such as price and availability data. This type of information is required by buyers to enable buying and is therefore categorized as buy-based. Unstructured information, on the other hand, is comprised of data that is not directly linked to the buying process and includes industry and supplier-specific information such as news and analysis, product descriptions, and demand forecasts. Figure 3 provides detailed examples of the various types of both buy-based and non-buy-based information. In general, information markets are migrating from providing strictly unstructured information to supplementing this content with structured data as they attempt to further segment their customers and diversify their revenue streams.

Figure 3

	Industry	Supplier	Product	Transaction	Collaboration
Non-Buy-Based	- Industry Content - Job Listings - Discussion Forums - Industry Performance Statistics	- Alternative Suppliers - Company Info	- Descriptions and Characteristics - Quality Statistics - Needs Identification / Matching - Warrantee Details		- Demand Information - Inventory Levels - Supply Chain and Product Design
Buy-Based		- Performance and Credit Ratings - Supplier Certification	- Alternatives - Availability / Lead Times - Pricing	- Order Information Transfer - Order and Payment Tracking - Contractual Arrangement Support - Shipping Alternatives / Optimization - Returns and Custom Management	- Production / Job Scheduling

Product Markets

Product-based marketplaces are becoming a necessary feature of on-line companies that are striving to justify their rich valuations. At the highest level, there are two types of product-based markets: physical good-based and service-based (including the sale of published information). However, within each type of market exists a variety of distinct 'sub-markets.' Within physical goods markets, for example, there are two primary sub-markets: production-based products and non-production-based products. Production-based products include primary raw materials, excess raw material inventory, and OEM parts utilized in the manufacturing process. Non-production-based products include custom-made equipment, standard equipment, used equipment, surplus equipment, and MRO goods. To simplify matters, we may differentiate production and non-production-based products along two dimensions: price per unit and ease of specification. Figure 4 overleaf outlines this more detailed physical good-type segmentation scheme.

Figure 4

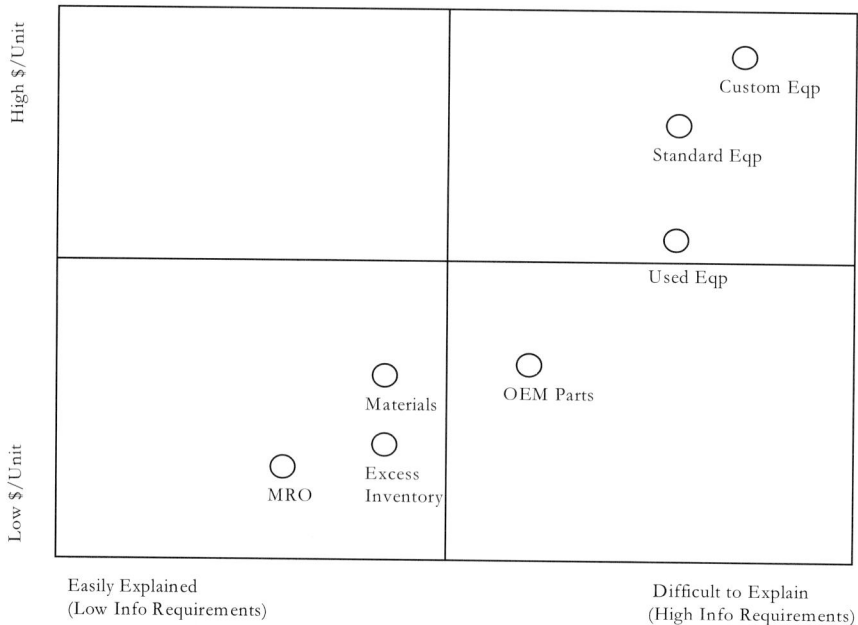

Traditionally, on-line marketplaces, which encompass a variety of selling processes (eg, catalogs, fixed-price auctions, dynamic-price auctions, directories, exchanges, etc), focused primarily on MRO goods, which were less expensive on a per unit basis and easily specified in print. However, they have evolved to include direct materials and, now, various types of equipment, some of which is extremely expensive and not easily specified in print.

As is the case with physical good markets, there are two primary sub-categories of service markets: organizational-focused services and product-transfer-oriented services. Organizational-focused services include offerings such as training and customer relationship management (CRM). Product-transfer-oriented services include offerings such as logistics management and credit. Figure 5 provides more detail on these service segments. Many on-line marketplaces today consider the provision of services as a key method of differentiating their offerings while generating additional sources of revenue. In many respects, offering services in addition to mere physical goods transactional capabilities will enable on-line marketplaces to establish the community aspect that is so crucial in facilitating solid buyer–seller relations. Those sites that do the best job of creating and maintaining community are the ones most likely to be able to drive additional transactions and create sustainable competitive advantages.

Figure 5

Organization-focused Services	Product Transfer-focused Services
Training	Logistics management
CRM	Insurance
Recruitment	Escrow
Legal and financial services	Credit
Planning and forecasting	Risk management
Marketing management	Receivables management
Consulting	Research reports

Market Tools

But what are the actual mechanisms used to facilitate these buyer–seller interactions? A variety of buyer–seller tools can be administered on-line, including requests for information (RFI), requests for quotes or proposals (RFQs, RFPs), auctions, catalogs, and exchanges. These tools provide the basis of a company's revenue streams, through advertising, sponsorships, and transaction fees. RFIs typically involve a potential buyer asking a seller to provide additional information, either on-line or off-line, on a product or process. RFQs involve a potential buyer requesting a specific price for a given item, while RFPs tend to include both a quote and a qualitative description of the work to be done. Each of these requests is important because it generates leads for suppliers. The ability of a site to spawn RFIs, RFQs, and RFPs in general typically translates into advertising revenues from suppliers who want to generate these requests and from advertisers who want to benefit from site traffic. However, today, many on-line marketplaces are beginning to translate RFQs and RFPs directly into transaction revenues.

Other tools such as catalogs, auctions, and exchanges are equally, if not more, important. Catalogs display structured information, including product specifications and fixed prices. They can involve one cataloger selling to buyers, or aggregated 'meta-catalogs' in which suppliers' wares are combined to provide more selection to buyers. Those catalogs that can be updated in real time by suppliers are often referred to as 'distributed catalogs'. In general, auctions are either fixed-priced or dynamic-priced. The former type of auction offers fixed, non-negotiable prices, while the latter involves bidding in a number of possible formats, including Dutch, English, reverse, etc. Standard Dutch and English auctions typically involve a supplier offering its goods to multiple buyers, while a reverse auction entails multiple suppliers bidding for one buyer's business. Exchanges such as the off-line New York Stock Exchange involve multiple potential buyers and sellers. Within these 'many-to-many' marketplaces, liquidity reigns and prices are established by supply and demand.

The variety of tools utilized by on-line markets can be diagrammed based on their technological and informational requirements. For example, RFIs require a low level of technology as well as a low level of information to facilitate the information transaction. On the other hand, RFPs require more complex technology as well as a greater amount of information. Figure 6 provides details.

Figure 6

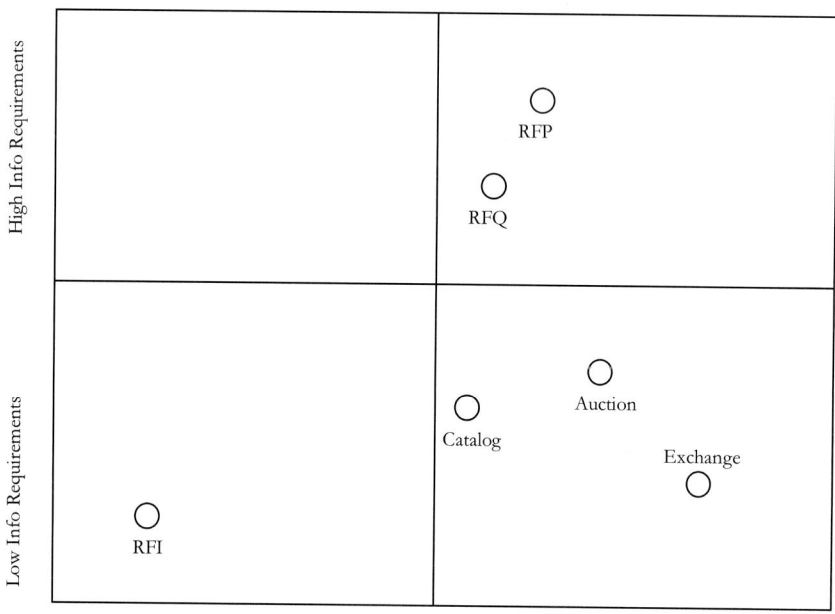

Examples

The variety of products, services, and information offered via unique formats and tools reflects either the distinct characteristics of the particular market, or the marketplace owner's perception of which ones offer the most revenue and profit potential. For example, various tools are more suitable for specific products and purchasing processes than others. As a result, OEM parts may optimally be transacted through spot market exchanges, while supplier product information can be best transacted through unstructured RFIs. In general, the existence of multiple marketplace attributes translates into hundreds, if not thousands, of possible variations of on-line marketplaces. Figure 7 lays out a schematic for segmenting the various types of markets in existence today.

Figure 7

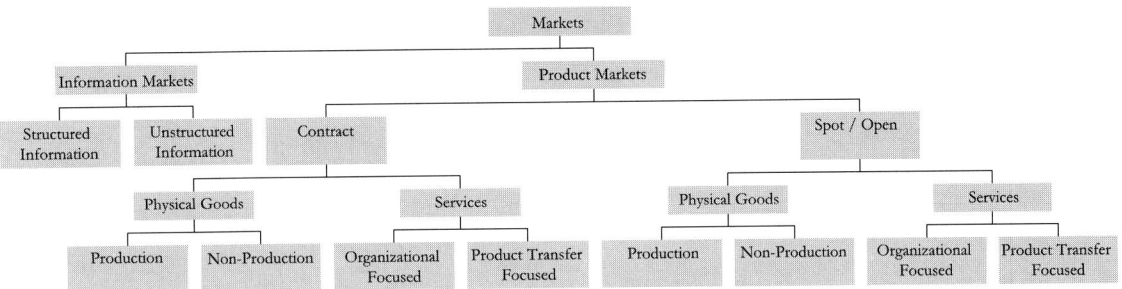

We can better understand the true variability in markets by examining several real-world examples from today's B2B landscape. Freemarkets, located in Pittsburgh, PA, is a creator of business-to-business on-line auctions for buyers of industrial parts, raw materials, and commodities and services. The company is primarily a buy-side open market mechanism, where pre-qualified suppliers transact business through reverse auctions. By contrast, VerticalNet, a Horsham, PA, company, owns and operates 57 commerce-enabled industrial communities. Unlike Freemarkets, VerticalNet is a sell-side market maker, which uses its industrial communities to build the market liquidity that its medium-sized sellers require to generate sales. VerticalNet operates a spot and open market exchange for production goods, as well as fixed- and dynamic-priced auctions and catalogs, across its communities. In turn, RightWorks, a privately held San Jose, CA, company, offers procurement software to large companies in order to help them streamline their purchasing processes. The company uses a combination of auction and catalog technology to facilitate buyers' contract purchase of non-production goods. Commerce One, of Pleasanton, CA, has a comparable procurement offering to that of Rightworks. However, Commerce One is also attempting to become a buy-side market maker by setting up large-company, non-production goods-buying consortia.

Conclusion

In this still relatively early stage of B2B e-commerce, marketplace owners and operators are experimenting with a variety of marketplaces. Given the high valuations placed on companies with distinctly different models, it remains to be seen which markets will ultimately emerge as the winners. However, it is likely that, given the value that can be added to both buyers and suppliers via very different information and product offerings, as well as through the use of very different transactional formats and tools, multiple players will ultimately survive and thrive in the B2B marketplace.

Blair LaCorte has served as VerticalNet's Senior Vice President of Strategy and Electronic Commerce since January 1999. Before joining VerticalNet, Mr LaCorte was an Executive in Residence at Internet Capital Group, specializing in B-to-B e-commerce companies. Prior to ICG, Mr LaCorte was the President of Internet Technology Group and Senior Vice President of Partnerhsips at CADIS, Inc., a software company specializing in electronic commerce and procurement in business-to-business markets. CADIS was later purchased by Aspect. In 1996, Mr LaCorte was named one of the top 10 business-to-business marketers of the year by Business and Marketing Age. He received a B.A. from the University of Maine and an MBA from the Amos Tuck School at Dartmouth.

Chapter 7:

Catalog Content Management

Trey Simonton, EVP, Business Development, ec-Content

Undoubtedly, one of the most high profile steps in establishing a business-to-business exchange is the selection and integration of the platform that powers the marketplace. However, the information that fuels the exchange is the supplier catalog content used by the buying organization to make its purchases. Buyers that are serious about migrating towards purchasing electronically believe that B2B exchanges enable them to have access to a broad range of suppliers in order to locate the items they need. The value the exchange provides will be determined by these buyers, and it is the quality of the content that will most directly impact the buyer's ability to locate and make informed decisions surrounding the items to be purchased. For an exchange to be successful, as well as differentiate itself as a viable procurement solution, it must fully address the issues surrounding the acquisition and maintenance of quality catalog content.

Despite their obvious importance, resources and expertise surrounding catalog content and ongoing catalog management have been underestimated by most B2B exchange initiatives. This chapter will help to define 'quality catalog content', as well as provide direction as to how an exchange should go about acquiring it. The chapter also establishes criteria surrounding the assembly of a solid content management strategy, profiles methods of managing content through supplier enablement tools and outsourced service providers, and documents issues in the supplier engagement process.

Content Management as a Foundation

B2B exchanges will spend millions of dollars buying and building the infrastructure to run an electronic marketplace. The strategy surrounding how supplier catalog content will be acquired, represented, managed, and maintained can provide a perfect roadmap for how to construct the overall solution.

Consider first the exchange community. Content in the context of the community can be defined as the supplier catalog information that is available to the purchasing organization. Traditionally, buyers have been able to locate the items they wish to purchase in a paper-based catalog. Detailed information surrounding the make-up of each item was contained in a long description or a detailed spec sheet that enabled buyers to make a selection and phone in a transaction. In an electronic procurement environment, static catalog content must be transformed into a 'transactive' state.

In order for catalog content to be considered transactive, the buyer must be able not only to locate the desired product within a catalog, but also validate the product based on a detailed description, compare products based on attributes and a uniform presentation, access availability, pricing, and configuration information, and ultimately send the purchase request to the supplier. In large supplier communities, accessing this type of quality catalog information has proven to be a difficult task and a key differentiator between emerging B2B exchanges. Integration of software and solutions that enable suppliers to provide robust catalog information and, in some cases, outsourcing the process of enhancing and cleansing the content can prove to be a key element in building an on-line community.

Once the quality of the content has been addressed, the capability to query the content, as well as to maintain its accuracy and support updates, drives commerce. How buyers query the content can drive the selection of a platform that has an advanced search engine that can configure items specifically to a buyer's preferences. Additional focus should be placed on the ability to customize catalog presentation to a specific buyer. Be aware that the functionality of various marketplace platforms is becoming more standardized surrounding workflow and transaction management. Leading B2B exchanges are selecting platforms that can be tailored to the type of catalog content that must be searched and based on the capability to integrate the content available to feed the transaction.

In both enabling the community using quality catalog content and selecting a platform based on its ability to integrate and make use of the supplier catalog, it is the content management strategy that provides a long-term vision for the requirements surrounding building the marketplace.

Varying Models for Managing Content

Exchange solution providers have outlined two basic approaches to managing content.

- A *'supply-side approach'* enables suppliers to provide a catalog representation via their website or through an ongoing catalog feed. Although this model is appealing, most suppliers do not have the technology or the resources to establish and maintain the high-quality catalog content required for the exchange to be successful. In addition, suppliers who can provide a quality representation of their catalog maintain their content in varying formats, and incorporate proprietary methods for searching, and processing an order. Multiple approaches to accessing supplier catalogs are very cumbersome and can quickly become frustrating for buyers within a B2B exchange.

- A *'buy-side approach'* enables B2B exchanges to establish an internal representation of supplier catalogs that can be hosted within the site. This model is most beneficial to buyers, because catalogs can be aggregated and normalized into a uniform presentation that can be easily searched and enables product comparison. Unfortunately, supporting this model requires a large amount of effort and sustaining the model can come at great cost to the exchange.

Selecting which model will be most beneficial to the long-term success of a B2B exchange is one of the key elements in building a content management strategy. The supply-side approach is most likely to provide speed-to-market, but unfortunately has proven to be difficult for suppliers with limited resources and technology. The buy-side approach provides the best catalog representation to buyers, but can be very costly to maintain for exchange providers.

The Importance of Quality Catalog Content

The primary purpose of a B2B exchange is to facilitate trading relationships between buyers and suppliers. Capable exchanges make it simple for buyers to quickly locate the items they want to buy and compare those items across a broad base of suppliers. To facilitate this process, supplier catalogs must be represented in a uniform manner, and the presentation of each item must be tied to attributes known to the buyer.

A quality content representation comprises a detailed extended description (no abbreviations), associated part numbers (including supplier, manufacturer, industry standards, etc), unit of measure, price, and associated images. Ideally, each item should have detailed attributes that break out various components of the item description. Attributes will vary across industries, but typically will include information like size, shape, color, or use. Attributes are the detailed components required to differentiate between similar items and are extremely important to buyers who must ensure the items they are purchasing fit or interact with an associated product. Based on the industry to which an exchange caters, attributes could prove to be a key method of differentiation and a crucial component surrounding ease of use.

If the items within a catalog are difficult to find and the search mechanism used by the exchange is not intuitive, the exchange is not likely to be accepted by the buying community. There are a number of practices that can be incorporated to make catalogs intuitive to the buyer.

1. A uniform structure for catalog information

Content can be organized across supplier catalogs using a taxonomy or commodity coding structure. This allows items within the catalog to be grouped based on industry, association, and use. For instance, a ballpoint pen would fall within an office supplies category, while a cordless drill might fall within a category focused on industrial supplies and equipment. Most taxonomies and commodity codes are organized in a hierarchical format that enables users to 'drill down' into detailed product groupings that will enhance search capabilities. Finding that same ballpoint pen mentioned earlier might include drilling down through categories starting with office products, then desktop supplies, then writing instruments leading to a long list of pencils, felt tip markers, and ballpoint pens. This makes it easy and intuitive for buyers to narrow their search by providing a structure for grouping of items within the catalog.

2. Content normalization

In most cases, computers and software are unable to compare items based simply on a long description. Both need items to be tied to a specific number or code for reliable comparison. The process of content normalization consists of mapping various item or part numbers to a specific number or code. The process can be very cumbersome, but the behind-the-scenes result can prove very beneficial to buyers. Suppliers work to brand items, by changing the description within their catalog. Multiple suppliers can offer exactly the same item, but buyers find it difficult to compare pricing based on the varying descriptions across supplier catalogs. It is the process of content normalization that delivers on the ability to establish an apples-to-apples comparison for buyers who want to locate the *right* item at the *best* price.

3. Personalization of catalog information

Although suppliers may be able to provide a catalog of tens of thousands of items, some buyers may only be interested in the items they purchase on a frequent basis. Further, when buyers view catalogs, they want pricing customized to their buying organization. B2B exchanges can do a lot to enhance the overall buying experience by limiting the amount of information buyers must disseminate, and by customizing or personalizing catalogs based on preferences established by the buyer.

Each of the practices presented above can offer huge benefits toward truly enhancing the buying experience within an on-line exchange. To provide a uniform structure for catalog information, content normalization, and catalog personalization requires additional investment by the B2B exchange and must be addressed early in establishing an ongoing content management strategy. It is important to note that although each practice can be established and administered on its own, the capabilities of the search engine and platform solution power the exchange that enables buyers to make use of these all-important benefits. This is one more reason why exchange providers are encouraged to establish a solid content management strategy prior to the selection of a platform to support the marketplace.

Understanding the Costs of Content Management

Content management is a complex task that has ongoing implications for a B2B exchange. Many exchanges naively assume that acquiring catalog content is a one-time task, and that once the catalogs are cleansed and available, updates can be managed easily over time. Further, blind assumptions are being made surrounding a supplier's capability to provide their catalogs in an electronic format with detailed descriptions and accurate, up-to-date information. Unfortunately, recent history has shown content management to be a much more difficult task than expected.

Most suppliers only have access to the very poor and abbreviated item descriptions held within their legacy inventory systems. The catalogs they currently furnish are paper-based and are represented electronically in a design layout for printing purposes, rather than in a structured database format for representation within an on-line exchange. The process for aggregating and enhancing catalog content can be very costly. Most B2B exchanges outsource this process in order to avoid the burden of having to establish an internal content management team.

Content and catalog transformation from traditional formats to a transactive electronic format requires a diverse set of skills. Skilled workers must have an in-depth knowledge of catalog feeds that come in varying data formats ranging from flat files, Excel spreadsheets, and Microsoft Access databases to complicated EDI and XML-based formats. These same workers offer domain expertise in specific industries to cleanse, categorize, and normalize product descriptions. Numerous software tools that enable this process have emerged on the market, making vast promises surrounding the automation of content management. The reality is that content cleansing continues to be a highly manual process that can be enhanced by software tools, but which requires expertise and human intervention for ongoing maintenance and support. B2B exchanges that acknowledge early that the expense and resources associated with content transformation represent an ongoing investment are best positioned to establish a plan for gradual growth tied to the acquisition and maintenance of supplier catalogs.

Suppliers are constantly updating both product and pricing information. Their legacy systems often change, requiring them to submit updates in varying formats. Since most supplier systems cannot provide a detailed change report, catalog updates arrive as complete replacement files. As a result, content that has been cleansed by the exchange must map prior enhanced descriptions to the new updates. Product and catalog content is seldom updated more than a few times a year. On the other hand, pricing updates occur much more frequently. Based on the industry and fluctuations in the market, pricing can change on a daily basis. In an ideal situation, suppliers would be able to provide these updates electronically and in a format specified by the B2B exchange. Unfortunately, the burden for being flexible and enabling suppliers to provide updates falls on the exchange, requiring the exchange to maintain adequate staff to process and manage the ongoing catalog feeds.

When evaluating whether to outsource the responsibility for content management, or to staff up to support the process internally, consider the focus of the exchange itself. Building content will establish content ownership and could be a long-term factor for differentiation. Exchanges that choose to take on the burden of managing content internally usually have to assemble a team solely focused on content acquisition and maintenance. Even with the benefits of content ownership, building a staff focused on content management can dilute the focus of the exchange and can become crippling to its prosperity if the team is not successful.

It has been estimated that as much as 30% of a B2B exchange's annual operating expenses could be associated with the ongoing management of content. No matter how content is acquired, updates and cleansing of catalog content are a never-ending process.

Getting Your Head Around Supplier Issues

Two key factors that help to assess the market opportunity for any B2B exchange are *fragmentation*, the high costs associated with transacting and communicating among trading partners, and *supply chain inefficiency*, the ability of suppliers to effectively support the transaction process. Although these factors indicate a very viable opportunity for the exchange to be successful, each is an even stronger indicator that both suppliers and buyers have only limited experience and resources focused on technology. The supplier community is likely to have a very difficult time providing even a small representation of quality catalog content. It is important for any B2B exchange to understand the reasons why a marketplace has remained fragmented.

1. *The importance of supplier relationships*

B2B exchanges that simply acquire, cleanse, and enhance supplier catalog content without establishing a contract with the supplier to define the trading relationship will face an inability to get orders fulfilled. This fact may seem obvious to some, but in an era when exchanges tout their ability to bypass the supplier, they often forget that the supplier is responsible for delivery and fulfillment of the product. In addition, many B2B exchanges assume that acquiring an electronic catalog from a supplier is as simple as calling up the supplier and asking for it. Suppliers are increasingly focused on data ownership and may be reluctant to give out their quality catalog content to unfamiliar exchanges. The distribution of the catalog is often controlled by someone in the corporate headquarters and finding the right individual to approve the release of the information could take a lot of time navigating a supplier's organization.

2. Establishing contract pricing

Once an exchange has access to a supplier's electronic catalog, pricing negotiations can begin. In most cases, B2B exchanges do not have the long-standing relationship or purchasing history required to negotiate the low prices and deep discounts needed to make an exchange truly attractive. B2B exchanges should approach suppliers like investors. A supplier must buy in to the value of the exchange, and to its long-term capability to offer increased revenue opportunities, before the supplier will agree to competitive pricing.

3. Suppliers can be reluctant to commit

It is important to recognize that suppliers are concerned about decreased profit margins and the inability to communicate directly with their buyers. In addition, most suppliers are being approached by numerous B2B exchanges, creating an increased number of customers to support. Maintaining quality catalog content that has to be customized and output to multiple exchanges can be cost-prohibitive to many suppliers. An increasing number of suppliers are pushing back stating that they are simply incurring additional costs by supporting so many on-line exchanges. New B2B exchanges should acknowledge the supplier's fears, and work with the supplier to incorporate new business processes that establish a win-win relationship for both parties.

4. Enabling suppliers to participate

As mentioned throughout this chapter, many of the suppliers currently being approached by B2B exchanges are burdened with antiquated technology and limited resources. There are many tools available that enable suppliers to submit their catalog content in varying formats for presentation in an on-line exchange. B2B exchanges can establish the most basic of tools by using an Excel spreadsheet or Microsoft Access database to provide suppliers with a template for presentation and submission of the content. In addition, there are a growing number of tools providers that have created a robust interface for suppliers to use to build their electronic catalogs. These tools can reside on the supplier's desktop or can be accessed via the Web. A combination of tools that enable suppliers to submit their catalogs electronically, plus the flexibility to receive catalogs in multiple formats, is an increasingly proactive way to get buy-in from the supplier community.

Issues surrounding the engagement of suppliers truly emphasize the importance of establishing the supplier relationship and provide evidence that, in some cases, the relationship with the supplier may be more valuable than the catalog itself. A large number of suppliers that are willing to participate in an on-line exchange may simply lack the ability to continually support their catalog content across multiple marketplaces. Once again, the burden falls back on the B2B exchange. In establishing a content management strategy, the exchange must take into account the costs associated with maintaining the catalog representation in a 'buy-side' model. It was recognized earlier that the 'supply-side' model could prove to be less expensive and quicker in the short-term, but issues surrounding the engagement of suppliers indicate that a 'supply-side' model could hinder broad supplier representation within the exchange.

Establishing a Content Management Strategy

After a thorough review of all the issues and costs associated with long-term content management, it becomes remarkably clear how difficult it is to accurately predict the time and resources necessary to get to market with a solid and sustainable catalog content representation. The target market will dictate the strategy a B2B exchange should take — both in the area of buyer expectations and supplier capabilities. When exchange providers begin to outline a content management strategy they must first make a few key decisions.

The Build vs. Buy Decision

In the area of content management, the build vs. buy decision establishes whether an exchange will assemble an internal staff to focus on content acquisition, enhancement, maintenance, and ongoing management, or will choose to outsource this portion of the business to a trusted partner.

1. *Building an internal content management team*

Building an internal content management team is likely to be the preferred solution in vertical industries that represent a limited number of products and services from a targeted supplier community. The benefits of building an internal content management team include ownership of the content and a greater level of control over the long-term use of that content. Many B2B exchanges that choose to develop an internal team focused on content management see the potential to re-sell the quality catalog content they create back into the supplier and manufacturer community.

It is important that when an exchange chooses to build and maintain its catalog content internally, it purchase tool sets to aid in the process. Currently, there are tools available for tracking and aggregating catalog feeds from suppliers, enabling suppliers to manage and maintain their own catalogs, as well as building taxonomies or commodity coding structures specific to a core industry for catalog content organization. The B2B exchange should be aware that the costs tied to purchasing these products, and target product selection are based on two criteria:

- the willingness of the targeted supplier community to adopt a prescribed tool set for maintaining its own catalogs; and
- the realistic requirements that the exchange will have to build and maintain the catalog content in-house.

When establishing a content management strategy that incorporates these tool sets, there are several things the B2B exchange should keep in mind. Many of these tool sets are rules-based. It can take a great deal of time to build the rules surrounding the aggregation and management of supplier catalogs. Once established, the rules for supplier-specific catalog feeds will provide a system for efficient management of item and pricing updates. It is important to note that although tool sets focused on the aggregation of catalog content provide tremendous capabilities surrounding organizing and formatting catalog feeds, human intervention will still be required to cleanse the content. On the other hand, tool sets that are focused on enabling the supplier are predicated on the fact that the suppliers within a target community are willing to invest the time and resources it takes to cleanse and maintain their own catalog information using the associated tool. Again, as mentioned above, the B2B exchange should research its target market segment before assuming that the supplier community will be willing to incorporate a prescribed tool set.

Problems arise in the *build* approach when the limitations of the internal content management team and its ability to rapidly establish, cleanse, and maintain quality catalog content are counterproductive to the success of the exchange. B2B exchanges that choose the build approach will have to factor in the costs associated with the purchase of content management tool sets and the ongoing costs associated with employee resources required to support this portion of the business.

2. *Buying or outsourcing content from a third-party content service provider*

Buying or outsourcing content from a third-party content service provider is the preferred solution in horizontal or vertical industries that require the B2B exchange to interface with large numbers of suppliers representing millions of products and services. Outsourcing the content management process is the ideal option for B2B exchanges that do not wish to dilute their focus on the core business of building an on-line trading community.

A content service provider (CSP) is an organization that is focused on the acquisition, normalization, management, and maintenance of large volumes of catalog content. Since CSPs are in the business of managing content, they are likely to have existing relationships with a large number of suppliers in target industries. Further, depending on the amount of time a CSP has been in business, it may have access to, or ownership of, large libraries of high-quality catalog content. This type of offering provides immediate liquidity for a B2B exchange, enabling the exchange to get to market quickly with a diverse catalog representation.

CSPs are also well equipped with their own tools for aggregating, cleansing, and normalizing content. Most CSPs have established routines surrounding the organization of content into specific taxonomies, as well as the attribution of content for specific industries. Also, truly capable CSPs place as much focus on engaging the supplier community as on managing the content. The requirements for being flexible with receipt of supplier catalogs in multiple formats, as well as providing tools for enabling suppliers to provide their initial catalog feeds, do not go away by simply outsourcing the problem to a third-party service provider.

When comparing multiple content service providers, a B2B exchange can use a number of criteria to qualify and select a long-term partner. Relationships with established suppliers, content libraries that offer immediate liquidity and speed-to-market, existing processes for aggregating, cleansing, and normalizing content, tools that enable suppliers to create and submit their electronic catalogs, the ability to accept catalog feeds from suppliers in multiple formats, scalability, and domain expertise in cleansing and categorizing content for an exchange's target industry, are all good standards for comparison. However, the most important criterion for comparing CSPs should be the quality of the content the CSP will provide and maintain on an ongoing basis.

The degree to which a B2B exchange outsources the content management process to a third-party service provider is the final component of the *buy* decision. Although the exchange wants to leverage as much as possible the strengths of the CSP, the exchange should never surrender the long-term ownership of the supplier relationship. In this chapter, we have repeatedly emphasized the establishment of the trading relationship as one of the key purposes of the exchange, and as a point of long-term differentiation.

Complete Content Management Strategy

A complete content management strategy should yield a detailed specification surrounding how catalogs will be formatted, organized, and displayed in the exchange. This specification will help in the selection of an exchange platform, as well as the selection of the search engine that will be used to query the catalog. It is certainly worth the time it takes to research how well content management tool sets, either purchased or provided by CSPs integrate with various exchange platforms.

The content management strategy will also establish a plan for growing the number of suppliers represented within the exchange over the course of the first year, as well as moving forward. B2B exchanges are encouraged to pilot their content management strategy with a limited number of suppliers for at least 90 days, and to be willing to modify the strategy if it is not successful. Although speed-to-market continues to be important, a lack of quality catalog content can be a devastating blow for an on-line exchange.

Finally, the content management strategy should outline a detailed program for engaging suppliers. B2B exchanges need to establish trading relationships with targeted suppliers, but once the supplier agrees to participate, what comes next? A detailed supplier engagement program will outline step-by-step instructions with flexible options for how the supplier should provide and update their electronic catalog. The quality of this information can be invaluable in making it easier for the supplier to be up and running quickly, as well as in alleviating many of the supplier's fears surrounding participation.

The core planning surrounding solutions required to build a B2B exchange can be derived from various components of the content management strategy. Based on the build vs. buy decision, a content management strategy will be established that outlines costs associated with both short- and long-term content management goals. Once again, these costs should not be underestimated and are an important factor in providing a strong foundation to ensure the success of a B2B exchange.

Conclusion

In a market that is highly focused on first mover advantage, the key to continuing success is the ability to deliver an on-line exchange that provides both pricing and procurement efficiencies. Today's B2B exchanges are discovering that the key to delivering on this promise is a solid content management strategy that drives many of the benefits to buyers within the marketplace. To summarize the points outlined in this chapter:

- Many of the existing B2B exchanges have underestimated both the costs and the resources associated with the acquisition of content, as well as long-term content management.

- B2B exchanges have the ultimate responsibility for turning information-based catalogs into quality transactive catalogs for use in their marketplace.

- B2B exchanges can enhance the overall buying experience by establishing a commodity coding structure or taxonomy which makes the content easier to search, normalizing the content so that buyers can find the *right* item at the *right* price, and customizing catalogs so that buyers are presented with their personalized catalog presentation and associated pricing.

- Most suppliers do not currently have the technology or resources to dedicate to establishing and maintaining quality electronic catalogs.

- In order to address supplier issues, B2B exchanges should focus on the relationship with the supplier, establish a personal trading relationship, acknowledge each supplier's fears, and provide tools and programs that better enable the supplier to participate.

- When establishing a content management strategy, the capabilities and expectations of both suppliers and buyers in the target market should drive the decision of an exchange to build its own content management team or to outsource to a third-party content service provider.

- Finally, in addition to establishing whether the exchange will build its own content management team or outsource to a third-party CSP, a complete content management strategy should specify how catalogs will be formatted, organized, and displayed in the exchange, create a plan for growing the number of suppliers that are represented within the exchange, and outline a detailed program that makes it simple and profitable for a supplier to participate.

In the race to establish a B2B exchange, high-quality content can be a noticeable advantage. Exchanges will differentiate themselves based on the quality of their catalog content, usability of their interface, and key relationships with suppliers. B2B exchanges that are willing to prioritize speed-to-market as a close second behind using content management as a strong foundation for building the marketplace will find that it pays huge dividends in mass market adoption, as well as long-term success.

Trey Simonton, EVP of Business Development, joined ec-Content, Inc in January 2000 and is responsible for providing leadership, vision and direction for the business development, sales and marketing departments. Trey provides business planning and strategy crucial to ec-Content's support of digital marketplaces, and drives strategic alliance partnerships tied to the provision of content management and maintenance services. Trey also establishes and oversees ec-Content's positioning and messaging in their marketplace, highlighting the company's business objectives and technology superiority.

Prior to working with ec-Content, Trey had a wealth of experience in the e-procurement industry. He has been working with processes, procedures and technologies focused on the enablement of suppliers since the early nineties. He assisted in the build-out of the one of the first digital marketplaces solely focused on government agencies which employed at AMBAC CONNECT, Inc., serving as their National Vendor Account Manager. There, Trey deployed a supplier catalog and content management strategy that supported electronic procurement for thousands of schools, cities, and municipalities in Texas, California, Missouri, and Pennsylvania.

Trey has also held numerous consulting and management-based positions within the e-commerce industry, where he has been involved with electronic procurement solutions and Internet operations across market segments. Trey held positions at Empower Solutions, a premier provider of software implementation solutions and led the Internet solutions practice in their work for the Treasury Department and Judicial System for the Government of Puerto Rico. Trey received a BA in Business Administration and International Business and Marketing from Baylor University.

Chapter 8:
Selecting the Right Trading Platform

Ramesh Patil, CTO, RightWorks Corporation

Throughout this book, industry experts have shared their views on the various conceptual and business challenges faced by exchange operators. Entire chapters have been devoted to the very complex issues of how to evaluate and incorporate content and supply chain management, logistics, and financial services. In this chapter, we move beyond concepts and ideas into implementation, exploring the technological aspects of building and deploying an exchange.

While there are many decisions to be made, none has greater consequence than the selection of a trading platform. The trading platform is the technological heart of an exchange. It provides the functional means by which the exchange enables participants to transact business, integrate with their back-end enterprise systems, and seamlessly access service offerings from external providers.

So, what is the 'right' trading platform? Before we can answer that question, it is necessary to explore the characteristics of successful exchanges to gain a complete understanding of the forces that drive users to participate in exchanges, ultimately leading to a self-sustaining exchange. In the latter part of this chapter, we describe the technical qualities necessary for the trading platform to enable these 'characteristics' of success, ending with a comprehensive list of questions to ask trading platform vendors.

But first and foremost, let's explore what we mean by 'trading platform'.

What is a Trading Platform?

Essentially, a trading platform is the combination of hardware and software components that run an exchange. Although the specific combination of components may vary based on the purpose and volume of the exchange, there is a core platform that all exchanges have in common. The core platform requires hardware components such as server machines, database servers, and networks to provide the electronic skeleton upon which the software components operate. The software components of the trading platform are those applications that power the nerve center of the exchange — not only supplying the functionality of the exchange to participants, but enabling integration with external services (such as procurement, financial settlement, or order fulfillment software applications hosted by Internet service providers).

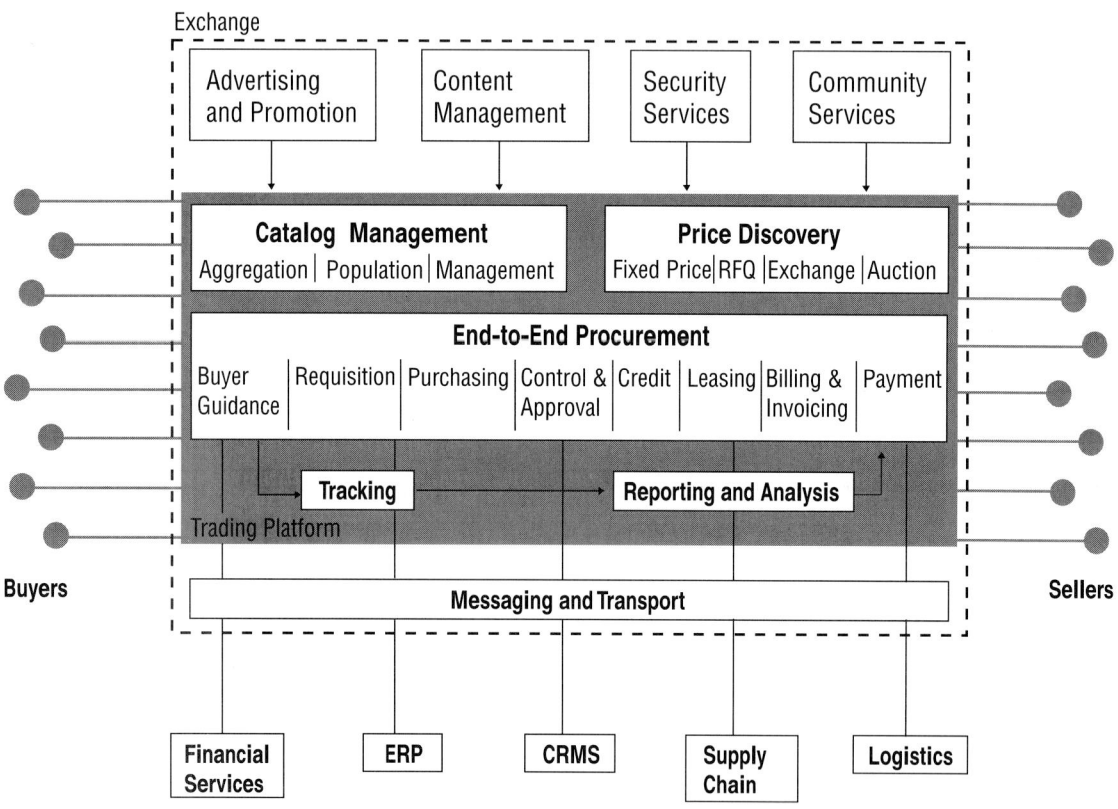

Figure 1. Trading platforms handle catalog management, price discovery, and the procurement life cycle, while enabling integration with service providers and back-end enterprise systems.

Just like other types of e-businesses, the core platform must pass the e-commerce litmus test of any system designed for the Internet — that is, security, scalability, performance, load balancing, and failover.

When selecting a trading platform, you must consider many issues, including the inter-relationship of the hardware and software required for the trading platform. For example, does the software require that the exchange operator purchase expensive high-end machines to run servers; or can the system be expanded using additional, less expensive systems? Another important consideration is how the trading platform integrates the platform's software components with the external software components of suppliers (such as catalog contents), buying organizations (such as ERP systems), and service providers (such as third-party logistics).

So, before delving into the numerous technical issues that must be considered when choosing a trading platform, let's first describe the characteristics that define a successful B2B exchange.

What are the Characteristics that Define Successful Exchanges?

Successful exchanges are those ventures that dominate their vertical market, sustaining enough participation that they cannot easily be overcome by a competitor. But how do successful exchanges build and sustain the participation necessary to be so resilient in the face of competition? By offering a differentiated set of services that maximizes the value for *each* market participant. Essentially, the value of the exchange can be measured by the extent to which exchange participants *incorporate* the exchange into their business processes. The more vital the exchange is to the business processes of its participating organizations, the more successful the exchange will ultimately be. The characteristics that define the value offered by successful exchanges can be described in terms of the following:

- **Ease of use.** Can users easily access and use the exchange without assistance?
- **Business adaptation.** Does the exchange seem as if it is an extension of the user's company? Does it use the same business terminology, and reflect familiar business rules and processes?
- **Full transaction life cycle.** Does the exchange support a full range of services necessary to close the loop on purchasing activities — from product selection, to order fulfillment, to financial settlement?
- **Full procurement support.** Can the exchange provide all the purchasing features that buying organizations require to conduct business as usual?
- **Global availability and reliability.** Is the exchange always up and running? Does it perform searches and complete transactions quickly? Does the exchange operate as a trusted third party?
- **Participant self-service.** Can users easily join and access the exchange *how and when* they want to?
- **Fast evolution.** Can the exchange innovate rapidly, adding new functionality that satisfies the needs of its participants?

- **Commerce intelligence.** Does the exchange provide its users with actionable insight — that is, the ability to determine how they are performing with regards to exchange activity?
- **Content.** Can exchange users seamlessly access content, whether it is hosted by the exchange or by a third-party provider?

The following sections examine each characteristic in turn to offer a more complete understanding of the forces that drive successful exchanges.

1. Ease of use

Ease of use is always a characteristic that users expect from an Internet-based business, including exchanges. As with business-to-consumer (B2C) e-commerce sites like amazon.com, the exchange needs to be easy enough to use that any authorized user, at any location, can use any Web-browser-capable client device to view a product catalog, select items, and submit their 'shopping cart contents' for purchase. Where exchange procurement differs from B2C e-commerce sites is what happens *after* the shopping cart is submitted — the shopping cart contents become the items on a purchase requisition or other type of purchasing transaction. This concept of self-service procurement is how buying corporations reduce operations expenses and improve user productivity.

2. Business adaptation

Business adaptation, or the characteristic that allows exchange operators to 'personalize' the exchange experience by adapting it to the needs and business processes of the participating organizations, is another critical characteristic for both buyers and suppliers. In this sense, personalization encompasses everything from branding elements (essentially, the look and feel of the exchange) to the operation of the exchange itself: what catalog items buyers can choose, the business processes that must be followed for trading activities, or how specific requisitions should be approved within an organization.

Business personalization is essentially made up of two elements. First, participating organizations must be able to define how they interact with the exchange. This includes how the exchange appears visually: the fonts and colors that are used, which buttons appear on which forms, and which languages are used. Procurement activities should also be customizable, including:

- How the exchange operates based on the user's role within the organization, the user's requisition authority, and the organization's internal processes for determining spending limits, budget tolerances, and approval processes.

- How the exchange filters the user's view of content based on the organization's preferred suppliers and the user's authorization to purchase certain types of items.

- How price lists are customized to capture unique arrangements between buyers and sellers.

Second, exchange participants must be able to define their own functional roles and responsibilities from the macro-organization level down to the requirements of groups within their organizations, and then to individual users. Because each user may have a different role with its own set of unique responsibilities, the exchange must be able to 'control' its interaction with users based on the permissions and authorities defined by those participating organizations. This means, for example, that content may be dynamically generated and delivered based on the user accessing the exchange. This may extend to a user's view of catalog items, his authority to execute various functions within the exchange (eg, submit requisitions or administer purchase orders), his spending authority, the approval process for his expenditures, and his ability to see the transactions of others within the exchange. For example, if a user is only authorized to view and purchase items costing less than US$5,000, the exchange filters the user's view of the catalog so items of greater value are hidden from view.

Not only must the exchange be able to adapt to the needs of buying organizations, it must meet the business needs of suppliers as well. Since each supplier organization uses a different catalog format, communication protocol, and business model for selling their goods and services, so must the exchange support this diversity and enable suppliers to customize, or brand, their participation with the exchange. Streamlining incorporation and maintenance of product catalogs also greatly affects adoption rates.

Realistically, to facilitate this degree of business adaptation, exchange operators must let each organization manage its own administration. Enabling self-service administration minimizes the exchange operator's costs by keeping the exchange processes efficient and streamlined, while giving exchange participants greater control. And although exchange operators may choose to vary the amount of 'personalization' they allow participating organizations to have, they need the flexibility to offer personalization capabilities on a variety of levels to meet the diverse requirements of the exchange community.

3. Full transaction life-cycle

As business increasingly moves on-line, the exchange will become the center of electronic business commerce and collaboration. This means that the exchange must 'enable' the full transaction life-cycle — from product comparison and selection, through purchasing to delivery.

However, this does not mean that the trading platform 'implements' all of this functionality by itself. Sticking to core competencies and outsourcing the rest to other service companies keeps the exchange focused on its primary goals, and prevents the costly 'reinventing-the-wheel' syndrome. There are many content and business services that can fulfill aspects of the transaction life-cycle for the exchange. For example:

- **Financial services**. Just like any other e-commerce site, exchanges need to supply built-in payment processing to buying organizations. This means integration with third-party providers that assist buyers with credit management for establishing lines of credit or escrow lines of credit. In the case of global exchanges, international lines of credit will also be necessary. Automated banking is another benefit exchanges can offer users — helping them to establish credit and transfer funds on-line. Other types of financial services that can be integrated with an exchange include credit verification, settlement, trade financing, insurance, escrow, cash management, and tax calculation.

- **Logistics services** such as warehouse management, load consolidation, drop shipment, and event synchronization. For example, an exchange should be integrated with carriers (such as UPS, FedEx, Airborne Express, and the United Postal Service) for shipment tracking so that buyers can see the status of order delivery.

- **Content services** from outside content catalogs, content aggregators, or other exchanges.

- **Supply chain services** such as transportation management, supply planning, collaboration, and demand forecasting.

These types of services have been fully discussed in other chapters — the key point to consider here is that a trading platform must be able to accommodate the integration of these services.

4. *Full procurement support*

In addition to *enabling and supporting* full transaction life cycles, an exchange should be equipped to handle all aspects of the purchasing life cycle itself. The exchange must furnish multiple options for how buyers can purchase items from suppliers, including the types of procurement transactions summarized in the following table.

Type of Transaction	Behavior of the Exchange
On catalog purchasing	Provides multi-vendor catalog viewing. Combines items from multiple catalogs into a single purchase.
Special requests	Enables purchases from catalogs other than 'approved' catalogs. Enforces the same business rules and approvals processes as for on-catalog purchasing.
Purchase requisitions	Automatically forwards purchase requisitions through an organization according to the defined purchasing rules, approvals processes, budgetary limits, and catalog restrictions of that organization (on a per-user basis).

Type of Transaction	Behavior of the Exchange
Request-for-quote (RFQ)	Automates the request-for-quote process by electronically contacting appropriate suppliers, and then converting approved quotes to purchase requisitions.
Project-bound purchasing	Enforces defined project-bound purchasing rules as authorized users make purchases against a project budget. Notifies project owners of procurement activity.
Blanket purchase order	Automates decrements against a blanket purchase order between a buying organization and a supplier.
Credit card purchasing	Interfaces with payment processors (such as Network Commerce Inc. or VeriSign Payment Services), to enable real-time financial processing.
Auctions	Automates the auction process to enable real-time bidding from multiple buyers on supplier-listed items.
Reverse auctions	Automates the reverse auction process to enable real-time competitive sales from multiple suppliers with regards to a buyer's desired purchase list.
Spot buys	Based on the fluctuation of the market, enables organizations to buy large quantities of a commodity outside of normal purchasing procedures.

Further details about these types of procurement transactions are provided in the following sections.

On catalog purchasing

Every buying organization must be able to determine which vendor catalogs their users can browse to purchase items. When purchasing items from these approved catalogs, users should be able to perform extensive searches to find the items they require. Since suppliers offer different types of products or services that a user may need, the ability to combine items from multiple catalogs into a single purchase is essential.

Special requests

Although many purchasing organizations prefer to restrict buying to approved catalogs, when a user cannot find an item in the catalog he or she must be able to create a special request for the item. This is essential for helping users obtain the items they need for their jobs. Likewise, when new items or services are added to the exchange, or when new suppliers join the exchange, users must have the option to purchase off-catalog items. The same business rules and approvals processes should be maintained for special requests as for standard catalog requests.

Purchase requisitions
When users 'purchase' the items in their shopping carts, this action should generate a purchase requisition (PR). The PR acts as the control over the selections users make and, based on budgetary constraints or vendor preferences, is approved and forwarded to the appropriate supplier for purchase.

To meet these requirements, buying organizations must be able to define purchasing rules, approvals processes, budgetary limits, and catalog restrictions on a per-user basis. The exchange must then be able to use this information to modify the automated execution of the order in real time. For example, purchase requisitions should be automatically forwarded through the buying organization according to the pre-configured approval process for that organization. Once approved, purchase requisitions should then automatically become purchase orders, and routed to suppliers according to the organization's preferences.

Request for quote
Typically, the request-for-quote (RFQ) process is manual. Buyers create an RFQ that lists the items for which they want price quotes from suppliers, and submit it to their purchasing departments. A purchasing agent then conducts an analysis manually with one or more suppliers to obtain quotes. The best quote, usually from a price perspective, is then selected and the RFQ is updated with this quote and returned to the requestor. If accepted, the RFQ becomes a purchase requisition. Enabling electronic request-for-quotes to be automatically converted to purchase requisitions affords a useful value-add.

Project-bound purchasing
Buying organizations typically set up budgets by project, letting authorized users make purchases of approved items for the project, up to the budget assigned for the project. Exchanges that automate this process by allowing buying organizations to define project-bound purchasing rules, and by enforcing these rules as authorized users purchase items for the project, provide a valuable service to buying organizations. For example, granting project owners complete ownership of the project budget, and empowering them to set control points (for example, 75% of budget) that determine when automatic e-mail notifications will alert them of procurement activity.

Blanket purchase order
Sometimes buying organizations use blanket purchase orders for frequently purchased items. In this case, the buying organization establishes a contract with a supplier to purchase a certain quantity of a commodity over a period of time in exchange for a discount or special price. Once the purchase order is established, decrements against the purchase order are issued for purchases against the blanket purchase order. Exchanges that provide this functionality offer added convenience to buying organizations.

Credit card purchasing

Sometimes, organizations may want to purchase items with a corporate credit card. By interfacing with payment processors (such as Network Commerce Inc. or VeriSign Payment Services), exchanges supply a great service to buying organizations by enabling real-time financial processing. These types of organizations help customers and merchants safely and easily buy and sell merchandise online by offering secure, reliable, and affordable credit card, debit card, purchase card, and electronic check processing services.

Auctions

With auctions, a supplier lists the items they want to sell, and multiple buyers bid for purchase. For example, a company may have excess inventory or plant equipment that still has value, and the company would like to dispose of the inventory in the most economical way. The company identifies the items they are auctioning, determines the rules of the auction and the time frame, and runs the auction — selecting the best bid at the close.

Reverse auctions

Sometimes, users know what items they want to purchase, but they do not know which vendor they want to purchase from. In this case, reverse auctions may be used. With reverse auctions, a user can list the items they want to buy and set a deadline for purchasing each item, and multiple suppliers can bid competitive sales prices. Users should be able to make the process transparent (open-bid process) so that suppliers can see the best bid for each item, or choose to hide bids from suppliers (closed-bid process).

A deviation on the reverse auction occurs when buyers do not know potential suppliers of the items they want to purchase. In this case, the purchasing organization determines the suppliers and conducts the reverse auction for the buyer. Since reverse auctions are becoming more popular in markets where there are price fluctuations (for commodity markets such as gold, silver, or steel), exchange operators may decide to support them for their exchanges.

Spot buys

Some organizations regularly need certain commodities necessary for their business, and will buy them on a periodic basis when prompted by their ERP systems. But when prices are low, it behooves these organizations to buy large quantities of the commodities they need all at once. Spot buying is a dynamic process based on the fluctuation of the market, and typically occurs outside of standard corporate purchasing procedures. Some organizations also use spot buys to process one-time purchases of commodities. An exchange should give organizations the flexibility they need to enable spot buying while maintaining budgetary control.

5. Global availability and reliability

Just like any other e-business, exchanges must exhibit the classic e-commerce definitions of high availability and reliability — this means 24x7 availability and 99.9% uptime. Also, the faster the exchange executes transactions, the more users will enjoy the speed and ease of using it, and the more frequently they will use the services of the exchange.

Fast response time can be measured in two different ways: by transaction, or by user interaction. We commonly think of fast response times in terms of transaction time — how quickly can the exchange execute a transaction (for example, 'submit a requisition')? However, the time it takes to complete a user interaction is another measurement to consider. Significant studies show that the usability of a system and user satisfaction is influenced heavily by the time it takes the system to respond to a user action (like clicking on a link). If the request for showing a new item in a catalog takes 200ms, the user will browse the catalog. But if it takes a minute, the user will be reluctant to wait that long, and may use alternative methods to identify buying needs.

There are other aspects to availability and reliability by which exchanges are measured. Exchanges are expected to operate as a 'trusted third party'. This means the exchange must be a neutral party that reliably conducts its operations — providing a fair trading environment for all exchange participants, assuring equal and transparent access to the exchange, guaranteeing accurate transaction execution, and maintaining the privacy of each user's and organization's data.

In the most granular sense, trusted third-party requirements stem from transactional integrity. For example, sellers' products and pricing must be posted correctly, and buyers' bids and orders must be executed exactly as specified. For organizations to trust the exchange enough to make it part of their business process, the exchange must assure accuracy in its execution of transactions as well as the workflows that support it.

Lastly, exchanges can further increase the positive or 'reliable' impression of participants by first ensuring that buyers and sellers are qualified to complete the transactions to which they agree, and then providing mechanisms for handling complaints and resolving disputes.

6. Participant self-service

One of the most effective ways to drive adoption of an exchange is to grant participants control over their own registration, content, business processes, users and groups, and administration. Exchange operators should be able to give participants the freedom to use the exchange how and when they want to. This, in turn, drives user participation because it is faster for users to get started using the exchange.

However, empowering exchange participants does not mean that the exchange itself 'gives up' control. What it does mean is that the exchange operator must decide what levels of self-service it will permit participating organizations to have. Often, the level of self-service granted is based on the importance of the organization to the exchange.

But once participants are given control over certain aspects of the exchange, it is essential that the user interface is easy to use (remember that ease of use is one of the major characteristics that determines a successful exchange). So keep in mind that all kinds of users will likely participate in the exchange, including employees, managers, purchasing agents, suppliers, and administrators — some technical, some not — and that the interface to the exchange must be accessible to all of them without requiring a great deal of training.

For suppliers as well, self-service can play a very important role in how the exchange attracts and retains participants. For example, exchanges may want to grant their suppliers control over the presentation of their content as well as the freedom to update catalogs whenever necessary — including applicable business models, catalog formats, pricing structures, and branding (as discussed earlier).

7. Fast evolution

It's a given that the Internet has accelerated the pace of change in many ways. Internet standards are rapidly evolving to accommodate new technological innovations. With greater competition, business requirements for exchanges are increasing as new functionality generates new user expectations. And as exchanges strive to attract and retain users with improved functionality, the marketing requirements for exchanges are evolving as well. To 'survive and thrive,' exchanges must be highly adaptable — and the key to adaptability is ensuring that the trading platform adheres to open standards and architectures.

8. Commerce intelligence

Helping participating organizations to evaluate different aspects of their usage of the exchange is another way in which exchanges can enhance their value proposition. For example, letting suppliers evaluate their exchange-driven sales affords an opportunity not only for the supplier to alter operations to enhance future sales, but illustrates the value of the exchange to the supplier's business. Likewise, providing analysis capabilities to buying organizations helps those organizations to assess the performance of various suppliers relative to past orders, analyze vendor utilization, or determine how many orders are outstanding and when those orders will impact payables — further integrating the exchange into their business processes. However, it is important to note that it is the exchange operator that controls these capabilities, thus securing each organization's private information — granting access only to authorized users.

There are a number of other ways that exchanges can accommodate commerce intelligence. For example, incorporating scrolling tickers to display live bids and offers for auctions, or to show price information for various featured products. Live news feeds, or alerts that notify companies when prices change or when a supplier adds a new product to the catalog, are other possibilities.

9. Content

Offering seamless access to a wide diversity of items from many popular suppliers can be one of the most effective ways of encouraging exchange participant activity. 'Content'— and lots of it — will drive exchange business (and the resulting margins). However, simply enabling large quantities of content will not generate the participation that exchanges need to become self-sustaining. The success of an exchange is much more likely to be driven by *how* the exchange integrates content from its suppliers and presents content to its buyers. The exchange must be able to:

- integrate content from hundreds of thousands of suppliers, resulting in millions of stock keeping units (SKUs);
- provide effective comparison shopping with the information necessary to make educated buying decisions;
- enforce buying rules, including the ability to hide items from view based on authorization levels;
- flexibly import catalogs and modify them to add other organizational attributes;
- provide easy-to-traverse HTML catalogs that can be viewed from standard Web browsers; and
- allow for multiple ways of navigating and searching content, including multiple drill-down hierarchies (organized by supplier, commodity, or other logical organization), parametric searches, keyword searches, or text searches.

To encourage supplier participation, exchanges may want to allow suppliers to control the appearance of their catalog to consumers. For example, suppliers may wish to create catalog items with colored, formatted text and tables, colored graphics, sound, URL links (for linking to reference information on an intranet or a supplier's website), PDF files, or other types of attached files. Exchanges may also want to support supplier-defined parameters (or attributes) for different types of commodities. For example, light bulbs have wattage, socket type, and voltage, whereas computers have processor type, memory, and expansion slots. And, of course, these parameters should be fully searchable as well.

Qualities to Look for in Your Trading Platform

Now that we have a better understanding of those characteristics that underlie the value proposition for a successful exchange, it's time to take a look at the qualities that the trading platform must possess. In this discussion, a 'quality' is essentially an attribute that the trading platform should exemplify. By first exploring what the exchange must be able to *do* to be successful, we know what *qualities* the trading platform must possess to bring these characteristics to fruition. And these qualities, or attributes, will form the basis for the trading platform's technical requirements. For example, is the platform configurable — does it allow exchange participants to 'configure' the exchange interface to meet their needs without 'customizing' software? The following qualities are essential when selecting a trading platform to power your exchange:

- **Multi-organization capability.** Is the trading platform organized around a 'many-to-many' architecture, supporting the needs of all its users?
- **Configurability.** Can the trading platform be configured to meet the needs of its participating organizations and users, or does it require software customization?
- **Security.** Is the trading platform secure — is its transactional integrity preserved and does it protect each user's information from unauthorized access?
- **Interoperability.** Can the trading platform interoperate with external services and systems — can it integrate with systems controlled by participating organizations or services provided by third parties?
- **Adaptability.** Does the trading platform support near real-time updates to exchange information, and can it be evolved quickly to offer new functionality to exchange users?
- **Scalability.** Can the trading platform support an increasing number of participants and services, scaling hardware and software components easily and cost-effectively to meet performance requirements?
- **Globalization.** Does the trading platform support multiple languages and currencies, and deal with different tax structures, customs, and settlement issues?

1. *Multi-organization capability*

Exchanges are fundamentally 'many-to-many' and, as such, must accommodate the needs of buyers, suppliers, and the exchange operator. As discussed, exchanges must adapt their appearance and operation according to the business and e-procurement requirements of their participating organizations. Many of these customization capabilities must extend to groups and individuals within these participating organizations.

What this really means is that each exchange user interacts with the exchange differently, and this interaction is based on the user's role and the business rules defined by that user's organization. This many-to-many capability allows the exchange operator to gear the behavior of the exchange to the user accessing it. From a technical standpoint, this quality requires dynamic HTML generation, server-based execution, role-based authorization and authentication, and form-based configuration for organizations to administer users, groups, processes, and content. A workflow engine is also required if the trading platform is going to implement organization-specific business rules and approvals processes. Multi-organization capabilities are typically organized into the categories described in the table overleaf.

Multi-organization capability	Description
Branding	Gives organizations the power to customize the presentation of the exchange, including the layout, fonts, and colors used.
User interface	Lets organizations customize the user interface elements that appear on various pages within the system — for example, the buttons or fields that appear on the purchasing requisition page.
Catalog views	Based on a user's role and associated access privileges, allows organizations to filter a user's view of the items within the catalog, without needing to create separate catalogs. Organizations should also be able to filter the catalog to only show items from their preferred suppliers.
Transaction views	Enables organizations to restrict a user's view of the procurement transactions to those for which they have access privileges.
Pricing	Lets organizations change the prices shown in the catalog to reflect special negotiated agreements with suppliers.
Catalog content	Gives suppliers control over the content and presentation of their catalog as well as their pricing schemes, without impacting overall exchange performance.
Preferences	Permits users to determine the language used to present information.
Account codes	Enables organizations and groups to define and use their own internal account codes when purchasing items.
Organization hierarchies	Lets organizations use their corporate chain of command as the basis for procurement approvals.
Roles	Based on a user's role within the organization, allows organizations to shape the behavior of the exchange. For example, organizations should be able to restrict the activities the user can perform using the exchange, and the amount of money the user can spend without authorization.

Multi-organization capability	Description
Business rules	Empowers organizations to implement their internal procurement rules within the exchange. For example, organizations should be able to handle special cases like designating a single approver for all computer purchases.
Approvals processes	Gives organizations control over their exchange-based purchasing by allowing them to enforce internal approvals processes via the exchange.

Many-to-many capabilities have a broad reach, impacting all of the functional areas of an exchange. To make these capabilities technically feasible, the trading platform must meet one fundamental requirement — all many-to-many capabilities must be handled from a single instance of the software (ie, a single website and database combination).

There are two key reasons why exchange operators should insist on running the exchange from a single instance of the platform. First, as a single instance of the trading platform is 'scaled out' to support many organizations through the addition of multiple redundant components for each function, it is less susceptible to failure in a single component, and is thereby more reliable and easier to administer. Second, to gain full efficiency of the exchange, the exchange operator should be able to aggregate the data from all participating organizations for processing and analysis. This is easily accommodated when all organizations are using the same instance of the trading platform. What happens if the trading platform does not support a single instance? In that case, it would be far more difficult to provide comprehensive business adaptation for participating organizations. The exchange operator would have to support individual instances of the exchange to accommodate the special needs of each organization that requests adaptations (significantly increasing the operational burden), or simply deny the requests (potentially jeopardizing business with those organizations). Additionally, using multiple personalized instances of the trading platform makes it difficult to:

- Aggregate orders from different buying organizations to gain better pricing from suppliers.
- Aggregate reporting across participating organizations. Many different database instances must be created and data from them aggregated for operational analysis by the exchange operator.
- Maintain exchange software in a cost-efficient manner. For example, the catalog for each buying organization must be maintained separately — as a result, a simple price change would have to be propagated to each exchange instance to which it applies.
- Integrate the exchange with customer services. CRM systems must be integrated with each instance of the exchange, and customer service representatives must connect and re-connect to individual buyer systems to respond to customer inquiries.

Aside from enabling the fully personalized exchange to run from a single instance of the trading platform, it is also helpful, from a performance standpoint, that the trading platform uses a separate deployment server. Incorporating a separate deployment server in the platform architecture gives suppliers a way to freely update content, while letting exchange operators retain full control over when those updates are deployed to the production server of the exchange.

A multi-organizational view also allows the exchange to provide integrated data as well as analysis tools to participating organizations, offering valuable insight into their exchange participation while illustrating the value they reap from the exchange. Such analysis tools should include powerful keyword-based and text-based searches, queries, drill downs, charts, graphs, and pivot capabilities. And participating organizations should be able to integrate their exchange-based analysis with data from their own back-office systems for a comprehensive understanding of their purchasing activities.

2. Configurability

As noted throughout this book, there will only be one major winner in each vertical sector. To have competitive staying power, exchange operators must be able to grow their exchanges, rapidly adding innovative services and functionality that will differentiate them from their competition.

This kind of fast innovation requires a trading platform that handles customization via configuration — not coding. Why configuration? Because exchange upgrades must be deployed in weeks, not months, and innovation must be rapid and frequent. Meeting these time-to-market pressures mandates technology that does not require additional coding or customization efforts, because customized solutions need to be built and then rebuilt for each subsequent phase of the exchange's life. Coding takes time, building takes time, and testing takes time — time that exchange operators simply cannot afford.

Instead of 'hard coding' customization solutions, look for a trading platform that enables customization through configuration. And look for configuration solutions that are as simple as making selections from a Web-based form. Web-based forms should be used to perform administrative tasks, such as changing the branding of the exchange, customizing the elements of different portions of the user interface, selecting a common currency, and controlling catalog content. And selections made in these configuration forms should take effect immediately upon submission of the form. As a result, reconfiguring the trading platform is as simple as making different selections in a configuration form and clicking 'submit'.

Obviously, a trading platform that is configurable to this extent can easily enable multi-organization capabilities because participating organizations use these Web-based forms to configure the operation and look and feel of the exchange in real time to meet their business purposes. The exchange operator does not implement these changes — the participants do. This does not mean that the exchange operator loses control of the exchange; rather, the exchange operator exercises control by determining which configuration capabilities should be 'given' to participating organizations.

3. Security

The very nature of the exchange's role — as intermediary between its exchange participants — means it has access to and control over confidential data. Market participants expect that their confidential data will be safe with the exchange. To ensure security, choose a trading platform that keeps each company's information secure from intruders and from other participating organizations — especially if participating organizations are given self-service administration privileges to the exchange.

Purchasing organizations require a further level of security from the exchange, because they need to restrict information views or purchasing activities according to the authorization levels of their users.

In addition to exchange-specific security issues, the trading platform must also address the security concerns faced by most types of Internet business, including:

- **User authentication.** User authentication is a major security issue for exchanges, and the costs of misidentification are high — resulting in unauthorized access to internal confidential data or, worse yet, to a competitor's confidential data.
- **Data encryption.** The encryption of data between systems is a focal point for exchange participants, as the exchange must be able to integrate with the back-end systems of many different purchasing organizations, supplier content systems, and systems in use by service providers or other digital exchanges. The trading platform must keep the data exchange between systems secure from unauthorized interception.
- **Single sign-on.** The proliferation of authentication systems has resulted in another administrative concern — single sign-on. Users want to log on to the exchange once, and then use multiple applications without needing to log on to each application separately. Single sign-on can provide this capability, making it easier to integrate with best-of-breed applications such as those supplied by catalog, financial, supply chain, or logistics service providers (or even other exchanges).

4. Open interoperability

The trading platform acts as the integration point for the set of services that make up the full transaction life cycle. As such, the platform must be highly interoperable, with diverse applications and systems.

To accomplish this, the trading platform should support open industry standards that enable plug-and-play components and services, while leveraging existing IT infrastructures and systems. Adherence to such standards keeps the trading platform from becoming obsolete as new technologies emerge, promoting seamless relationships with commerce partners, facilitating stable links to other digital exchanges, and easing integration with content from suppliers or content service providers.

Because the trading platform is, by virtue of the role it plays in the exchange, very complex, interoperability must be ensured on several levels, including content, transactions, and business systems. In terms of content, the trading platform must provide open, integrated access to all content — including vendor catalogs originating in Oracle Exchange, Ariba IBX Suite, TPN Registry, C1 Marketsite, and ec-Content. To integrate with many supplier catalogs, the trading platform must support prominent Internet standards for e-commerce content, including Open Buying on the Internet (OBI), RosettaNet, and Extensible Markup Language (XML).

In terms of transactions, the trading platform must *enable* the full transaction life cycle. This means empowering the entire procurement life cycle from the perspective of buying organizations (discussed earlier). It also means closing the loop with supplier systems once items have been ordered; this requires that the platform support XML, EDI, and fax. If the exchange integrates with service providers such as financial or logistics services, the trading platform must also assure XML integration with these services for tax and freight calculation, credit card processing, shipment tracking, and additional payment services. And if the exchange integrates with providers of external services such as news feeds, analytics, and research, the trading platform must support common data interchange formats such as XML.

In terms of business systems, the trading platform must *support* integration with the back-office systems used by participating organizations — for example, internal accounting and ERP systems, as well as databases where valuable enterprise data is stored.

In terms of providing the widest possible access to users, open interoperability also means that the platform is able to dynamically generate content and deliver it to the user's browser in standard HTML format that can be read across client devices — this concept is known as the *zero-client footprint*. Zero footprint means that users will be able to access the exchange with just a Web browser.

5. Adaptability

Exchanges share a common maxim — rapid change. This means that the trading platform must be able to easily adapt to evolving business requirements, allowing exchange operators to painlessly reconfigure the exchange to support new functionality or incorporate new services. As we discussed previously, look for a trading platform that offers configuration with easy-to-use HTML forms.

Adaptability also applies to maintenance and upgrade issues. A trading platform that follows object-oriented software design principles allows new technologies to be integrated in a short amount of time, impacting only those areas that require change. Why? Because each component of an object-oriented trading platform contains a discrete bit of functionality so that upgrades are contained. This means that upgrades only affect a few small areas of the platform, rather than the entire trading platform.

Another benefit of an object-oriented trading platform is that it keeps integration points very stable, facilitating third-party application integration. By supporting stable integration points, upgrade issues are minimized, making it easier for organizations to integrate the exchange into their business processes.

6. *Scalability*

The trading platform must be scalable, capable of handling thousands to hundreds of thousands of concurrent transactions from exchange participants while guaranteeing fast transactions to all users — no matter where they reside in the world. To deliver fast transaction time, the platform must deliver high throughput for sub-second response times. Entries, queries, selections, page downloads, and transaction confirmations should all execute with sub-second round trip times, ensuring a high-performance exchange.

Even more important than fast response times, exchanges cannot afford failures that cause downtime or lost purchases — especially in dynamic trading situations such as auctions or reverse auctions. In all cases, transactional integrity must be preserved as the trading platform scales. Buyers should be able to access the exchange, even in the case of a hardware failure, while suppliers should be able to update catalog data at any time — without impacting the performance of the exchange. These are difficult, but not impossible, expectations to meet. Ultimately, scalability comes down to how the trading platform is architected.

Platforms based on n-tier architecture demonstrate the scalability and performance necessary to support hundreds of thousands of users concurrently accessing the exchange and executing transactions. Why? Because n-tier architectures use multiple servers to execute transactions, and can balance user loads across these servers to improve availability and performance for exchange participants. Furthermore, n-tier architectures support failover: if one server goes down, the system can transparently transfer its load to another server, ensuring the uninterrupted operation of the exchange. Look for a trading platform that enables scaling up and out — up in terms of adding processors to existing servers, and out in terms of adding server boxes to the exchange architecture.

Also choose a trading platform that offers staging and production servers — this will allow the exchange to support self-service by global users 24x7. The staging and production systems, extend self-service to each user without jeopardizing the integrity of operational systems, as changes are first 'staged' on the staging server before going into production mode. This eases the maintenance burden while allowing the exchange to control the changes entered by others before those changes are published. Automated tools that apply these changes to operational systems are critical for eliminating potential errors in the process.

With staging systems, suppliers and buyers can make updates at any time to the content of the exchange without impacting the performance of the exchange. This is because the content of the staging system is updated, and the content of the production system is then synchronized with the content of the staging system so that all exchange users have access to the same information at the same time. Be sure to choose a trading platform that performs automated synchronization between staging and production systems as well — the less administration, the less overhead.

7. *Globalization*

As companies become increasingly global, exchanges will need to accommodate different locales, foreign currencies, and different languages. To accommodate these global requirements, the trading platform should be able to handle different locales easily and instantly, based on the user's preferences. For example, if a user changes his language preference, all exchange fields and contents should reflect the new language.

This means that the trading platform should support a variety of languages and multiple jurisdictions (including the associated currency, weights, and measures). Currency support not only includes the ability to handle the market currencies of the suppliers and buyers, but the trading platform must support triangulation of the Euro as well as non-symmetric exchange rates (for example, to build in the cost of exchanging money between currencies).

With each new release of the trading platform, language and jurisdiction support should be close behind — a few weeks, rather than months. And once again, for ease of administration, multiple jurisdictions should be managed with a single instance of the trading platform — providing various views to an international audience from a single exchange.

Summary

The issues driving selection of a trading platform are complex, as you must first determine what it is you would like the exchange to functionally *do*, and then look at those *qualities* of a trading platform that will enable you to provide those capabilities. However, once you fully understand the issues, setting technical requirements is a relatively simple process. The following matrix summarizes the technical issues presented in this chapter. Use it as a starting point for discussing the capabilities of trading platforms provided by different vendors.

Characteristic of successful exchange	Quality of the trading platform	Questions to consider
Ease of use	Configurability	Does the trading platform offer customization via configuration?
		Can the exchange operator and participating organizations configure Web-based forms to change the branding of the exchange, customize the elements of different portions of the user interface, select the common currency, and control catalog content?
	Security	How does the trading platform assure single sign-on?
	Open interoperability	Does the trading platform support dynamic HTML generation and server-based execution so that all users require is a standards-based Web browser?
	Globalization	How quickly do entries, queries, selections, page downloads, and transaction confirmations execute?
Business adaptation	Multi-organization capability	What sorts of multi-organizational capabilities does the trading platform offer for participating organizations?
		For groups within those organizations?
		For individuals within those groups?
		Do these capabilities include: branding, user interface, catalog views, transaction views, pricing, catalog content, preferences, account codes, organizational hierarchies, roles, business rules, and approvals processes?
		Does the trading platform include a workflow engine that implements organization-specific business rules and approvals processes?
		Can suppliers control the content of their own catalogs, including look and feel, and pricing structures?
	Configurability	Does the trading platform support form-based configuration for organizations to administer users, groups, processes, and content?
	Security	Does the trading platform support role-based authorization and authentication?

Characteristic of successful exchange	Quality of the trading platform	Questions to consider
		Does the trading platform dynamically generate its interface based on the role of the user accessing the exchange and the business rules defined by their organization, gearing the behavior of the system to the user accessing it?
		How does the trading platform keep each organization's exchange information private from other participating organizations?
		How does the trading platform filter content views and control application access to ensure that users within a participating organization only see information and execute actions for which they have permission?
		How does the trading platform keep the data exchange between systems secure from unauthorized interception?
	Open interoperability	How does the trading platform integrate with back-office systems such as financial and ERP systems used by participating organizations?
	Adaptability	Do upgrades to the trading platform affect integration points where third-party applications tie into the exchange?
	Scalability	Does the trading platform handle all multi-organizational customizations from a single instance of the database and website?
	Globalization	Does the trading platform support a variety of languages and multiple jurisdictions (including the associated currency, weights, and measures) from a single instance of the platform?
Full transaction life cycle	Open interoperability	Does the trading platform enable the full transaction life cycle via open integration with external service providers for services such as tax and freight calculation, credit card processing, shipment tracking, and additional payment services?
		Does the trading platform facilitate open, integrated access to all content, including vendor catalogs originating in Oracle Exchange, Ariba IBX Suite, TPN Registry, C1 Marketsite, and ec-Content?
		Does the trading platform close the loop with supplier systems once items have been ordered using XML, ED1, and fax?

Characteristic of successful exchange	Quality of the trading platform	Questions to consider
	Security	How does the trading platform keep the data exchange between systems secure from unauthorised interception?
		How does the trading platform assure single sign-on so that users can move smoothly between trading partner applications?
	Adaptability	Do upgrades to the trading platform affect integration points where third-party applications tie into the exchange?
Full procurement support		Does the trading platform empower the full procurement life cycle, including: • on-catalog purchasing; • special requests; • purchase orders; • request for quote (RFQ); • project-bound purchasing; • blanket purchase order; • credit card purchasing; • auctions; • reverse auctions; and • spot-buys.
	Globalization	Does the trading platform support a variety of languages and multiple jurisdictions (including the associated currency, weights, and measures) to enable the international locations of participating organizations to use the same procurement system (the exchange)?
Global availability and reliability	Scalability	How quickly do entries, queries, selections, page downloads, and transaction confirmations execute?
		Does the trading platform use an n-tier architecture with load balancing and failover?
		Does the trading platform use staging and production servers to provide 100% uptime while still allowing self-service updates by participating organizations?

Characteristic of successful exchange	Quality of the trading platform	Questions to consider
Global availability and reliability (cont.)	Globalization	Does the trading platform support a variety of languages and multiple jurisdictions (including the associated currency, weights, and measures) from a single instance?
		How long after a release does it take the trading platform vendor to release languages and associated jurisdictions?
Participant self-service	Multi-organization capability	Does the trading platform use staging and production servers to allow self-service updates by participating organizations?
		Can participating organizations configure Web-based forms to change the branding of the exchange, customise the elements of different portions of the user interface, select the common currency, and control catalog content?
	Security	How does the trading platform reliably authenticate users to establish their true identities?
		How does the trading platform keep each organization's exchange information private from other participating organizations?
		How does the trading platform filter content views and control application access to ensure that users within a participating organization only see information and execute actions for which they have permission?
	Globalization	Does the trading platform support a variety of languages and multiple jurisdictions (including the associated currency, weights, and measures)?
Fast evolution	Configurability	Can the exchange operator and participating organizations configure Web-based forms to change the branding of the exchange, customize the elements of different portions of the user interface, select the common currency, and control catalog content?
	Adaptability	Does the trading platform use an object-oriented design to minimize maintenance and upgrade issues?
		How extensive are upgrades within the trading platform?

Characteristic of successful exchange	Quality of the trading platform	Questions to consider
Fast evolution (cont.)	Globalization	How long after release does it take the trading platform vendor to release languages and associated jurisdictions?
	Scalability	Can the architecture of the trading platform scale both up (in terms of the size of the server) and out (in terms of the number of servers)?
Commerce intelligence		Does the trading platform provide integrated OLAP analysis capabilities?
		Do these capabilities include powerful keyword-based and text-based searches, queries, drill downs, charts, graphs, and pivot capabilities?
	Security	How does the trading platform keep each organization's exchange information private from other participating organizations?
	Open interoperability	Can organizations easily integrate their exchange-based analysis with data from back-office systems?
	Multi-organization capabilities	Does the trading platform handle all multi-organizational customizations from a single instance of the database and website, enabling comprehensive reporting across the exchange?
	Globalization	Does the trading platform support a variety of languages and multiple jurisdictions (including the associated currency, weights, and measures) from a single instance of the platform, enabling organizations to report on the procurement activities of the entire global enterprise?
Content	Open interoperability	Can organizations integrate their exchange-based analysis with data from back-office systems?
		Does the trading platform facilitate open, integrated access to all content, including vendor catalogs originating in Oracle Exchange, Ariba IBX Suite, TPN Registry, C1 Marketsite, and ec-Content?
		Does the trading platform enable integration with supplier catalogs using prominent Internet standards for e-commerce content, including Open Buying on the Internet (OBI), RosettaNet, and Extensible Markup Language (XML)?

Characteristic of successful exchange	Quality of the trading platform	Questions to consider
Content (cont.)	Multi-organizational capabilities	Can suppliers control the content of their own catalogs, including look and feel, and pricing structures?
	Security	How does the trading platform keep the data exchange between systems secure from unauthorized interception?
	Scalability	Does the trading platform use staging and production servers to provide 100% uptime while still allowing self-service updates by participating organizations?

Ramesh Patil has more than 20 years' experience in research in knowledge-based systems, applications of artificial intelligence, and Web-based collaboration tools. Prior to joining RightWorks, Dr. Patil served as project leader at the University of Southern California's Information Sciences Institute. He also served as assistant and associate professor at the Massachusetts Institute of Technology. He is a fellow of the American Association for Artificial Intelligence and American College of Medical Informatics. He received a Bachelor's degree in Electronics and a Master's degree in Electrical Engineering from IIT Kharagpur and a Ph.D. in Computer Sciences from the Massachusetts Institute of Technology.

Chapter 9:
Taking a Successful Exchange Public

Christopher E. Vroom, Managing Director, eCommerce Equity Research, CSFB

Building a business is tough. Articulating a persuasive business plan, attracting growth capital to fund expansion, and putting together a top-notch team to successfully execute the vision are formidable hurdles that few companies surmount. In fact, fewer than 3% of all businesses receiving venture funding actually develop a viable model and achieve the important recognition associated with completing an initial public offering.

When we assess a company's IPO prospects, we gauge the size of the total market opportunity and its growth characteristics as the foundation upon which success or failure rests. Bigger potential and faster growth is better. Of course, the size and growth of the market does not alone predict success. Just as important, we analyze the specific business model employed to exploit the potential, and determine how well management is executing against the promise. We gauge execution upon both quantitative and qualitative factors. Regarding the former, management credibility is crucial, especially for early stage companies who must convince investors that rapid growth can be effectively controlled, while quantitative measures such as revenue run rate, margin structure, and capital intensity of the business all figure large in our analysis.

When building a B2B e-commerce company, management must first consider the opportunity, and then articulate a persuasive business model to exploit the potential. Once the early signs of liquidity in the marketplace have been demonstrated, public investors will take notice and the exciting process of preparing for an initial public offering can be undertaken.

Assessing Market Opportunity: B2B is Real, It's Big, and It's Happening Now!

Increased adoption of the Internet as a medium of communication, information, and commerce promises to alter forever the competitive landscape across nearly $55tn in global economic activity. From bookselling to metals trading, community building and even voting, smart Internet entrepreneurs will profoundly reshape business, consumer, and government behavior.

The speed and degree of Internet adoption as a medium of exchange will, in our view, rest entirely upon the value derived by network participants. Consumers, for example, will assess the Internet value proposition along the same measures that have predicted success in the physical world — price, selection, service, and convenience. On-line operators who best their bricks-and-mortar competitors on these criteria will enjoy market share gains and solid economic returns. Similarly, businesses will gauge the promise of B2B initiatives against the costs associated with their implementation and the economic benefits conferred by network adoption.

The lesson is simple — compelling value, supported by economic returns that exceed the cost of capital, wins every time.

With respect to B2B e-commerce, here we find the most persuasive evidence arguing for a radical transformation of the economic order. Exploiting the power of .com will confer upon those singular visionaries who embrace the promise, unassailable competitive advantages, an operating edge that will drive faster revenue growth, higher profitability, and superior economic returns in even the most prosaic of industry segments. Executives who ignore the transforming power of this new channel will face an ever-tightening cycle of market share erosion and profit collapse as more nimble, forward thinkers wrest away customers with superior performance and value-added services.

1. Sizing the potential

Predicting long-term B2B potential on an aggregate basis necessarily rests upon an assessment of both global economic activity and supply chain dynamics. With respect to the former, total business-to-business economic activity worldwide approaches $47tn, with the United States accounting for roughly 34% of the total, or $16tn. This figure encompasses not only the value of finished goods and services but also incorporates activity through intermediate stages of the production process, including manufacturing and wholesale distribution. Insofar as B2B initiatives promise to improve efficiency throughout the supply chain, gauging total economic activity seems an appropriate starting point to determine the magnitude of the opportunity.

Long-term, we believe that nearly two-thirds of global economic activity — $30tn — will become electronically enabled and that 40% of these transactions, or $12tn will flow through third-party marketplaces, either industry-sponsored or independent.

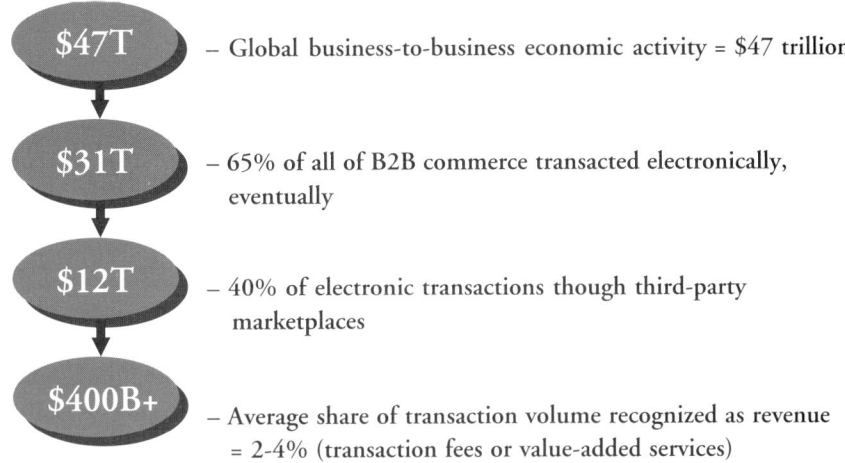

We believe that well-executed marketplaces that not only provide transparency throughout the supply chain, but also incorporate value-added services into the offering, will enjoy sizable transaction and ASP-based revenue. Indeed, we see B2B exchanges enjoying better than *$400bn* in high-margin, recurring revenues, or 2–4% of total transaction volume.

2. We see B2B exchanges creating better than $1 trillion in stock market value

The stock market implications of the B2B revolution are profound. As shown below, the generous profit margins and relatively low capital intensity of B2B exchanges should support a premium valuation for these companies, yet assigning only an average S&P500 EBIT multiple to the group suggests market value in excess of $1tn.

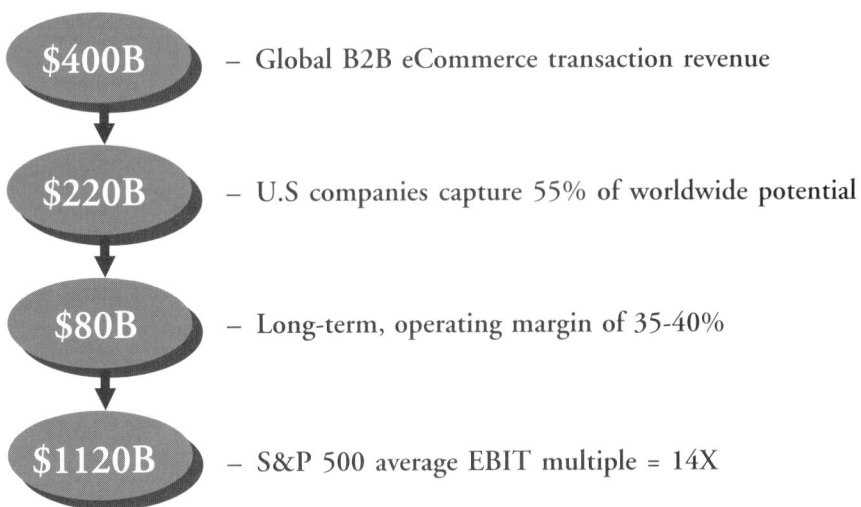

3. Value creation rests upon the economic benefits conferred by network participation

The substantial stock market potential of B2B marketplaces rests upon the economic benefits these solutions provide to their customers. As shown below, B2B exchanges provide substantial benefits that are realized by all channel participants. By aggregating large populations of buyers and suppliers, e-marketplaces introduce greater transparency into the supply chain, permitting greater price discovery.

At the same time, buy-side procurement applications, such as the solutions offered by Ariba and Commerce One, serve to automate the procurement process for both direct and indirect goods. This workflow automation substantially reduces operating costs by eliminating manual or paper-based processes. Expenses are streamlined still further through the collaborative power of the Web, permitting greater capacity utilization through synchronization of production schedules. Finally, the long-term promise of B2B is demand optimization, as customer needs are more accurately defined and served.

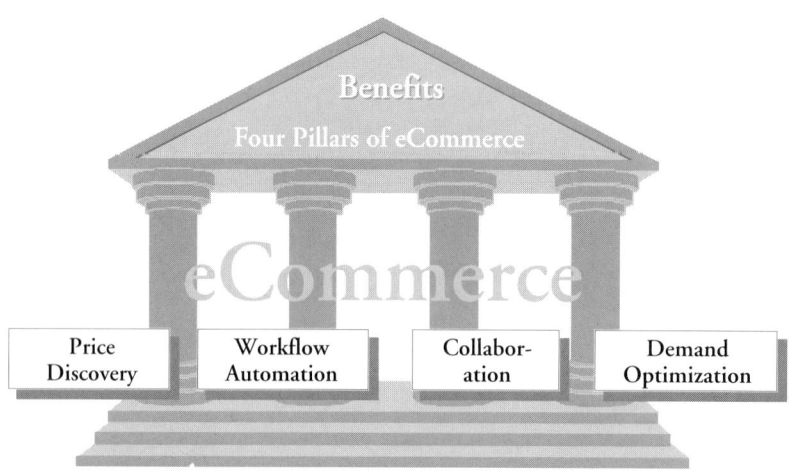

Greater price transparency, automation, collaboration, and demand optimization have important positive effects on enterprise income statement, balance sheet, and cash flow characteristics.

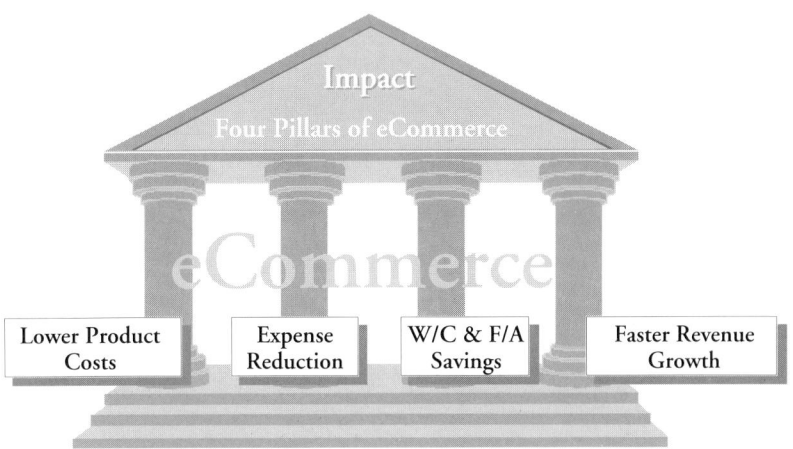

In our view, these benefits — ranging from demand aggregation and better price discovery to faster inventory turns and lower transaction costs, among others, will prove persuasive for both buyers and sellers, thereby ensuring broad-based adoption.

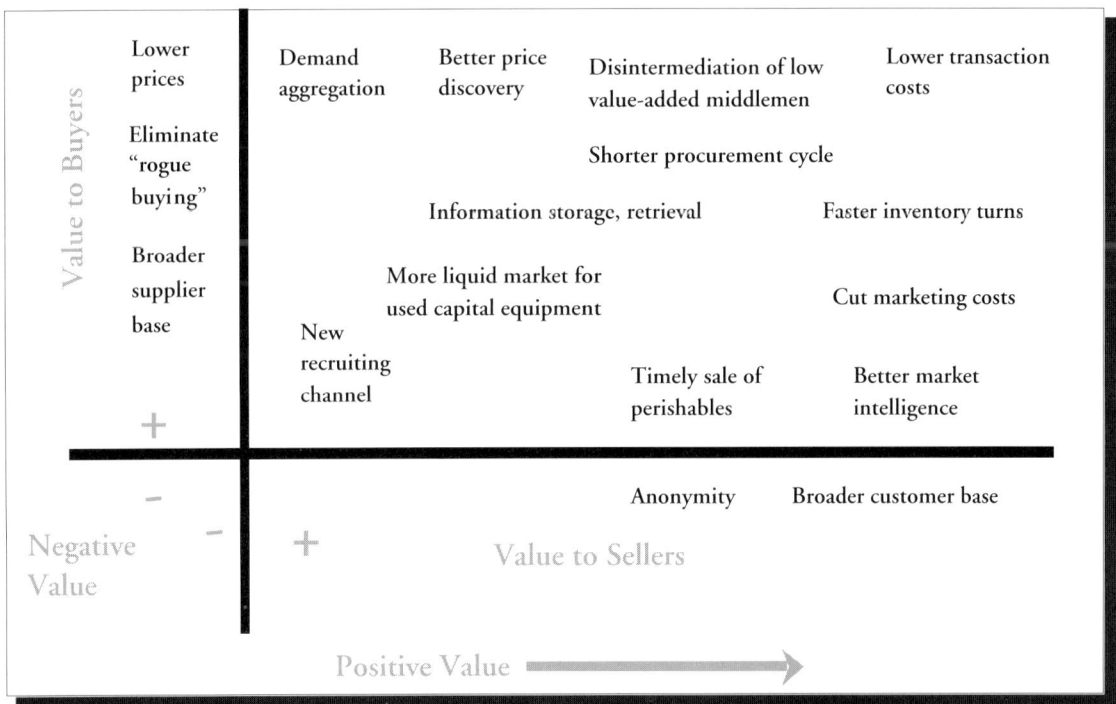

Executives across global industries have embraced B2B solutions — over the past six months alone, more than 300 of the world's largest corporations have announced their intention to participate in one or more exchange — recognition of the transforming power of .com. We believe that the efficiencies arising from B2B will radically improve the profit profile of those organizations that successfully adopt. Indeed, setting aside the substantial balance sheet and cash flow efficiencies from e-solutions, we see marketplace adoption conferring upon network participants better than 1,000 basis points of operating margin improvement. This degree of margin expansion will drive non-believers out of business. We segment the gains from B2B adoption into product and process cost savings, as depicted below.

Buyside Benefits Are Substantial

	Pct. Of Sales	Pct. Savings	Operating Margin Improvement
Product Savings:			
Direct Goods	44%	6.5%	2.8%
MRO	11%	20.0%	2.2%
Process			
Direct Goods	5%	15.0%	0.8%
MRO	10%	50.0%	5.0%
Other SGA	15%	10.0%	1.5%
Totals	84.5%		12.3%

Source: Credit Suisse First Boston Technology Group

The preceding table predicts potential B2B efficiencies for the average S&P500 company. Procurement of direct goods — products such as steel or rubber that are used in the production process — is generally pretty efficient. We see 5–8% savings here, mostly through the use of auctions and greater supplier choice. While direct goods procurement is relatively efficient, spending on indirect goods — items such as office products that are not used to produce the product itself — is highly inefficient, with off-contract buying and decentralized purchasing creating significant opportunity for cost reduction. We have assumed 20% savings on overall indirect product costs, savings which we believe will be realized through a combination of reduced off-contract buying — ensuring contract compliance adds, in our estimation, better than 10% alone to margin potential — and by identifying additional suppliers through aggregation.

Product cost savings for both indirect and direct goods will yield significant operating margin improvement, profit gains that will be augmented by process cost savings as workflows are increasingly automated.

4. Monetizing liquidity

B2B marketplaces promise to confer upon network participants important cost savings and higher profitability. The distribution of these economic benefits will inform the value of the exchange itself. Drawing analogies from physical world distribution models, we believe that well-executed exchanges that achieve liquidity will comfortably retain revenues — defined as transaction fees plus fees for value-added services — equal to 2–4% of total trading volume; this reflects roughly 20% of the aggregate economic benefit created by the marketplace. For mega-exchanges such as Exostar, the aerospace and defense exchange powered by Commerce One, this suggests revenue potential in excess of $3bn.

5. B2B solutions fundamentally alter information flows between channel partners

Widening use of B2B solutions promises to substantially alter supply-and-demand chain dynamics across virtually every sector of the global industrial and service economies. While automating the procurement process behind the firewall yields important cost benefits, the true promise of B2B e-commerce lies in the potential to facilitate collaboration throughout the supply chain. In many industries today, information flows are linear between trading partners. Component suppliers communicate supply trends to the manufacturer and in turn rely upon that manufacturer for demand assessment. In this context, it can take days or weeks for changes in supply or demand trends to become transparent throughout the channel.

Conversely, marketplaces alter the manner in which information is communicated among partners, permitting demand and supply signals to propagate up and down the chain with little delay. The financial implications of true channel collaboration are significant — capacity utilization can be improved through better demand assessment and, relatedly, buffer inventory stocks — protection against unanticipated change in demand patterns — can be sharply reduced, thus providing not only sizable expense efficiencies and greater revenue growth but also working capital savings.

6. Articulating the model

B2B business models have the potential to radically impact the competitive landscape across global business by introducing cost structure-altering efficiencies throughout the supply chain. In our view, the gains available through these B2B solutions will prove so compelling that businesses that fail to embrace the promise will find their viability challenged by more forward-thinking competitors.

In order to realize optimal value, the business model employed must reflect the specific characteristics of the industry — domain expertise is crucial. From a stock market standpoint, investors prefer, and will reward most highly, those business models that yield fast-growing, high-margin revenue that scales with liquidity and requires relatively little capital to sustain.

B2B marketplaces promise to rank among the most productive of all technology business models, with license, subscription, and transaction-based revenue streams combining to power rapid growth and outstanding returns on capital. In the figure below, we have outlined the potential return characteristics of a mature exchange relative to the typical S&P500 manufacturing concern that will utilize the marketplace to drive efficiency.

	S&P 500 Inc.	B2B Exchange
Sales	100	100
Gross Margin	35	90
Operating Expenses	20	50
Operating Profit	15	40
Net Assets	100	25
Return on Net Assets	15%	160%

As shown above, B2B marketplaces, because of their relatively efficient use of capital and high margin structure, promise to generate economic returns well in excess of their cost of capital. We have summarized the various business models employed by B2B exchanges in the table below.

	Drive Adoption	Scale with Liquidity	Revenue Today	Stability/ Predictability	Score
Transaction fee	★★★	★★★	★	★★	9
Margin on sale	★★★	★★★	★	★★	9
Subscription/ASP	★	★★	★★★	★★★	9
Collateral services	★★★	★★	★★	★	8
Licensing/maintenance	★★	★	★★	★★	7
Market intelligence	★★	★★★	★	★	7
Consulting	★	★	★★★	★	6
Advertising/slotting	★★	★	★★	★	6
LT fixed contracts	★	★	★	★★	5
Referral fee	★★	★	★	★	5
Percentage of savings	★★	★	★	★	5

The models that score big are those that scale with increased liquidity and which are characterized by a high component of recurring revenues — these increase the stability and predictability of the business. However, transaction-based approaches lag when it comes to instant gratification, as altering embedded business practices takes time.

The Road to IPO: The Why, When, and How of Going Public

With smart management in place, technology and implementation partnerships forged, and early signs of marketplace liquidity validating the model, many companies will attempt to tap the public markets for growth capital. The IPO process can be mysterious even to those executives who have already taken the plunge and can be segmented into three distinct steps: selecting underwriters, due diligence, and marketing the deal.

1. Selecting underwriters

Before the IPO process begins, an underwriting team must be selected. During this period, executives will discover new friends and more favors owed than ever thought possible, as a motley crew of clean-cut bankers with studied research analysts in tow compete for the lucrative assignment of leading the transaction.

That this competitive frenzy can become brutally personal is unsurprising given the amount of dollars at stake. Indeed, initial public offerings are highly profitable, with gross spreads averaging 7%, or $7mn for an offering of $100mn. The lead manager is the firm that supervises the undertaking, from spearheading drafting sessions and the due diligence process, to scheduling an effective roadshow. Most importantly, the lead manager plays a defining role in positioning the company to potential investors. Thus, the credibility and experience of the research analyst should be one of the key criteria employed in the selection process. To recognize the unequal division of responsibility in preparing a company for the IPO, the lead manager realizes the lion's share of the total fees generated by the deal — generally 50–60% of the total, while the co-managers, selected mainly for the quality of research, divide the remainder.

We have mentioned research as a key criterion that should be carefully considered when selecting a lead underwriter, and this facet of the process bears elaboration. Analysts at the major Wall Street firms specialize in one particular industry segment — B2B e-commerce, for example — and are responsible for articulating to institutional investors not only the important industry trends and themes, but also specific investment opinions on the public companies within the segment. In addition to guiding clients towards the long-term winners, research analysts help to identify, and establish relationships with, the most promising private companies within a sector. By building an extensive network of industry contacts, the analyst develops superior insights that enhance his or her institutional credibility. In addition, many analysts can be helpful in a business development context, making introductions to potential partners and providing a trusted perspective on new initiatives. In short, the relationship with the research analyst can be critical, extending as it does from working through the roadshow presentation, to marketing the deal, to supporting the stock through the vagaries of daily trading in the aftermarket.

While we believe that research firepower is paramount in the selection process, banking support and the firm's distribution capabilities should be weighed as well. With respect to the former, the best bankers are relationship — rather than transaction-driven — don't expect that the banker who shows up for the first time two weeks before the beauty contest will be there after the IPO to opine on issues of great strategic import. We have recognized that we can best leverage our sector insights by developing fewer relationships, but ones that are broad and deep. In short, the best bankers don't want to be all things to all people, but rather seek to become trusted advisors to the most influential companies in each major technology sector.

The last, but by no means least, important piece of the puzzle relates to how the transaction will actually get done. Distribution matters a lot — placing the shares with quality buyers who will not only buy the deal but will continue buying to support the stock after the transaction are all critical. In this regard, experience and industry knowledge make a real difference. Partnering with a firm whose salesforce understands technology and maintains strong relationships with key tech buyers is crucial. It is important to recognize that the lead manager of the initial public offering will be a key business partner for many years to come. As such, the selection process should be managed with the same degree of analytical rigor that governs partnerships in the core business.

Having appropriately prioritized the different factors that will add the greatest value, companies often invite a number of competing firms to make presentations to senior management and often board members. These 'beauty contests' are generally conducted over a two- or three-day period with two-hour slots allocated to each firm. During the presentation, the investment bank will argue its merits with supporting evidence in the form of graphs and charts, outlining the firm's track record, how successful past deals have been, distribution capabilities, and research prowess. CEOs will find it unsurprising that virtually every firm worth its salt can find a way to present exactly the same data and end up beating the competition. It is for this reason — the relatively short time period within which this critical decision must be made and the many ways to manipulate the same performance data — that management really needs to establish relationships well before the offering so that the selection ritual becomes really a formality.

2. Due diligence

After the underwriting team has been selected, the process of preparing both filing documents and marketing materials begins. An organizational meeting is called at which time management presents key elements of the business strategy to both bankers and analysts. Financial assumptions are tested rigorously and customer checks conducted. This first phase of the process takes approximately three weeks, after which time the registration statement, or S-1, is filed with the Securities and Exchange Commission (SEC).

While the SEC is reviewing the document, management and the underwriting group prepare the roadshow, typically a 25-minute presentation that is designed to encapsulate the key strategy and business model advantages and to persuade an investor to buy the stock. Typically, the Chief Executive Officer kicks off the discussion, articulating the long-term vision of the company, and then introduces the Chief Financial Officer for a financial and business model review.

The SEC review process generally takes 30 days when the SEC's workload is normal, but can stretch to 45 days or more when the offering calendar is heavy. Following their review, additional information, or requests for clarification of business relationships or accounting standards, may be forthcoming which are responded to in the form of amendments to the S-1. After the amendments have been filed, the prospectus is printed and the roadshow to institutional and retail investors begins.

3. The roadshow

Establishing early momentum is crucial to the success of any technology offering. We generally conduct pre-marketing, one-on-one meetings with key technology buyers prior to launching the deal, and facilitate management meetings with thought leaders in the institutional investor community before the roadshow even begins. By doing so, we hope not only to season management to the key strategic questions they will face on the roadshow, but also to build demand.

We then augment this early demand with an international roadshow to visit key buyers in London, Geneva, Frankfurt, Milan, Amsterdam, and other financial centers — all in three days. As is the case in the United States, it is critical that the firm leading the transaction have long-standing, strong relationships with the major buyers of technology stocks. With demand building and excitement mounting, the roadshow team returns to the US for as many as 90 'one-on-one' meetings and group lunches with major institutional investors across the country. The schedule can be arduous, as depicted overleaf.

By focusing on key accounts in a highly targeted roadshow, we hope to build demand to ensure a successful offering. Extending the same example from one roadshow we managed last year, the company was able to generate demand for the stock that substantially exceeded the total offering.

This 'oversubscription' gave us and the company the flexibility either to increase the number of shares offered, in order to meet demand, or to raise the offering price. In this instance, we did both, raising substantially more growth capital than originally anticipated. Successful pricing of initial public offerings requires a lot of information and a great deal of experience. In this instance, we were able, because of the strong relationships that research and the salesforce had forged with key accounts, to accurately assess demand and target the specific investors who really wanted to own the stock long-term.

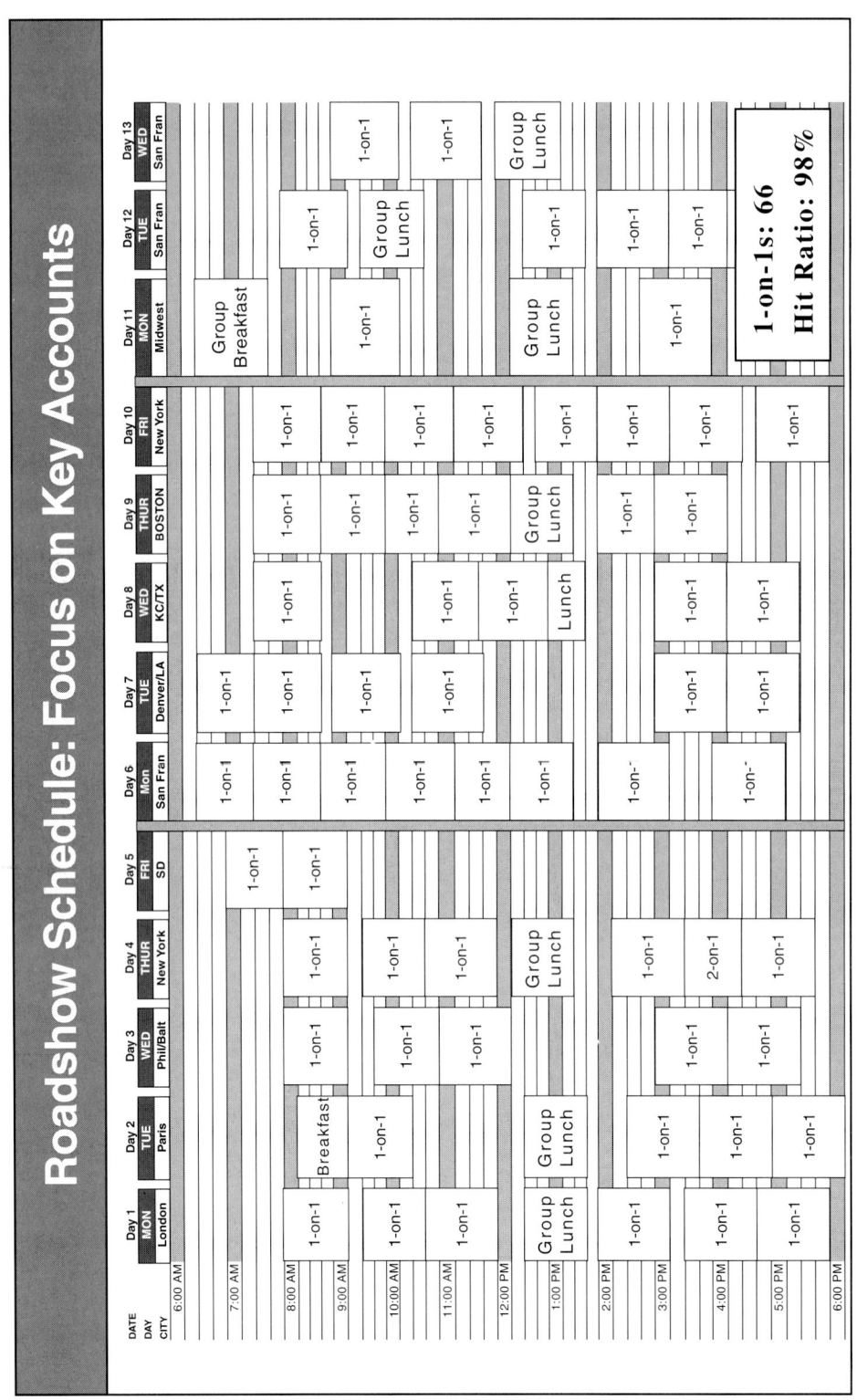

144 - Taking a Successful Exchange Public

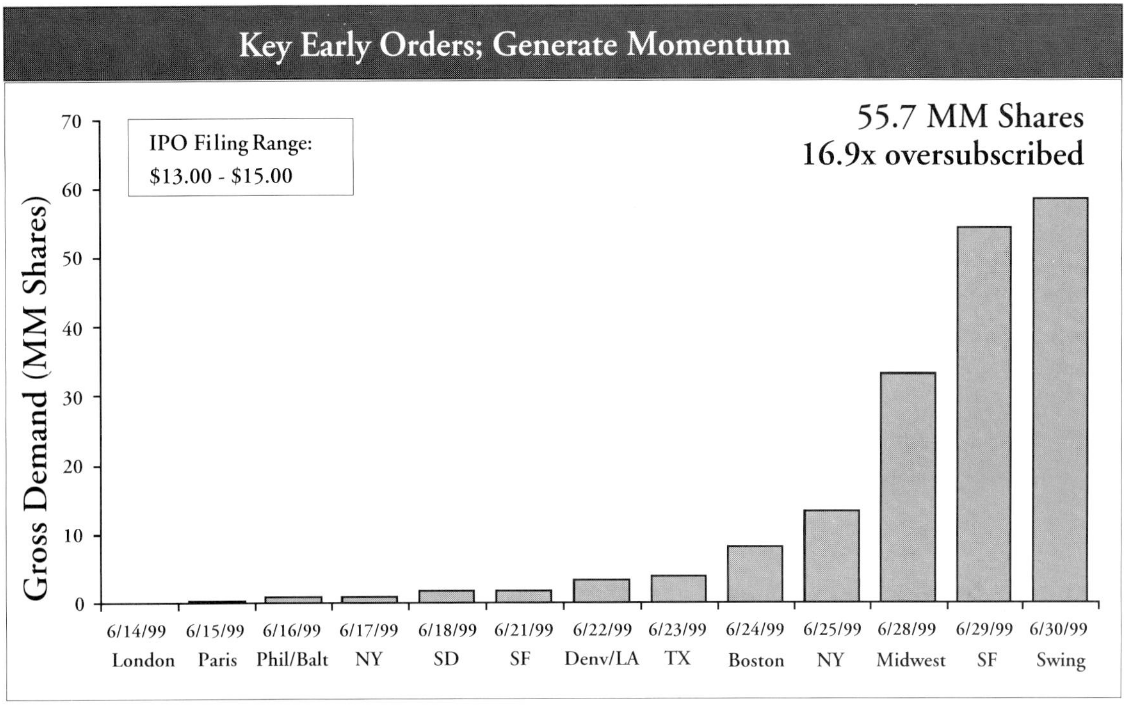

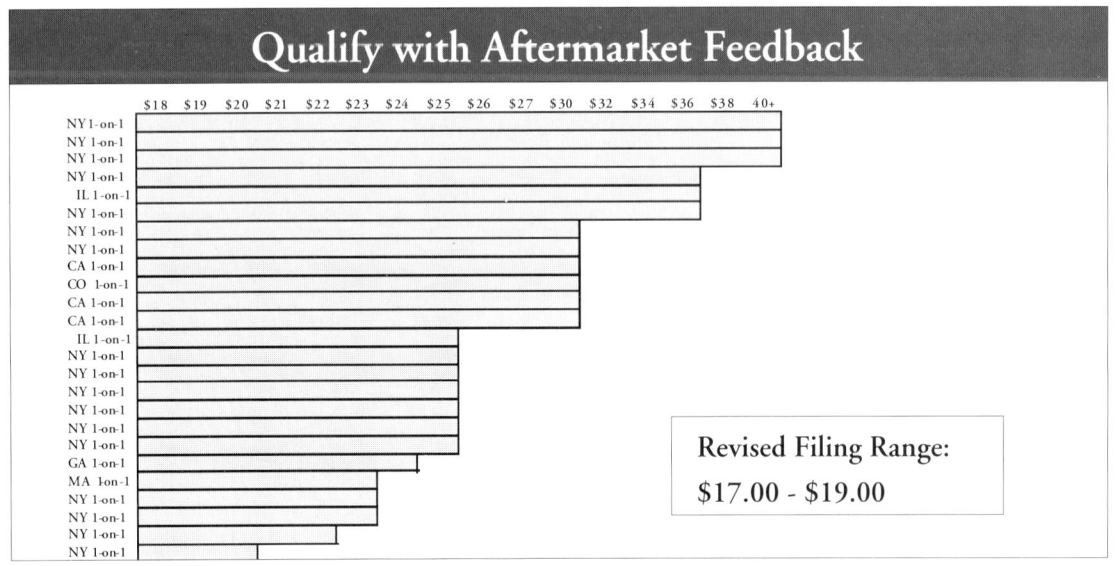

145 - Taking a Successful Exchange Public

As shown above, we were able to determine exactly which accounts were willing not only to buy the deal, but also to place aftermarket orders up to a specific price level. By gauging interest this precisely, we were able to make certain that the buyers who knew the story and who were committed to accumulating additional shares in the aftermarket were allocated a big enough position on the IPO to induce more buying even after the stock had moved up strongly following its debut.

The IPO is Just One Step in a Long Journey

Many factors figure large in taking a successful exchange public. First and most important, is the market opportunity, the business model employed, and the management firepower to execute the vision. Selecting the right firm with research credibility is critical as well. Acute strategic insights from the bankers help to cement partnerships and may shed light on new opportunities that might be overlooked or under appreciated. A strong salesforce focused on technology is essential, as is a capital markets team with deep experience and knowledge of institutional buying behavior globally.

In the end, the initial public offering is just one, albeit exciting, step in a successful company's growth. For senior management, it is an opportunity to interact with smart people in the investment community, professionals who have watched growth companies come and go and thus can provide valuable insights into business strategy and relevant parallels with the past. For research analysts, the opportunity to develop a partnership with great entrepreneurs who take the time to explain their experiences and visions of the future is a great privilege that few positions offer. And for public investors, the opportunity to participate in the early stages of what could become a great growth story is not only exciting, but the best-tested way to long-term wealth creation.

Christopher Vroom is a Managing Director of eCommerce Equity Research at the Credit Suisse First Boston Technology Group where his coverage includes business-to-business e-commerce companies. He joined the firm in January 2000 from Thomas Weisel Partners where he was a partner and head of the firm's Electronic Commerce research group. Prior to joining TWP, Mr. Vroom was a Managing Director at Alex Brown and Sons for 12 years, where he was head of the firm's retail industry research effort and co-head of Electronic Commerce research.

Chapter 10:
Entrepreneurs vs. Industry Consortia

Arthur B. Sculley and W. William A. Woods

As we emphasized in the first chapter of this book, 'liquidity is king' for B2B exchanges. A successful exchange must attract as many buyers and sellers as possible, and ensure that the largest buyers and the largest sellers use its central market space. Two different approaches to this issue are currently being explored.

Entrepreneurial Markets

Many B2B exchanges are being developed as dot.coms, independent companies established by experienced vertical industry professionals who have seized the opportunity to leave their Industrial Age corporations and start up a B2B exchange. Their former corporate employer would find evolving into a B2B exchange difficult to do because of the perceived lack of neutrality when a major player owns the market space. These entrepreneurs have a deep knowledge of their particular industry and strong relationships with the main buyers and sellers in that vertical space. Entrepreneurial exchanges have the following advantages:

- perceived neutrality;
- speed — quick decision-making is essential;
- independence;
- dedicated, motivated, and professional CEO/management team; and
- the ability to refine and change their business model in real-time. A good example of this is AviationX, which started out as the B2B exchange for the whole aviation industry. When several major airlines announced their own consortia approach, AviationX was nimble enough to re-focus on smaller regional airlines and adjust its business plan to make it more of an Application Services Provider for those airlines.

However, not all dot.com exchanges raise enough capital to survive through the long build-up phase, and some of them haven't made it.

In addition, dot.com exchanges need to build up sufficient liquidity to make the exchange a winner. As we stated in Chapter 1, this may include strategic partnerships with the largest bricks-and-mortar players in that vertical market space. One way to do this is to attract the largest buyers and sellers on to the exchange with special deals — such as reduced fees or an equity stake (eg, Ventro). This has raised some questions about the continuing neutrality of these exchanges.

We believe that a dot.com exchange must embrace the biggest buyers and sellers in its market space and this may require relinquishing some equity. As long as the exchange continues to operate as a neutral market and retains the other elements of neutrality that we highlighted in Chapter 1 — such as objective standards for new members, fair and equal access to the trading system, and an independent compliance team that reports directly to the advisory board — then the exchange can still demonstrate the necessary level of neutrality to attract other players.

Industry Consortia

Not to be left out of the B2B revolution, a number of large bricks-and-mortar companies have decided to form their own B2B exchanges. Competitive pressures are now forcing even the largest manufacturers to work together to launch such exchanges. For example, GM, Ford, DaimlerChrysler, Nissan, and Renault are working together to create an auto exchange called Covisint. These types of exchange are being called 'industry consortia plays' because they are formed by a consortium of existing buyers or sellers in a particular market space.

There are now over 40 such industry consortia. Other leading consortia plays include:

- *Exostar* — Boeing, BAE Systems, Lockheed Martin, and Raytheon in the aerospace and defence industries;
- *MyAircraft* — United Technologies and Honeywell International in the aerospace industry;
- *GlobalNetXchange* — Carrrefour Supermarche, Sears Roebuck, Kroger, and J. Sainsbury in the retail supermarket space;
- *The WorldWide Retail Exchange* — a B2B retail store procurement exchange being set up by Target, Kmart, Safeway, Walgreen, DairyFarm, and 13 others;
- *e2open* — Acer, IBM, Hitachi, Matsushita, LG Electronics, Nortel Networks, Seagate Technology, Solectron, and Toshiba in the computer, electronics, and telecommunications industries; and
- *Transoria* — a consumer products exchange (food, beverages, and household consumable products mainly) being set up by several leading consumer brand manufacturers.

These consortia plays are either representative of the buy-side (eg, Covisint) or the sell-side (eg, Transoria). In either case, industry consortia have the major advantage that they are well funded by their bricks-and-mortar parents. However, these attempts to start a B2B exchange face the same challenges that the entrepreneurial exchanges face. In particular, they must:

- **play to win** — liquidity is king, so the exchange with the most trading will dominate;
- **operate as a neutral exchange** — so that they attract the maximum number of potential buyers and sellers to generate the most efficient prices; and
- **operate as a 'virtual' company** — so that they can be fast, flexible, and change the business plan quickly.

An enormous advantage for consortia plays is that they bring tremendous natural liquidity to the exchange in the form of combined buying or selling power.

The largest problem that consortia face is how to establish the operating neutrality of the exchange. One of the most hotly-debated issues in B2B is whether consortia plays can retain sufficient neutrality to attract other buyers and sellers.

The key issue is not necessarily ownership — but how the exchange is operated and controlled. Independent ownership and neutrality in operation are not the same thing.

The main things that an industry consortia must focus on to demonstrate its neutrality are:

- establishing objective standards for new members;
- maintaining fair and equal access to the trading system;
- appointing an independent CEO and management team with entrepreneurial incentives to develop the exchange;
- having an advisory board and user committee structure which brings representatives from all the user groups into the management of the exchange; and
- setting up an independent compliance team that reports directly to the advisory board and enforces the rules and regulations of the exchange fairly against all members.

Every industry consortia must be staffed with dedicated, independent, management. Right now, most industry consortia are seconding existing staff into these proposed new exchanges. This does not tend to work very well. The seconded staff don't have the right motivation to make the business succeed, recognizing as they do the cost to some of the owners' core existing businesses. Similarly, seconded staff don't tend to have the 'career at risk' or bottom-line responsibility that enables them to change the business plan as frequently and as dramatically as may be required to succeed.

Upcoming Convergence

We believe that there will now be a period of intense competition between entrepreneurial B2B exchanges and industry consortia plays in various vertical markets. Ultimately, however, the winner-takes-most effect will drive mergers and consolidations, and one dominant exchange — with the greatest liquidity — will emerge in each vertical.

B2B exchanges are being judged on how well they serve all their members and how fair and equal they are. The winner is likely to be the exchange which demonstrates that it is operated in a neutral way so that all buyers and sellers feel comfortable in joining that market — irrespective of the equity ownership structure.

Anti-trust Issues

In the first chapter of this book, we identified the potential for these many-to-many markets to bring together buyers and sellers from all around the world. The results can be a highly competitive virtual market with on-line auctions creating dynamic pricing, reducing manufacturers' costs of raw materials, parts, and supplies. In addition, these net markets have the capability to tie together the manufacturer with its suppliers (Tier 1) and its suppliers' suppliers (Tiers 2 and 3). This can lead to greater efficiencies in the design of products, and ultimately to a 'build to order' business model that dramatically reduces manufacturing time, inventory levels, and distribution costs.

On the other hand, we accept that virtual markets can still create the opportunity for collusion, unreasonable restraint of trade, abuse of market power, and, in the case of buy-side led exchanges, the power to drive purchase prices below free market prices (ie, monopsony power).

Pro-competitive Structural Features

However, we believe that there are a number of structural features that can help ensure that these dynamic new businesses are used to create the significant pro-competitive efficiencies that they promise to deliver.

1. *Trading system design*

The new feature of all these B2B exchanges is that they are using the ubiquitous connectivity standards of the Internet to enable companies to communicate with each other, to connect to the exchange's central market, and to power their electronic trading systems. By definition, no B2B exchange has a physical trading floor or relies on brokers communicating by telephone or fax to execute trades.

The direct result of this is that B2B exchanges have electronic pricing mechanisms which provide a full audit trail of all activity in the system and which can be 'hard-wired' to ensure that anti-competitive activities don't occur on the exchange. The centralized pricing system is the most important function of an exchange, and the exchange must seek to ensure the integrity of that pricing mechanism. The key elements of a fair system for qualified members are:

- equal access;
- the order with best price has highest priority;
- first in, first out (FIFO);
- effective procedures to ensure that each seller's products are posted correctly and that buyers' bids and orders are transmitted accurately; and
- trades are consistently executed in accordance with the published rules of the exchange.

With a fully electronic, auto-matching system, these rules can be hard-coded into the system software using sophisticated algorithms. The rules of a successful B2B exchange will require members to honor the integrity of the exchange's pricing mechanism.

To the extent that the exchange's trading rules cannot be 'hard-wired' into the trading system, the exchange must introduce and enforce the trading rules against the members.

2. Ownership structures

Most traditional stock exchanges were set up by stockbrokers and are still exclusively owned by the brokers — eg, the New York Stock Exchange (NYSE) and the London Stock Exchange. This type of exchange operates rather like a 'mutual society' or private club.

It was mainly due to the fact that the NYSE is, and has acted as, a private club, that the US Government passed the Securities Exchange Act of 1934, which requires all National Securities Markets to be registered by the Securities and Exchange Commission. In the 1920s, for example, the NYSE would protect members who were trading whilst insolvent, if they were long standing-members, rather than kicking them out immediately.

By way of contrast, B2B exchanges are all being set up as 'for profit', neutral market spaces. This follows from their objective of bringing as many buyers and sellers together as possible in order to create dynamic pricing and to lower the cost of procuring supplies for buyers and expand the range of potential buyers for the suppliers. Some are being set up by independent entrepreneurs, such as the Stojka brothers who founded PlasticsNet. Some are being set up by a group of large players in that industry, such as MetalSite, which was set up by Weirton Steel, LTV Steel, and Steel Dynamics, or Covisint, which is being set up by a group of the largest auto manufacturers. But in all cases they are seeking to be neutral and independent markets with open access to all players in that industry.

B2B exchanges that are truly open have objective criteria to determine who may have access to the centralized, electronic marketplace and provide equal access. Equal access means that every trading member has equal access to the exchange's trading system, irrespective of size or duration of membership.

Monopsony Power

The main objective of B2B exchanges is to bring the maximum number of buyers and sellers together, to create dynamic pricing and thus lower the cost of procuring supplies. As such, they empower the buyers by enabling them to contact more potential suppliers and by creating the potential for 'reverse' auctions — where the buyer sets a price and the suppliers have to bid on it (with prices falling as the auction progresses). They also benefit suppliers because sellers from all over the world can access the whole range of potential buyers for their products. The use of traditional auctions allows the sellers to get buyers to bid competitively for their products.

What is fascinating about the Internet revolution in B2B e-commerce is that it has created a 'once in a lifetime' shift in the balance of power from the supplier to the buyer. This is illustrated by the industry consortia which are being formed by the buy-side. These buy-side consortia are working together to combine their procurement operations to create one central, on-line marketplace. In each case there are a group of buyers realizing that in the networked economy they can lower their procurement costs by creating a central exchange. In these B2B exchanges, all the potentially suitable suppliers can link into the exchange over the Internet and the buyers can create dynamic pricing by getting those suppliers to bid in on-line auctions for some contracts (reverse auctions).

On the other hand, by combining their purchasing power through an exchange and restricting suppliers' access to that exchange, the buyers may be able to exercise monopsony power and force the suppliers who are members to quote prices below those that would prevail in a freely competitive market. This danger is particularly prevalent in industries which are already dominated by a relatively small number of large purchasers, rather than those which are more fragmented.

However, providing these exchanges are set up as 'for profit' commercial entities with open access, then these B2B exchanges would be in breach of their financial responsibility to maximize shareholder value if they were to subjectively restrict access to their markets. Imagine if the WorldWide Retail Exchange (the B2B retail store procurement exchange being set up by Target, Kmart, Safeway, Walgreen, DairyFarm, among others — www.worldwideretailexchange.org) decided to restrict access to a limited number of suitable suppliers/vendors. It would be immediately self-defeating.

Initially, the retailers might be able to extract cost savings from those vendors which it admitted, but by limiting access to a small number of potentially suitable suppliers, the retailers would actually be reducing their chances of securing food, drugs, general merchandise, and textiles of the right quality at a lower price and with the right after sales service, etc. In such a scenario, the retailers would risk driving their limited number of selected suppliers to depress output and ultimately to go out of business as they forced the prices down. Open market forces therefore dictate that this B2B retail store exchange will be open to the widest range of potential suppliers that prove that they can deliver goods of the quality, in the quantity, and with the other service attributes that the retail stores require.

Conclusion

Calls for nascent B2B exchanges to be regulated are, in our opinion, premature. One of the reasons why the Internet has been such a driving force in the New Economy and has helped improve US productivity is because, to date, the US government has taken a relatively 'hands off' approach to both regulation and taxation. B2B exchanges are still at a very early stage of development and should not be burdened with over-regulation.

The key issue is that B2B exchanges can increase competition and promote efficiency, and they should be given the opportunity to prove that. The Internet has created a 'once in a lifetime' shift in the balance of power from the supplier to the buyer. In the face of such a dramatic reversal of the economic metrics, it would be detrimental to rush in and apply Industrial Age regulatory structures to these emerging new B2B e-markets. It is free markets, low barriers to entry, and easy access to start-up capital — and not governmental regulation — that will ensure all B2B exchanges preserve open and equal access to their market spaces.

Many B2B exchanges are also global in scope, so any regulation, which we don't recommend at this time, needs to be co-ordinated with other major governments in Brussels and Tokyo.

We therefore hope that the Federal Trade Commission (FTC) in the US and the European Union will refrain from premature regulation. This now appears likely after the FTC ended its preliminary investigation of Covisint, and the European Commission has authorized the creation of MyAircraft.com.

However, we also believe that the regulators should maintain a watching brief to ensure that successful B2B exchanges don't change their open structures in order to support anti-competitive features. At this stage, the regulators should focus their attention on those marketplaces where there is already a concentration of power in a small number of bricks-and-mortar buyers or sellers, rather than on the more fragmented markets.

William Woods is the CEO of the Bermuda Stock Exchange. Arthur Sculley is a partner in Sculley Brothers LLC. Together they have co-authored the best-selling book B2B Exchanges: The Killer Application in the Business-to-Business Internet Revolution *(ISI Publications). William can be reached at william@b2bexchanges.com and Arthur at arthur@b2bexchanges.com.*

Chapter 11:
What's Next? e-Marketplaces Set the Stage for New Business Networks

Bruce Temkin, Director, B2B Research and Advisory, Forrester Research, Inc.

e-Marketplaces such as ChemConnect and gofish.com will continue to pop up across industries — connecting buyers and sellers in new ways over the Net. While these venues represent a significant shift in the business trade landscape, today's players are still in their infancy. To understand the impact of these young firms, it is important to take a look at how these early-stage markets — and their participants — will evolve toward the next generation of e-business.

This chapter starts with a look at how bricks-and-mortar corporations adopt the Net. This shift represents a critical input to the growth of e-marketplace trade. Why? Because on line markets cannot take off until big buyers and sellers beef-up their e-business aptitude.

The next section describes how e-marketplaces will mature. These market makers will expand well beyond transaction facilitation. Over the next three years, successful on-line markets will establish deep interconnections with participants and significantly bolster their current service offerings.

Finally, we will jump ahead five-plus years and examine how the next generation of e-marketplaces will help to create an entirely new market structure — 'eBusiness Networks'. In this environment, firms will form relationships quickly, share information broadly, and create value by making assets fully available on-line.

Corporate America Embarks on an e-Business Voyage

Henry Ford's first car didn't have much impact. It was merely a trophy for the dentist who bought it in 1903. But the automobile ultimately reshaped society — moving city dwellers en masse into newly formed suburbs. What changed? People learned how to leverage this new transportation mode as the supporting infrastructure such as paved roads and gas stations matured. Lesson learned: technology adoption is a multi-stage process. So, let's put the Internet in perspective — as a B2B channel, it's less than five years' old. While the Net combines a unique set of characteristics (see Figure 1: The Net Offers Unique Capabilities), businesses will need many years before they can fully leverage these new capabilities. During this period, companies will evolve their operations through four phases:

- **Phase 1 — Experiment: Adapting Existing Business to the Net.** In the first steps toward Internet adoption, firms adapt existing operations to the Web. For the most part, they pragmatically go after cheap, quick, and obvious ways to use extranets or Internet sites to simplify or reduce the cost of reaching sizable segments of existing partners and customers.

- **Phase 2 — Deconstruct: Preparing for the Interconnected World.** Based on their own — and their competitors' — experiments, companies gain deeper insights into e-commerce threats and opportunities. They dig through their full portfolio of business relationships and manufacturing processes to pinpoint strategic advantages and disadvantages. By analyzing, untangling, and reshaping everything from customer service metrics to distribution channels into configurable building blocks, firms create a platform for leveraging the true capability of the Net.

- **Phase 3 — Re-invent: Transforming for the Internet Economy.** As firms are positioned for maximum flexibility in the re-invent phase, business-as-usual traverses company boundaries. Net-based business models have migrated from the periphery to the core of the operations, enabling corporations to plan and execute in real time based on market demand and prices.

- **Phase 4 — Breakaway: Thriving in New Business Networks.** Once a critical mass of firms re-invent their operations, companies will operate in a more networked manner — connecting with each other in a more dynamic environment. Companies that succeed at this stage will learn to innovate quickly and to fluidly leverage partners.

Figure 1: The Net Offers Unique Capabilities

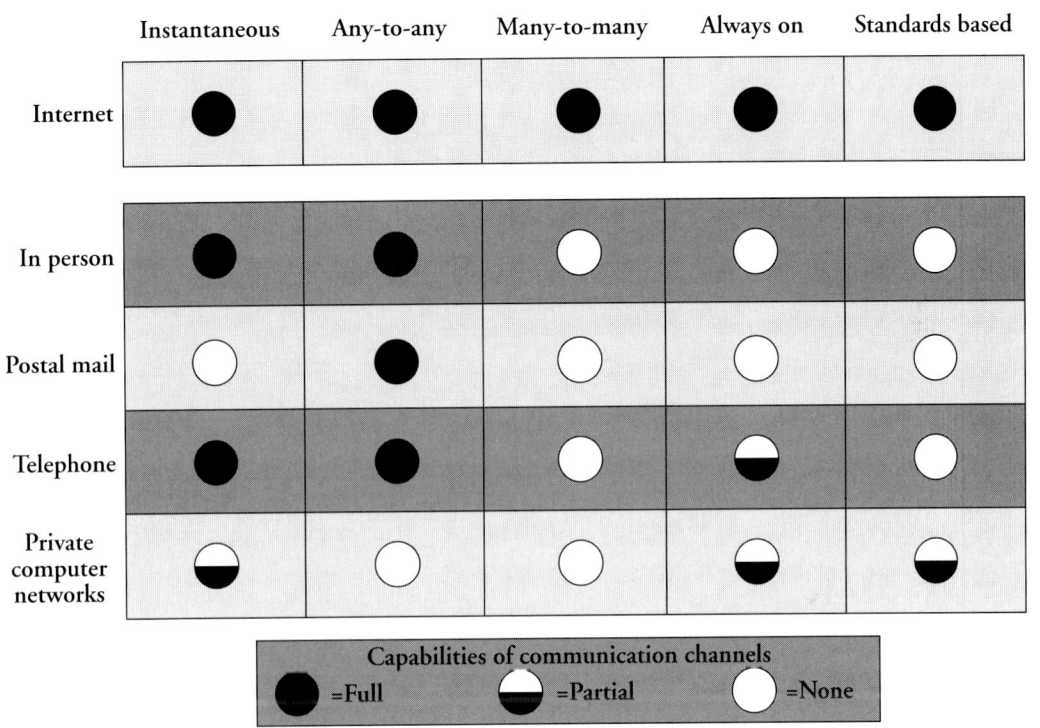

157 - What's Next?

The Net Creates a New Environment

As businesses move their operations on-line, long-held operating principles will begin to crumble. This transition will test how firms operate, affiliate, and organize as:

- **Performance is exposed.** As they participate in open venues such as e-marketplaces and partner with multiple service providers, companies will suffer intense scrutiny. Sites such as Open Ratings or CNET, which make it easy for customers to compare products and services, will continue to pop up. In this open setting, firms will have no place to hide. Financial services companies like The CIT Group or GE Capital, for example, will be forced to confront any shortcomings — from slow loan turnaround to high closing costs.

- **Relationships unravel.** A swelling crowd of e-marketplaces, such as e-STEEL in the steel industry and Chemdex in the laboratory supplies market, are redefining entire supply chains. These new venues are enticing firms to rethink long-standing trading relationships in favor of dynamic market models such as auctions and exchanges.

- **Vertical integration invites attack.** Because the Net amplifies business reach, even firms that perform just one narrowly focused task can thrive. HotDispatch, for instance, is succeeding in getting software vendors to offload technical support by pairing answer-seeking customers with a global panel of programming experts. Highly integrated firms will feel increasing pain as these specialized businesses run circles around their internal groups.

Firms Confront the New Business Realities

To survive the move to e-business, firms will concede that they:

- **Can't do it all.** The Net forces companies to get real about their strengths and weaknesses. Winners pull away from the pack by acting on these insights — exploiting the Internet to put partners on the critical path. Cisco Systems, for instance, offloads manufacturing of more than half of its units to highly wired partners like Celestica. Eastman Chemical, on the other hand, has spun off its entire chemical transportation department to form ShipChem.com — hoping to turn this world-class cost center into an on-line profit center. Smart movers will use the Net to shed cost centers and focus their efforts on genuine added value.

- **Can't hoard information.** Enlightened corporations have ditched 'need to know' thinking and have empowered their employees. The next step — a leap — extends the same philosophy to partners and customers. A case in point: Wal-Mart's retail success tracks right back to its supply chain domination, which rests on its partners having the information they need to act as if they 'own' the retailer's shelves.

- **Can't stockpile assets.** Large firms such as DuPont and Sears are beginning to see the fallacy of reserving assets for their exclusive use. These corporations are moving into the frontier by striking equal-to-equal deals with young firms like Ventro and Commerce One — New Economy enterprises that can more effectively bring valuable off-line assets into the new Net business environment.

e-Marketplaces Grow Up

While traditional firms wrestle with their e-business evolution, e-marketplaces fanatically leverage the Internet as their primary channel. These Net-native venues, however, are still in their infancy. Since these young firms pull together groups of buyers and sellers, their growth is constrained by the adoption of new processes by bricks-and-mortar participants. As the Net penetrates deeper into the operations of established firms, however, e-marketplaces will up the ante on their capabilities — evolving from basic transaction-enablers to full-service matchmakers that:

- operate hands-free;
- integrate participants;
- weave-in transaction services; and
- configure trading rules

See Figure 2: e-Marketplaces Evolve into Matchmakers.

1. Operate hands-free

Corporations today have launched e-business projects such as on-line selling and procurement with old processes dressed up in a new browser interface. What's wrong with this approach? Legacy procedures for handling returns, checking on-hand inventory, or routing procurement requisitions translate to the Net as poor service and make-work, because they:

- **Replay old mistakes in an exposed new channel.** When a retailer brings a bad off-line returns policy, such as the inability to return catalog purchases to a retail outlet, to the Net, it turns away on-line shoppers — a lesson learned painfully by Toys 'R' Us. And if a procurement project stalls because critical suppliers don't put good content on-line, users revert to off-contract buying.

- **Preserve manual tasks that struggle under on-line volume.** Manual steps like individual invoice matching will grind to a halt when they are overloaded by the sheer number of on-line transactions. This problem worsens as a firm's customers retain off-line practices, such as auto-faxing orders that must be rekeyed. This will bog down under the onslaught of smaller, more frequent on-line purchases.

Figure 2: e-Marketplaces Evolve Into Matchmakers

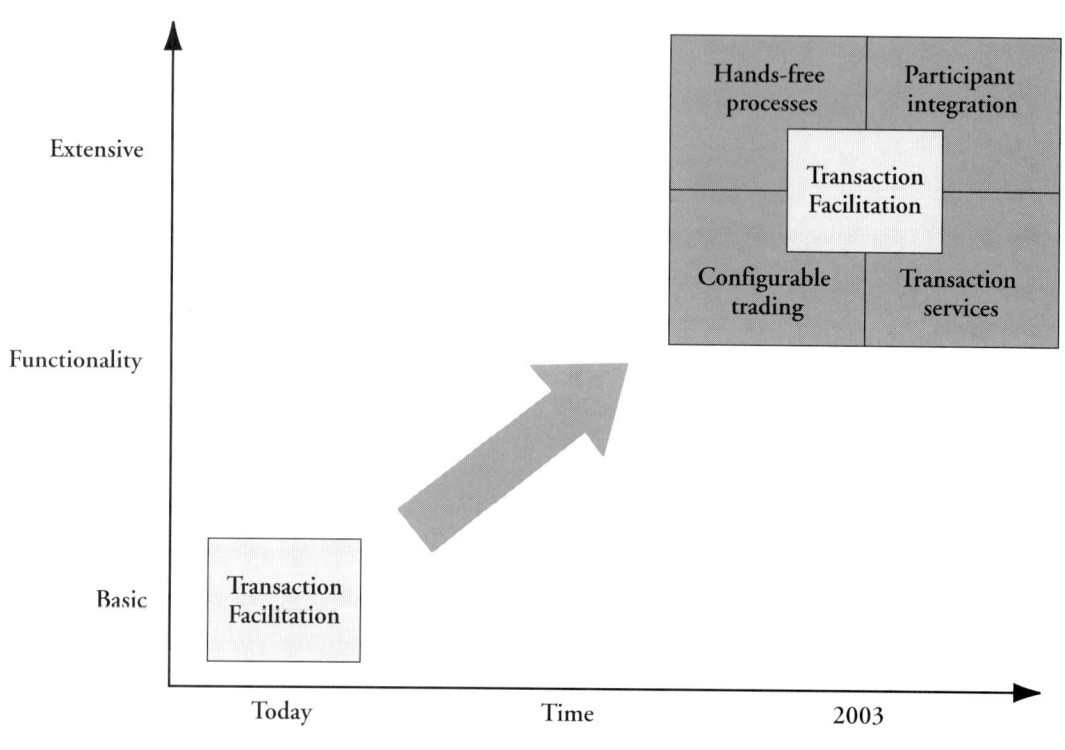

Source: Forrester Research, Inc.

Instead of reproducing legacy processes in a new technology, e-marketplaces will rearchitect their processes — and those of their participants — to take advantage of the Internet's unique characteristics. In this environment, firms benefit when their work with all parties — both inside and outside the firm — is fully automated. These processes, which Forrester calls hands-free, will adhere to three principles:

1) **Designed for the Internet.** The Internet is becoming richly populated with business services. Hands-free processes will tap these services to eliminate manual steps and offload responsibility. For example, instead of holding up an order while waiting for validation from the credit department, a hands-free process will use the authorization service of a credit bureau such as Escalate.com.

2) **Managed by exception.** In hands-free processes, rules-based decision engines replace most manual decisions. For example, tiered procurement authorizations can be implemented as an automatic approval based on an employee's title. The rules engine will 'throw' an exception into the manager's work queue only if a requisition cost is out of bounds.

3) **Analyzed and optimized continuously.** Hands-free processes are instrumented for quality of service, outcome trends, and recurring exceptions so that they can be monitored and managed. This helps procurement managers to negotiate a new contract based on a supplier's delivery performance. Process owners can optimize their efforts by analyzing the exception trends and adjusting the business rules.

2. Integrate participants

Today's e-marketplaces do little to foster intimacy between trading partners. To succeed, e-marketplaces will build a suite of real-time collaboration tools that tie together participants, allowing them to integrate the processes across these different firms by:

- **Picking standards for entire communities.** e-Marketplaces' format and protocol choices for automated trading will become *de facto* standards within these trading communities. Client companies will embrace these decisions, relieved to be out of the maze of competing XML schema proposals. More sophisticated about integration technologies and standards than their customers, e-marketplaces will mix and match pieces from framework proposers like CommerceNet, ebXML, RosettaNet, BizTalk.org, OAG, and OASIS.

- **Automating connections to firms' buy/sell systems.** e-Marketplaces will add programmatic interfaces that let participants transact automatically based on 'commerce APIs'. To create these interfaces, e-marketplaces will deploy data transformation products from vendors such as webMethods and OnDisplay to translate between partners' divergent vocabularies.

- **Hosting real-time conferencing.** Hands-free procurement still requires intervention when an automated process fails. Market makers should turn to vendors such as Optika who host resolution hubs that capture the context of a failed e-marketplace transaction — including ERP and customer relationship management (CRM) content. These hubs let trading partners resolve the problem using real-time collaboration tools like Web conferencing.

- **Developing intelligent workflow.** e-Marketplaces won't build customer loyalty if they fail to keep their capable-to-deliver promise. Sites need an intelligent purchase order rerouting mechanism that automatically fulfills undeliverable orders through an affiliate without ever involving the user. Emerging Internet standards like the Workflow Management Coalition's Wf-XML will help enable workflow routing across e-marketplaces.

- **Embedding supply chain planning tools.** To co-operate more effectively, companies must share data about factors like production capacity, scheduling, assembly, transportation, and warehousing. e-Marketplaces will add support for communicating this information and for monitoring and choreographing shared processes, using software from vendors such as Vitria, Extricity, and i2.

3. Weave-in transaction services

To meet the new demands of Net-enabled markets, globalized trade, and Internet time, companies will embrace a new generation of offerings — Internet transaction services (ITSs). This new class of services, which are priced by the transaction and delivered in the network, will help bridge the buyer–seller trading gaps within e-marketplaces. Who will offer these services?

- **Transaction underwriters will guarantee safety.** To answer the question 'Who am I doing business with?', companies will look to e-commerce underwriters. These on-line services will provide the electronic equivalent of a bank's letter of credit by verifying identities, qualifying partners, and providing guarantees. Transaction underwriters such as the Swiss firm Société Générale de Surveillance (SGS) will use VeriSign and eccelerate to help score the non-performance risks associated with a given transaction — and then guarantee those transactions for a per-transaction fee.

- **Regulatory watchdogs will simplify decision-making.** Doing e-business means trading in new regions and unfamiliar jurisdictions — and understanding the legal and tax implications of doing so. Regulatory watchdogs will help to navigate the minefield of local regulation by informing the decision process and minimizing the tax burden. When examining an offer for salmon in an e-marketplace such as gofish.com, how is a firm to know whether it can legally enter into the transaction — or what the true landed cost of the salmon will be? Regulatory watchdogs like ClearCross will provide definitive answers to these questions in real time over the Internet — before a firm commits to the deal.

- **Deal expediters will streamline financing and settlement.** Meeting a new trading partner and striking a deal is worthless without the ability to finance it. Deal expediters help to streamline e-commerce by connecting customers and financiers and turning receivables into cash. New Internet services like eCredit.com already link companies to dozens of financial institutions, including many firms that few companies have done business with before. By providing an on-line marketplace for credit, deal expediters deliver two benefits — lower prices and the ability to obtain financing in seconds.

- **Customer experience monitors will assess quality of experience.** On-line venues fail to measure — or even understand — participant satisfaction levels. Customer experience monitors will help firms to gain an outside view of their customers' quality of experience by providing both objective measurement and subjective feedback. Firms such as BizRate and Open Ratings will collect subjective customer experience data at every step in e-marketplace transactions.

4. Configure Trading Rules

The combination of next-generation e-marketplace technologies and smarter participants will catalyze an entirely new trading environment. In these highly evolved venues, firms won't just haggle over price — they'll tailor every interaction with:

- **Automated bidding.** Firms will automate recurring bidding decisions. How? By codifying rules about product specs, price parameters, and delivery timeframes. A publisher like Gannett will continuously monitor several paper exchanges, bidding on deals for newsprint up to a defined price ceiling, and setting rules to increase that ceiling by 10% when its internal inventory falls below a 10-day threshold.

- **Multi-attribute trade-offs.** Companies will optimize their purchases by factoring in critical elements such as quality, warranty service, and credit. Buyers will specify their preferences across these individual product attributes — kicking off automated matching algorithms at e-marketplaces that will compare these specs with the collection of supplier bids. For Johnson & Johnson's purchases of adhesive glue, for instance, the firm might specify requirements that weight level of quality twice as heavily as price or delivery time.

- **Customized invitation lists.** For every deal, firms will create a tailor-made list of participating sellers. Buyers will either individually invite particular vendors or automatically qualify a set of suppliers based on established criteria such as historical delivery metrics and integrated order processing capabilities. When buyers at Cargill want to get bids for sending six tons of coffee from Bogota to Miami, for instance, they might turn to their favorite three shippers as well as six others with refrigerated containers and on-time delivery records of at least 85%.

- **Preferential partnering.** Firms will give some vendors special treatment while keeping them competing for their business. A buyer like ConAgra might give a highly-valued chicken supplier the ability to 'pre-bid' in advance of the public market opening, or to place a final bid after the official close of the exchange. A buyer of bearings may provide The Timken Company with a 15% incumbency advantage — making this manufacturer's $300,000 bid appear more competitive than Kaydon Corporation's $275,000 offer.

e-Business Networks: The Future Market Context

As e-marketplaces mature into deeply integrated matchmakers, they will facilitate an entirely new set of business interactions. The combination of these interconnections and the evolution of corporations into e-businesses will set the stage for a new market context — what Forrester calls eBusiness Networks, defined as:

Resilient structures of interdependent players co-operating in real time over the Net.

This isn't just a shift — eBusiness Networks turn current practices upside down (see Figure 3: eBusiness Networks Will Redefine Business Relationships). In this topsy-turvy environment, long-held beliefs erode because:

1) **Links are free.** Today, deliberate negotiations yield carefully crafted contracts that lock down partnerships. But Net initiatives like RosettaNet, which is driving down the cost for firms to hook up in sectors of the electronics industry, set the stage for near-frictionless relationships between suppliers and partners.

2) **Information diffuses instantly.** Firms currently protect information as a matter of competitive necessity. But in eBusiness Networks, facts about a market will be easy to come by. With corporate systems linked up and transactions flowing through evolved e-marketplaces, real-time supply-and-demand data on goods, services, and human capital will become ubiquitous.

3) **Assets live on-network.** Firms will find that putting vital resources on the Net makes it much easier to get partners and customers to use those resources to the hilt. Companies will stop hiring workers and building plants for their own exclusive use. Instead, they will maximize returns — and boost their market caps — by putting these key assets in play over eBusiness Networks.

Figure 3: eBusiness Networks Will Redefine Business Relationships

	Today	eBusiness Networks
Data strategy	Own and hide	Share and exploit
Partner-switching costs	High	Low
Basis for trust	Relationship	Performance
Process focus	Intracompany	Intercompany
Industry evolution	Consolidation	Specialization
Decision-making	Computer-assisted	Human-assisted

Source: Forrester Research, Inc.

Principle 1: Links are free

Today, businesses spend months vetting potential partners — and then even longer hooking up with their new partners' disparate processes and incompatible systems. But Net-centric technologies that permit rapid, low-cost connections are maturing fast. A new infrastructure, built on XML and HTTP, will let companies form and disband connections quickly and at zero marginal cost. How will partnering change?

- **Partnerships will be brokered in real time.** Information in eBusiness Networks will go far beyond searchable lists of suppliers and products — it will include a critical mass of information about companies, services, capabilities, and prices. Hubs will feed this valuable data into advanced brokering technology to instantly 'network' potential partners at low cost to the participants.

- **Complex negotiations will yield to rules engines.** Standards-based platforms will enable firms to codify common contract terms in software templates, first within narrowly framed vertical markets and later across industries. Software will be able to automatically draft agreements to the point where people simply have to tweak the language and approve the contract.

- **Business processes will live in the network.** Processes such as customer care that span manufacturer, distributor, and retailer can be shared in eBusiness Networks. Rather than design captive business processes, companies will plug into shared systems provided by third-party specialists — like residential delivery provider Webvan. With these external bonds, firms will be able to dynamically adjust their services or product design processes to meet market demands.

Principle 2: Information diffuses instantly

Currently, companies work hard at keeping plans from leaking to competitors. But in the process, they starve their partners. In eBusiness Networks, this conventional practice will be turned on its head. As firms come to rely deeply on external providers for key services and products, their daily operations can be easily observed and decoded by third parties. What happens to corporate secrets?

- **The firm becomes an open book.** In eBusiness Networks, information gains value as it is shared among interdependent firms. The most evolved players — including some virtual dot.coms such as HoustonStreet Exchange — already act this way, sharing all but 'need to hide' information in order to give their partners the data they need to act quickly and in concert.

- **Market data will be common property.** Interactions that play out digitally and funnel through hubs are easy for software to observe, aggregate, and disseminate. What's the result of this openness? Market trends such as hyperdemand for Beanie Babies or short-term DRAM shortages in Southeast Asia are broadcast early, and to all participants.

- **Information decay will accelerate.** With fresh data continuously flowing, competitive advantage will shift to those companies that master advanced technologies such as neural networks to discern patterns in the data. These companies will distribute their insights because information will have little value until it is shared with partners in an eBusiness Network. As the network adjusts to this new information, those actions instantly become part of the broader data set — and the value of the initial insight falls to zero.

Principle 3: Assets live on-network

Conventional investment decisions revolve around buying or building — for internal use. This prudent thinking won't work in eBusiness Networks. Firms will instead grapple with a much broader trade-off: hoarding their resources versus sharing them with partners and customers over the network. Vanguard firms will resolve this dilemma by putting their key assets — say distribution capacity or product design documents — in play, because connected companies will attract smart partners and innovate faster. How will this work?

- **Firms with on-network assets will win more business.** eBusiness Networks will offer infinite partnering possibilities. To manage this opportunity glut, network participants will dynamically sort potential partners with a new metric — what Forrester calls return on connection (ROC). With ROC, companies will focus their finite resources — people, time, money — on the most productive partners. They will reject businesses that offer inflexible off-line assets, such as manually dispatched trucking fleets, linking up instead with suitors that offer a rich array of network-accessible resources.

- **Wired firms will innovate faster.** As switching costs shrink, businesses will swarm to value — the best products and services at the best business terms. Firms that reach out across the network to offer — and consume — best-in-class services will become more nimble, outpacing vertically integrated businesses. By maximizing on-network assets, these companies will be able to continually refine their products and services — in essence, out-innovating the competition. They will thrive by compressing and reshaping product life cycles, even as they cannibalize their own offerings in mid-cycle.

The Implication — Focus or Die

Poor-performing firms won't have any place to hide. Using the data-rich interconnections of eBusiness Networks, buyers won't settle for anything less than best-of-breed offerings. Why? The Net's reach will provide those purchasers with instant access to better proposals. The upshot: eBusiness Networks will pressure firms to specialize — surviving only by intensely focusing on their core value-add and learning how to interoperate with other top-notch specialists. As this specialization imperative proceeds:

- **B&S (breakups & selloffs) will eclipse M&A.** Today, merger mania continues to produce conglomerate behemoths. This trend will peak, as firms in eBusiness Networks rely more on partners than on wholly-owned resources. As businesses pare down, they will spin off viable departments, business units — even processes and intellectual property — into new stand-alone ventures. The result: capital flow will swing from megalithic corporations to virtual companies — and IPO spin-offs from existing corporations will look as cool as dot.coms.

- **Sellers will market their trading attributes**. To leverage multi-attribute interactions, buyers will quickly uncover the elements of their purchases. This discovery period is critical for sellers. Instead of waiting for characteristics to appear, smart suppliers will take an active role in helping their customers to define these important attributes. Why? Because the right set of criteria will help sellers to rise to the top. A firm that consistently hits delivery targets will make sure that buyers rate distribution highly.

- **Component brands will take off.** eBusiness Networks will bring good news to marketers: they will no longer be captive to internal product development, because they can snap together offerings from best-of-breed elements. The bad news: as component brands rise in importance, the firms that make the branded components or subsystems will assert themselves through 'Intel Inside' types of marketing campaigns. This noise will spawn new disciplines — like virtual brand management — and new matchmakers that help to assemble brands and assist buyers in selecting composite products.

- **Products will come to life — or die — in nanocycles**. With all of the free-flowing information available in eBusiness Networks, early feedback on new products becomes critical. Who will want to buy a product if everyone knows that 75% of the initial buyers weren't happy — and why they weren't? As this feedback mechanism becomes institutionalized in the network, new products and services will suffer the same fate as movies: they will be made — or broken — based on the 'box office' results of the first weekend. Successful firms will respond by increasing their innovation clockrates — cannibalizing their own products before someone else in the network does it for them.

A Quick Summary

The Net will do much more than just shift the flow of transactions — it will ultimately force firms to re-invent how they operate. These changes, however, won't happen overnight. Existing businesses will take several years to fully adopt the Net — evolving through a multi-step e-business voyage. During this transitional period, companies will redefine how they are structured, what they focus on, and how they interconnect with other firms. In this context, today's e-marketplaces represent just the beginning of a structural shift. As these Net-native players evolve, they will help to set the stage for an entirely new market structure that Forrester Research calls eBusiness Networks.

Bruce Temkin leads Forrester's research into the Internet's impact in reshaping B2B relationships. He is a recognized industry thought-leader in the areas of eBusiness strategy, restructuring of distribution channels, and the evolution of Internet-based business models. Bruce provides strategic advice to leading B2B eMarketplaces, technology vendors, and Fortune 1,000 firms. Bruce has extensive experience with technology-based business ventures — managing high-tech efforts in both large and small firms. Prior to joining Forrester, Bruce was an executive officer at several dot.com firms. Before those start-up experiences, he held various management positions at General Electric, Stratus Computers, and Fidelity Investments.

Chapter 12:
Financial Services for B2B Exchanges

Content provided during a series of interviews with
Steve Ellis, Executive Vice President, Internet Banking, Wells Fargo Bank

Financial services that integrate with sophisticated end-to-end fulfillment, tracking, and payment processing represent the next frontier for developing B2B exchanges.

While e-commerce providers have worked hard to automate many of the processes for conducting business on-line — from making catalog content accessible to facilitating auctions and negotiating sales agreements — to date, very little has been done to automate end-to-end financial services. For most exchanges today, e-commerce ends when you execute the 'buy' command. In fact, at least 50% of all US transactions (including consumer) are still paper-based (*The Nilson Report*, December 1999). And even when electronic invoices are exchanged, companies typically print and manually route or re-key the invoices into back-end ERP (enterprise resource planning) systems for off-line payment. This means that while the volume of purchases on B2B exchanges is growing dramatically, most payment and financing is still conducted off-line.

But this is changing. In this chapter we will look at some of the financial services available to exchanges today and who offers them. Then we'll explore some of the financial service platforms under development that will help to usher in the next wave of high-value B2B exchanges. We will conclude with a discussion of some of the authentication considerations that we believe will drive systems in the long term.

Why is it Important for B2B Exchanges to Include Financial Services?

As recently as January 2000, industry pundits projected that the number of B2B exchanges would grow to 10,000 and then consolidate. But as the same year draws to a close, most now believe that there will never be that many and that the industry will more likely consolidate to between 50 and 200 exchanges in the near term. What will cull the exchange winners from the losers will be the kinds of business services offered. Shipping, inspection, assembly, and other logistics functions will all help to make the B2B exchange easier to run and more cost-effective. But perhaps the most crucial offering for an e-market to increase its transaction volume today, is electronic payment and financial services.

Imagine getting a great price for steel or sodium bicarbonate, but then having to go off-line to verify credit, generate a purchase order, invoice the sale, insure it, transfer the money, create escrow accounts, and route authorizations. Important value could be created by B2B exchanges by bringing payment processing and financial settlement on-line. This greatly improves the automation of transactions. The e-services will be more efficient than paper processes; they will save time and money and will also reduce re-keying errors. They can also reduce the risk inherent in buying and selling on-line. Since the risk of doing business in a faceless medium like the Internet is potentially greater than in the physical world, reducing this risk remains a crucial factor in encouraging on-line purchases.

What Types of Financial Services are Relevant for Exchanges?

Any time companies conduct business transactions, risk is introduced. Simply put, buyers want to know: 'How do I know that I'll receive the goods on time, in good condition, and that they'll be of high quality?' Sellers worry: 'Will I be paid for my goods or services?' Financial products and services can help guard against these risks. For unacquainted partners, for example, financial institutions can hold payments in escrow until goods are received. For established trading partners, financial institutions can verify whether someone is authorized to complete a transaction, and can offer lower interest rates and fees to reflect lower risk. Financial institutions can also provide insurance to cover losses or damage incurred in shipping, as well as safe and secure transfer of funds.

Financial institutions literally offer hundreds of services for businesses that can be included on-line. Below we provide very brief descriptions of some of the first services to be e-enabled.

1. Credit cards

In the B2C arena, where small-dollar transactions are typical, credit cards are dominant. Wells Fargo has nearly 13,000 merchants accepting credit cards as of 3Q00 and — with the number growing rapidly — is one of the largest enablers of on-line credit card acceptance. But, given the large dollar size of B2B transactions, credit cards are less appropriate for the B2B arena since fees are charged to merchants as a percentage of the transaction. Recognizing this, American Express, MasterCard, and Visa have recently started forming partnerships with e-procurement companies to enable B2B payments. American Express is partnering with Ariba, Commerce One, and Concur; MasterCard is partnering with e-commerce Cubed; and Visa is partnering with Ariba, CyberSource and iCat.

2. Purchasing-cards (P-cards)

A P-card is a credit card-like program that a bank sells to a company, therefore giving the company more control over employee purchases and providing richer information about the credit card transactions. On a per-employee basis, a company can restrict the types of purchases an employee can make as well as set dollar value limits for transactions. Additionally, the company receives valuable reporting on company-wide spending.

3. Escrow

For exchanges that bring together unacquainted parties, or buyers and sellers who wish to remain anonymous, escrow can be an excellent service. For example, I-Escrow provides an escrow service on ECNet, an exchange where manufacturers can off-load excess inventory, such as semiconductors, without their competitors knowing who is doing the selling. When a buyer in this exchange makes a purchase, he pays the escrow company — a neutral third party. When the buyer confirms they have received the goods as promised, the escrow company releases the fees to the seller for a small fee.

4. Letters of credit and documentary collections

Financial institutions provide letters of credit and documentary collections to assure that importers will receive the goods they have bought from overseas, and that exporters will receive payment for goods they have sold to foreign parties.

5. Factoring

When sellers are crunched for cash, they can sell their receivables to a 'factor' at a discount. The factor then takes on the responsibility for collecting on the invoice from the buyer. Industries such as transportation and temporary employment are frequent users of this type of service.

6. Automated clearinghouse

Automated clearinghouse (ACH) is a batch-driven payment process built on a network of virtually all domestic financial institutions. It is used by literally millions of companies for services such as payroll and cash concentration. Settlement occurs in one or two days. Typically, transactions are inexpensive (about $0.25 per transaction), high volume (average 100 items/file), and relatively small dollar ($2500 on average) when compared to wires.

7. Wires

Compared with ACH, wires are more expensive per transaction, but provide same-day delivery. As with ACH, the funds are transferred electronically between banks domestically or internationally and are very secure. As a result, wires are appropriate for large-dollar transactions.

What Types of Companies Offer Financial Services to Exchanges?

Today, financial services are offered piecemeal to exchanges by banks and lenders, insurance companies, and other businesses that may specialize in specific markets, or by services such as I-Escrow that offer only one product, only on-line. The goal in the future will be to integrate these and other services into an exchange's overall workflow which is where we will begin to see tremendous efficiencies arise.

Traditional bricks-and-mortar financial services companies have an advantage in providing financial services to exchanges. In many ways they are the natural e-commerce enabler. Financial institutions have been dealing with business risk for centuries, and are best positioned to act as a trusted on-line intermediary between trading partners. They bring a full array of the products and services referenced above. This is important as a trading relationship grows between buyers and sellers from unknown vendor to strategic partner, because different financial services are appropriate. Financial institutions have long-standing relationships with financial regulators, strong relationships with their merchant customer base, and the financial strength and discipline to deliver comprehensive programs. And some have shown the strategic flexibility to pair with dot.com innovators for quick development and delivery of services.

Initially, financial institutions are e-enabling their treasury management and transaction-related services. *WellsXchange*^{R} service — for example, provides marketplaces with the ability to offer letters of credit, documentary collections, and lines of credit within their marketplace. Gradually, financial institutions are beginning to play an important role in eliminating off-line processing with electronic bill presentment and payment (EBPP) and other on-line payment and credit services. Through Wells Fargo's *Commercial Electronic Office*^{SM}, existing Wells Fargo customers can transact in foreign exchange, view account information, initiate ACH, and organize letters of credit and wire transactions.

1. Electronic transaction payment providers

Electronic transaction payment providers bring electronic and Internet-based payment solutions to billers, banks, and consumers. In September 2000, two major players merged: CheckFree and Transpoint. CheckFree was founded in 1981 and has been considered the leader in the electronic bill payment (EBP) marketplace. Together they design, develop, and market services that enable customers to make e-commerce payments and collections, automate recurring financial transactions and conduct secure transactions over the Web. Their EBP product aggregates bills from many billers to one website. It is used by over 350 banks and 1100 merchants to process over 60% of electronic bills in the US. The company's EBPP service is in use by 20 billers, including Bank One, First Union, and Morgan Stanley, and its APL investment services are the leading portfolio management system used by 225 money management institutions.

Clareon is another player in this arena. Clareon has designed a service to manage wire transfers between banks using the Internet. Clareon's service is built on research originally conducted for the Treasury Department to convert its paper-intensive payment process into an electronic process. The result is an on-line payment service for high-value transactions which works easily with any bank or enterprise system. Clareon transmits both payment and remittance information over the Internet to any bank. No prearrangements are required.

2. Electronic procurement software companies

E-procurement software companies provide Internet-based procurement solutions that link buyers and suppliers to automate the purchase of non-production goods and services. Prominent companies are Ariba, Commerce One, and Intellisys, with growing competition coming from Captura Software, Clarus, Concur Technologies, Extensity, GE Information Services, Netscape Communications, RightWorks, and TRADE'ex Electronic Commerce Systems, to name a few.

3. ERP vendors

The leading enterprise resource planning (ERP) software companies with an eye on B2B e-commerce are Oracle, PeopleSoft, BAAN, J.D. Edwards, and SAP. These companies have provided the legacy transactional systems for many companies and are poised to be the providers of information management solutions as their customers move part or all of their transactions onto the Web. For the most part, these companies are focused on B2B procurement solutions for mission critical business operations. Some ERP companies already offer B2B e-procurement solutions for non-production goods between businesses.

So, Where is it all Going?

Financial services for B2B exchanges today are still fragmented and very new. Some of the financial services available to B2B exchanges were originally developed for B2C e-commerce and are only now evolving to address the more complex needs of B2B e-commerce. Some services will easily evolve. Others will need to be created anew. Financial institutions are also e-enabling their existing products and creating new products and services to serve the diverse financial service needs arising in the New Economy.

Most financial services available today focus on payment processing and EBPP, with many companies offering individual financial services such as sourcing credit, escrow or payments authentication and processing. But a new generation of integrated financial services platforms is in the making.

FinancialServicesMatrix.com, Inc. is an example of the comprehensive integrated financial services platform you will likely see more of in the future. FinancialServicesMatrix.com was created as a new company by Wells Fargo & Co, Citicorp, Inc., and three technology firms: Enron Broadband Services, i2 Technologies Inc., and S1 Corporation. It will allow on-line trading partners to access services from any of the participating financial services providers, helping to reduce the financial risk of B2B e-commerce. Additionally, it will help address a significant obstacle to the growth of on-line exchange volume — the ability to safely make payments on-line and provide access to a wide range of payment options. The site will offer a comprehensive array of financial products and services, including, but not limited to, electronic payment (ACH, wires, p-check, credit/p-cards, etc), credit and risk management (trade credit, access, escrow, receivables management and factoring, foreign exchange, etc), information services, and infrastructure.

Financial Services for Next-generation B2B Exchanges

Ultimately, financial services will become more than simply a cost of doing business. As the market for B2B goods becomes more seamless, where price comparisons are easy to make, well-integrated financial services can give an exchange a competitive advantage. As exchanges grapple with ways to encourage Web stickiness — that is, how to attract *and* retain exchange participants to achieve liquidity — value-added financial services could become the difference between the winners and the losers. The winners will be the ones that figure out how to save companies time and money by providing on-line business processes that are secure and reliable. These exchanges will help employees buy on exchanges and sellers settle their accounts. The exchanges that distinguish the quality of their offerings will find they are in a better position to protect themselves from price erosion as well.

In the future, financial services in an exchange will encompass much more than payment settlement and reconciliation. Beyond integrated financial services platforms, we will also be seeing more sophisticated user authentication schemes that enable 'true' on-line credit management services. On-line trading partners will find that they need to inspire trust by reliably assuring one another of their identities and payment execution capabilities.

User Authentication — a Necessity for Credit Management On-line

Conducting financial services on-line necessitates that trading companies find a way to authenticate who their buyers are and what they are authorized to buy. Today, exchanges typically use two credentials — user name and a password — for buyer authentication. When large companies are involved, three-factor authentication becomes necessary — company name, user ID, and password. However, this type of authentication does not provide any additional form of security beyond 'what you know'.

The next level of security, which is now emerging, looks at not only who you are, but 'what you have'. Token cards provide a randomly-generated number on a physical device that you would hold in your possession and use in conjunction with your user name, password, and PIN. While the token card can only reside on a physical device, an emerging tool — digital certificates — may also be stored on the browser. The digital certificate is an electronic form of identification that enables a user to have the same level of authentication as with a token card. The digital certificate can be housed in two forms — in your browser software, or on the chip of a smart card, which is digitally read by a card reader that could be hooked to a PC, cell phone, your PDA, or other devices. Wells Fargo, for example, will use digital certificate technology for Virtual Purchase Connection, an on-line payment solution for businesses available in late 2000.

Summary

In this new on-line economy, tying together information from disparate sources provides us with powerful new value propositions. For example, authenticating a buyer, understanding what they are authorized to buy, and coupling that with their available credit, gives a more complete financial picture. Systems that tie the authentication process to the buying process of the company and credit availability are a winning combination for the spontaneous purchase. For buyers with pre-existing arrangements with sellers, credit is often extended, with settlement done once a month. To move this kind of relationship onto an exchange requires a new layer of tools to help the exchange track all on-line buying, generate an e-invoice, and account for purchases and payments made through a multitude of traditional and electronic channels.

Next-generation exchanges, if they are to achieve the scale of efficiency they are capable of, will need to integrate their financial systems and their trading partners' back-end ERP systems. This will greatly facilitate credit verification, purchase order generation, invoicing, shipping, delivery, payment, and adjudication. And just like the traditional systems in place today, these on-line systems will have to handle partial shipments, returns, and the like, electronically. Any company that wants to remain competitive will make solving these challenges a priority. Success in this will fuel transactions at the exchange, and will drive up the exchange's liquidity — the key to creating value. As exchanges continue to look at ways to increase on-line transaction volume and keep buyers and sellers on their sites, those exchanges that provide this type of integration will be the winners in their market space.

Business 2 Business

Aerospace • Agriculture • Auto • Chemicals • Electronics • Construction
Energy • Financial • Food & Beverage • Travel • Industrial Equipment
Transportation • Media • Printing • Real Estate • Food Service • Retail

Exchange Profiles

Business 2 Business

Aerospace • Agriculture • Auto • Chemicals • Electronics • Construction
Energy • Financial • Food & Beverage • Travel • Industrial Equipment
Transportation • Media • Printing • Real Estate • Food Service • Retail

Profile *i*: Arbinet-thexchange

Contact information		
	Name:	Chris Reid
	E-mail address:	creid@thexchange.com
	Phone number:	(212) 797 9060, ext. 2026
	Mailing address:	33 Whitehall Street, 19th Floor, New York, NY 10004

Name	Arbinet-thexchange
URL	http://www.thexchange.com
Target markets	Telecommunications
Summary of business goals; achievements to date	Arbinet-thexchange is the full-service, on-line exchange for on-demand transactions, automated physical delivery, and settlement of trades of telephony bandwidth. Thexchange is neutral, favoring neither buyers nor sellers, and allows participants to trade anonymously. Automated delivery is accomplished by employing advanced trading software and a set of patented processes to link the web-based trading platform with carrier-grade telecommunications switching equipment. Arbinet-thexchange handles all settlement,

collection, and payment for trades effected on its exchange, and provides continuous monitoring and on-line rating of the service quality of each seller's network.

Arbinet-thexchange estimates the total global market for telephony bandwidth measured in minutes at $706bn in 2000. This market is characterized by both falling prices and a high level of SG&A expense, which at 25% of revenues is 9% higher than the US corporate average. Use of Arbinet-thexchange's full-service, automated trading solution helps members cut costs and maintain profitability by providing the opportunity to generate incremental revenues, as well as lowering the cost, risk, and transaction time required to complete transactions for telephony bandwidth.

Our Solution

Our members trade the use of telephony bandwidth, which can carry voice, fax, and Internet Protocol (IP) traffic, and is metered in minutes. Our members move this traffic across traditional telecommunications (PSTN), packet data, voice over Internet protocol (VoIP), and wireless networks. The minute of telephony bandwidth is a commodity with a standard unit of trade, large numbers of buyers and sellers, and high trading volumes.

Our solution integrates a central on-line exchange with telecommunications switching equipment, to which all members are interconnected. This architecture eliminates the need for buyers and sellers to establish separate direct connections. Our patented proprietary software monitors the rates posted on the exchange, and the quality of each call passing through our switching equipment, and automatically sends members' calls via the lowest-cost path, that satisfies their specified routing and quality of service parameters. Arbinet-thexchange provides a single invoice or payment to each member. Our exchange is neutral, and all members trade anonymously.

Our Technology: Carrier Grade, Web-Tone Quality

Every aspect of thexchange has been painstakingly designed to ensure each trade, each call, each transaction, and each call record is precisely processed.

Arbinet-thexchange operates a state-of-the-art systems platform, which was designed with an emphasis on scalability, performance, and reliability. Our platform consists of three main components: the trading implementation platform, the rating, reconciliation and settlement platform, and the global delivery layer. These systems are connected through patented and proprietary technology, which automatically routes members' traffic in accordance with member orders placed via the on-line market. The operating support system manages all billing and settlement functions.

Our switching platform is the Nortel GSP switch, which is fully redundant with capacity to 100,000 DS0 circuit equivalents. Arbinet uses integrated technology manufactured by 3 Com, Cisco, Clarent, and Vocaltec to support and process VoIP transactions. Our carrier-grade infrastructure supports all major signaling standards, including C7, SS7, ISDN, and PRI. Our systems are located in our own facilities in New York, and our staff provides 24-hour monitoring and engineering support to all of our systems.

Benefits of Arbinet-thexchange

Arbinet-thexchange eliminates the inefficiencies involved in buying, selling, and provisioning network capacity. Specifically, our exchange allows providers to reduce SG&A and network operations costs, shorten price discovery and market reaction time, and reduce market and credit risk, and offers an anonymous alternate channel with increased market reach to generate incremental revenue. The ultimate benefit is the ability for the member to enhance profit margins.

Our Members

Members of Arbinet-thexchange are telecommunications service providers seeking to buy or sell the use of minutes of telephony bandwidth. Buyers and sellers currently include multinational, international, national, and local telecommunication carriers and VoIP service providers.

Date founded	1996
Founder	Alex Mashinsky
Locations	New York, Virginia, Florida, Tokyo

No. of employees	90
Management team	Anthony L. Craig, *Chairman* and *Chief Executive Officer* (appointed December 1999; previously President and CEO of Global Knowledge Network, a global learning services company. Mr. Craig is a 33-year technology industry veteran, and has served as director of alternate channels marketing at IBM; President and CEO of GE Information Systems; President and CEO of Prime Computer; Senior VP of Oracle Corporation; and VP at Digital Equipment Corporation).

J. Curt Hockemeier, *President* and *Chief Operating Officer* (appointed April 2000; Executive VP and COO, Telephony Operations, AT&T Broadband).

Robert S. Vaters, *Executive Vice President* and *Chief Financial Officer* (appointed January 2000; previously Excecutive VP of Finance and Administration and CFO of Premiere Technologies, Inc., a global supplier of enhanced communications services).

Neil A. Torpey, *Executive Vice President* and *General Counsel* (appointed February 2000; previously a partner in the corporate department of Paul, Hastings, Janofsky & Walker LLP, an international law firm).

Norris M. 'Buddy' Hall III, *Senior Vice President, Network Operations and Development* (appointed March 2000; previously Senior VP of network operations at Talk.com, an Internet-based telecommunications services provider). |
| Board of directors | Alex Mashinsky, *Founder* and *Vice Chairman*
Anthony L. Craig, *Chairman*
Alex Mashinsky, *Vice Chairman*
Curt Hockemeier, *Director*
Douglas A. Alexander, *Director* (Internet Capital Group)
Philip Summe, *Director* (Flatiron Partners)
Paul G. Theunissen, *Director* (JP Morgan Capital)
Roland A. Van der Meer, *Director* (ComVentures)
Donna C. Redel, *Director* (The World Economic Forum) |
| Major investors | Amerindo Investment Advisors
BancBoston Ventures
Bedrock Capital Partners
Breakaway Capital |

	Chase Capital Partners CornVentures Internet Capital Group J.P. Morgan Capital Corportion Van Wagoner Capital Management
Strategic partners	Nortel Networks Cisco Systems Sun Microsystems Oracle Breakaway Solutions Architel ECTEL FiberNet Telecom PricewaterhouseCoopers Hitachi 3COM Taylor McKenzie
Major clients/members	Our members are anonymous. According to figures from Arbinet's S-1, as of March 2000, Arbinet-thexchange had 48 interconnected members, of which 27 had begun to trade actively on the exchange.
Summary of recent announcements	Milestones: - 16 August 2000 — Arbinet-thexchange appoints Donna C. Redel, Prudential, Divisional CTO and former Chair of Comex, to board of directors. - 10 August 2000 — Arbinet-thexchange completes implementation of full-service, dynamic bandwidth trading solution. - 9 August 2000 — Arbinet-thexchange and Nortel Networks Commission DMS-GSP switch in first web-controlled dynamic switching application. - 3 August 2000 — Arbinet-thexchange, certified by Taylor McKenzie, debuts the first objective quality of service ratings for on-line traded communications bandwidth. - 13 June 2000 — Arbinet-thexchange raises $41mn bringing total equity capital raised in past eight months to $75mn. - 31 May 2000 — Arbinet changes name to Arbinet-thexchange. New brand emphasizes end-to-end trading services for members.

- 27 April 2000 — Arbinet names J. Curt Hockemeier *President* and *Chief Operating Officer.*
- 20 December 1999 — Arbinet Names Anthony L. Craig, *Chairman* and *Chief Executive Officer.*
- 2 December 1999 — Arbinet raises $30mn from syndicate of global financial institutions.

Awards:

- ITU's Geneva '99 World Communications Award for Technology Foresight.
- AMR Research's Top 20 Independent Trading Exchanges.
- *InformationWeek*'s E-Business 100 Award.

Gross turnover for 1999 Arbinet-thexchange reports its end-1999 revenues as US$649,393. (According to the company's S-1, this amount does not include revenues from a business that was discontinued in 1999.)

Profile *ii*:
ChemConnect, Inc.

Contact information	Name: E-mail address: Phone number: Mailing address:	ChemConnect, Inc. info@chemconnect.com (415) 364 3300 44 Montgomery Street, Suite 250, San Francisco, CA 94104
Name		ChemConnect, Inc.
URL		http://www.chemconnect.com
Target markets		Buyers and sellers of petrochemicals, plastics and polymers, basic industrial chemicals, fine and specialty chemicals, and industrial gases.
Summary of business goals; achievements to date		ChemConnect developed and manages the World Chemical Exchange, with over 11,000 members from 7,000 member companies in more than 110 countries. In addition, 33 industry leading companies from around the world have designated the World Chemical Exchange their preferred third-party on-line exchange. Charter members include: Abbott Laboratories; Air Liquide; BASF AG; Bayer; Borealis; BP Amoco Chemicals; Celanese Ltd.; Crompton Corporation; The Dow Chemical Company; DSM N.V.; Eastman Chemical Company; Enichem; GE Plastics; The Geon Company;

	Huntsman Corporation; Hyundai Corp.; Imperial Chemicals Industries, PLC; Mitsui & Co. (U.S.A.), Inc.; Marubeni America Corporation; Mitsubishi Corporation; Nova Chemicals; Occidental Chemical Corporation; Owens Corning; PPG Industries; Praxair; Reichhold, Inc.; Repsol; Rohm & Haas; Saudi Basic Industries Corporation; Solutia Inc.; Sterling Chemicals, Inc.; Sumitomo Corporation; The Titan/Westlake Group.
Date founded	1995
Founders	John Beasley, Jay Hall, and Patrick van der Valk
Locations	Headquartered in San Francisco, ChemConnect has offices in Frankfurt, Houston, London, Paris, Philadelphia, Rotterdam, and Singapore.
No. of employees	176
Management team	John F. Beasley, *Chairman* and *Chief Executive Officer* Philip J. Ringo, *President* and *Chief Operating Officer* Robert E. Drury, *Chief Financial Officer* Linda Stegeman, *Senior Vice President, Marketing* Gary Cofran, *Vice President, Worldwide Sales* Raj Bhargava, *Senior Vice President, Product Planning & Engineering* Joseph Morrissey, *Senior Vice President, Global Operations* Peter Navin, *Vice President, Human Resources*
Board of directors	Tom Baruch, *General Partner*, CMEA Ventures John Beasley, *Chief Executive Officer*, ChemConnect Frederick J. Grede, *Chief Operating Officer*, Hong Kong Exchanges and Clearing Ltd. and *Chief Executive Officer*, Hong Kong Futures Exchange Philip J. Ringo, *President* and *Chief Operting Officer*, ChemConnect Chris Schaepe, *General Partner*, Weiss Peck & Greer Bill Tai, *Partner*, IVP J. Lawrence Wilson, *Retired Chief Executive Officer*, Rohm & Haas
Major investors	Abbott Laboratories; Air Liquide; BASF AG; Bayer; Borealis; BP Amoco Chemicals; Celanese Ltd.; Crompton Corporation; The Dow Chemical Company; DSM N.V.; Eastman Chemical Company; Enichem; GE Plastics; The Geon Company; Huntsman; Hyundai

Corp.; Imperial Chemicals Industries, PLC; Mitsui & Co. (U.S.A.), Inc.; Marubeni America Corporation; Mitsubishi Corporation; Nova Chemicals; Occidental Chemical Corporation; Owens Corning; PPG Industries; Praxair; Reichhold, Inc.; Repsol; Rohm & Haas; Saudi Basic Industries Corporation; Solutia Inc.; Sterling Chemicals, Inc.; Sumitomo Corporation; The Titan/Westlake Group.

ChemConnect's strategic investors include Andersen Consulting, Chemical Week Ventures, Chemical Market Associates Inc., Citigroup, Enron North America, and SAP Ventures.

Top-tier investment firms — including Goldman Sachs, Morgan Stanley Dean Witter, Institutional Venture Partners (IVP), Weiss, Peck & Greer, CMEA Ventures, Vulcan Ventures, and Highland Capital Partners — back the company.

Strategic partners	ChemConnect's strategic partners include Andersen Consulting, Chemical Week Ventures, and Chemical Market Associates, Inc.(CMAI).
Major clients/members	Abbott Laboratories; Air Liquide; BASF AG; Bayer; Borealis; BP Amoco Chemicals; Celanese Ltd.; Crompton Corporation; The Dow Chemical Company; DSM N.V.; Eastman Chemical Company; Enichem; GE Plastics; The Geon Company; Huntsman; Hyundai Corp.; Imperial Chemicals Industries, PLC; Mitsui & Co. (U.S.A.), Inc.; Marubeni America Corporation; Mitsubishi Corporation; Nova Chemicals; Occidental Chemical Corporation; Owens Corning; PPG Industries; Praxair; Reichhold, Inc.; Repsol; Roche; Rohm & Haas; Saudi Basic Industries Corporation; Solutia Inc.; Sterling Chemicals, Inc.; Sumitomo Corporation; The Titan/Westlake Group.
Summary of recent announcements	2 Aug 2000 — ChemConnect announces a new corporate member. On-line purchasing of chemicals grows as ChemConnect welcomes Roche as its 52nd corporate member.
	28 June 2000 — ChemConnect establishes two Japanese JV companies. Joint venture with Mitsui, Mitsubishi, Sumitomo, and Marubeni to operate an on-line chemical exchange, tailored for the Japanese chemical industry with access to — and for — 'global' market through the World Chemical Exchange.

19 June 2000 — Frederick J. Grede joins ChemConnect Board. Grede is Chief Operating Officer of Hong Kong Exchanges and Clearing Ltd., Chief Executive Officer of Hong Kong Futures Exchange, and a former Executive Vice President of the Chicago Board of Trade.

30 May 2000 — ChemConnect acquires Industrial Gas Exchange. Purchase of IGX brings new executive talent, product offerings, and clients to the World Chemical Exchange, a global Internet platform for chemicals and plastics.

Latest revenue summary for 2000	As a private company, ChemConnect does not disclose this information.
Certifications/awards	<ul><li>July 2000, ChemConnect is named to *Forbes* 'Best of the Web B2B List'.</li><li>3rd Quarter 2000, Dbusiness.com listed ChemConnect as one of the top 50 San Francisco companies to watch.</li><li>May 2000, *Red Herring* recognizes ChemConnect as one of the Herring 100 top companies.</li><li>Dow Jones refers to ChemConnect as '… *the eBay of the chemistry world.*'</li><li>1999 Golden Web Award winner.</li></ul>

Profile *iii*:
Commerx, Inc.

Contact information	Name: E-mail address: Phone number: Mailing address:	Jill Kouri jkouri@commerx.com (312) 464 7813 3 Westbrook Corporate Center, Suite 700, Westchester, IL 60154
Company name		Commerx, Inc.
URLs		http://www.commerx.com http://www.commerxplasticsnet.com http://www.commerxmetals.com http://www.commerxpackaging.com
Target markets		Industrial markets: plastics, metals
Summary of business goals; achievements to date		Commerx develops, implements, integrates, and hosts a suite of scalable software applications for e-procurement, auctions/exchanges, supply chain collaboration, and logistics. Designed to increase efficiency and eliminate waste from the industrial supply chain, Commerx can also integrate these solutions into its users' business processes.

Date founded	1995
Founders	Tim Stojka and Nick Stojka
Location	Chicago, with sales force nationally
No. of employees	165
Management team	Tim Stojka, *Chairman* and *Chief Executive Officer* Nick Stojka, *Executive Vice President* David Dill, *Chief Financial Officer* Jeff Garwood, *Chief Operating Officer* Richard Hay, *Vice President, Marketing and Strategy* David O'Meara, *Vice President, Corporate Development* Neal Ebert, *Chief Information Officer* Chris Borneman, *Chief Technology Officer*
Board of directors	Tim Stojka, Commerx, Inc. Nick Stojka, Commerx, Inc. Kenneth Fox, Internet Capital Group John Hamm, Internet Capital Group Timothy Ozark, AIM Financial Corporation Charles Fritz, NeoMedia Technologies, Inc.
Major investors	Capital Research and Management Eastman Ashland Internet Capital Group LLC (NasDAQ: ICGE) MC Capital Inc. Mitsui & Co. (U.S.A.), Inc. Palantir Associates Pivotal Asset Management
Strategic partners	Ariba Commerce One Commerce Quest Manugistics Schneider Logistics

Major clients/members	Nypro, Inc. Behr Metal Lawson Mardon Alberto-Culver, Inc.
Summary of recent announcements	• Signed agreement with Manugistics to provide hosted supply chain collaboration tools. • Introduced Commerx eBuy, our hosted e-procurement solution.
Gross turnover through Q3, 1999	US$2.7mn
Latest revenue summary for 2000	None: due to our quiet period, resulting from 26 January 2000 S-1 filing.
Rankings/Awards	Commerx PlasticsNet has been named a Computerworld Smithsonian Award Laureate, ranked a 'Top 5 marketplace' by AMR Research, and named to *Forbes'* 200 best website listing. Commerx Co-founder, Tim Stojka, was named to the *BtoB's* list of 'Top 25 E-Champions' and CTO Chris Borneman was named a 'premier 100 IT leader' by *Computerworld* magazine. In 1999, Commerx PlasticsNet was ranked a 'Top 5 B2B' website by *BtoB* (then *Advertising Age's Business Marketing*). Also, Commerx ranked in the 'Top 50' of *Information Week* magazine's first 'eBusiness 100' listing and received an Award of Excellence from the Society of Plastics Industry (SPI).

Profile *iv*:
ec-Content, Inc.

Contact information	Name: E-mail address: Phone number: Mailing address:	Trey Simonton, EVP, Business Development trey.simonton@ec-content.com (800) 978 6641 10996 Torreyana Road San Diego, CA 92121
Name	ec-Content	
URL	http://www.ec-content.com	
Target markets	Horizontal and vertical B2B exchanges, e-procurement, and suppliers across all industries.	
Summary of business goals; achievements to date	*When buyers Find, and when attributes and images Educate, users will Buy. That's Q-Centric.* Only ec-Content can bring over 80 years of content management experience to your on-line exchange. ec-Content is able to provide the most experienced content management specialists in the world — ready to bring liquidity to your B2B Net marketplaces and e-procurement exchanges. ec-Content provides over 5 million items from office and computer products, construction, and automotive parts and supplies for speed to market. In addition, ec-Content is	

able to deliver the scope of time-tested procedures, tools, and relationships surrounding catalog and content management that will translate to a better buying experience for your buyers' success. ec-Content — transforming Net marketplaces with quality catalog content solutions.

Date founded	July 1999
Founders	Trade Service Corporation
Location	San Diego, California
No. of employees	ec-Content has 39 employees in sales, operations, programming, and management. An additional 45 are dedicated to building technology enhancements.
Management team	Anthony Dubreville, *Chief Executive Officer* Tod Moore, *President* Trey Simonton, *Executive Vice President, Business Development* David York, *Executive Vice President, Operations* Brian Cassidy, *Vice President, Finance* Leslie D'Amato, *Vice President, Sales* Bob Brooks, *Vice President, Marketing*
Board of directors	Not disclosed
Major investors	ec-Content, Inc. is currently owned (11/99) and funded by Boston Ventures.
Strategic partners	Ariba RightWorks Poet Software Frictionless Commerce
Major clients/members	Alta Vista Buildpoint Buzzsaw Cephren Comdais Market Mile (American Express B2B Commerce Network) OpsExchange Planet HVAC Trade Power SourceTrack

Summary of recent announcements	1 May 2000 — E-markets tool up for e-business; *eWeek/PCWeek*.
11 May 2000 — Trading exchanges get catalog help; *InternetWeek*. Announces alliance with Ariba; *CNNfn*.
22 May 2000 — e-Market solutions abound; *eWeek*.
26 May 2000 — E-Procurement and B2B marketplaces; *PC Magazine*.
Latest revenue summary for 2000	Under US$10mn

Profile *v*:
Farms.com, Ltd.

Contact information	Name: E-mail address: Phone number: Mailing address:	Joseph G. Dales joe.dales@farms.com (877) 438 5729 855 Ridge Lake, Suite 600, Memphis, TN 38120
Name	Farms.com, Ltd.	
URL	http://www.farms.com	
Target markets	Farms.com focuses primarily on the US$180bn US agriculture market. The company has particular expertise in several key verticals, beef, swine, grains, and feed. Products and services are targeted to all players along the supply chain, which include input suppliers, producers, processors, distributors, and consumers.	
Summary of business goals; achievements to date	The Farms.com e-commerce hub services members of the agriculture industry with site components: the 'Marketplace'; 'Farm Store'; 'Ag Portal Website'; and 'Farm Manager'.	

- The Marketplace features exchanges and auctions for cattle, swine, and feed stuffs. A distinguishing feature of the Farms.com Marketplace is the use of proprietary bid/ask software (patent pending) to create instantaneous markets. Buyers and sellers pick their price in a real-time market, where bids and offers to sell are made and accepted at any time. The company operates on-line markets in feed commodities, cash grain, eggs and poultry products, ag-chemicals, alfalfa hay, animal health products, breeding cattle and genetics, feeder cattle, feeder pigs, and real estate. Farms.com addresses major inefficiencies and risks inherent in the supply chain of the agriculture industry. The e-commerce hub connects all players and results in a critical flow of information that provides a mechanism for price transparency, price discovery and liquidity, and maintaining the integrity of specialized product.

- The Farm Store sells inputs for crop protection and animal health, and features an ag-career site with classified ads and links to preferred suppliers.

- The Farm Manager provides farmers fee-based risk management and decision support services.

- The Ag Portal Website is a leading agriculture portal with a search engine. It is an on-line community where farmers can get weather reports, commodity prices, and agriculture-related news or share advice in chat forums.

Founders

Farms.com was founded in January 1995 by successful cattle farmer Ben Zaitz, and was one of the first e-commerce plays within agriculture. Mr. Zaitz has extensive experience in crop production, dairy farming, and the cattle business. Prior to establishing Farms.com, he operated a dairy cattle brokerage. Farms.com merged with eHarvest.com in April 2000. eHarvest was founded in 1996 as a B2B Internet company and features a portal with services, marketplaces, and links for players along the agriculture supply chain. The eHarvest founders combined their strong agriculture background to develop an e-marketplace for the hog vertical.

Locations

Company headquarters are located in Memphis, TN, with regional offices in Ames, IA, USA and London, Ontario, Canada.

No. of employees

60+

Management team

Robert Sparks, *Chief Executive Officer* (previously with Sparks Companies Inc.)

	Dennis Reeve, *Chief Financial Officer* (significant public (IPO) experience) Jay Gibbs, *Chief Technical Officer* (previously with Fedex E-commerce); Joe Dales, *Vice President, Marketing* (founder of eHarvest.com, 15 years in agri-marketing) Keith Canfield, *Senior Vice President, Business Development* (FIBX.com)
Board of directors	Robert Sparks, *Chief Executive Officer* of Farms.com Ben Zaitz, *founder* of Farms.com Joe Dales, *founder* of eHarvest.com Tom Thornton, divine interVentures Ejnar Knudsen, vTraction Shelby Massey, agriculture industry businessman
Major investors	Farms.com has key financial investors that are also ag-industry players. These investors possess valuable agriculture and Internet industry expertise, contacts, and credibility that Farms.com is leveraging into strategic partnerships, alliances, customer relations, and brand awareness. Key investors include vTraction.com and divine interVentures. • *vTraction.com* (www.vtraction.com) is the world's first e-co-operative. It is an independent operating company of Rabobank, which is intended to facilitate the development of B2B food and agriculture vertical exchanges. Based in the Netherlands, Rabobank has over 100 offices in 32 countries and total assets of US$290bn. This relationship promotes Farms.com to co-operative members worldwide, thereby driving liquidity. • *divineinterVentures* (www.divineinterventures.com) is a venture capital firm and an incubator for start-up B2B Internet companies.
Cash and commitments	Seed investors US$2mn vTraction US$10mn divineinterVentures US$32.2mn Total US$44.2mn

Strategic partners	Farms.com has strategic alliances that include media, e-commerce enablers, consultancies, and financial services. Alliances create cross-marketing opportunities and allow Farms.com to offer a broader range of services. *Agribiz.net* (www.agribiz.net) is a key ally and leading e-commerce enabler in the agri-food industry. Agribiz incubated eHarvest.com.
Major clients/members	Farmers and agri-businesses.
Summary of recent announcements	15 March 2000 — appointed Robert D. Sparks, formerly Vice Chairman of Sparks Companies, Inc., as *Chief Executive Officer*, and Jay Gibbs, a FedEx veteran, appointed as *Chief Technology Officer*. Gibbs most recently served as *Vice President* and *Chief Technology Officer* for Sparks, the e-commerce initiative of Sparks Companies, Inc. 7 March 2000 — Farms.com announces merger with eHarvest.com. to create the premier agriculture on-line exchange. For a collection of press releases, print articles, and videos, please visit our website: www.farms.com/inthenews.cfm
Gross turnover for 1999	US$15mn, US gross revenue
Latest revenue summary for 2000	US$45mn, US gross revenue
Traffic levels	Current: 8,000 unique users per day; 1,200,000 page views per month. Rate of growth: 20% per month.
Members	Current: 40,000. Rate of growth: 12% per month.

Profile *vi*: HoustonStreet Exchange

Contact information	Name:	Kim Salem
	E-mail address:	ksalem@houstonstreet.com
	Phone number:	(603) 766 8703
	Mailing address:	2 International Drive, Suite 370 Portsmouth, NH 03801

Name HoustonStreet Exchange

URL http://www.houstonstreet.com

Target markets Energy (electricity, crude, refined products, and natural gas)

Summary of business goals; achievements to date

- HoustonStreet aims to be a model for how energy companies do business. In order to achieve this, HoustonStreet needs to position itself as a global brand for on-line energy trading.

- To build the company and launch the website in Internet time, HoustonStreet established the *web for the Web* business model as a rapid-development network of strategic partnerships with companies that have expertise in specific fields, rather than building its own departments in-house. Drawing on its partners' core competencies, HoustonStreet is able to execute quickly and effectively in a rapidly changing environment. HoustonStreet has also forged strategic liquidity partnerships with key energy companies that offer domain knowledge and a commitment to drive activity on the site.

- The company has launched four separate trading platforms for different products in less than a year, with a fifth planned for Fall 2000.

- HoustonStreet will use XML (extensible markup language) to link trading information with a company's mid- and back-office systems to streamline business processes and allow trading organizations to operate efficiently in a paperless environment.

Date founded	27 April 1999
Founder	Frank Getman
Location	Portsmouth, NH
No. of employees	50
Management team	Frank Getman, *President* and *Chief Executive Officer* Tom Zikas, *Vice President* and *General Manager* Kevin Sluder, *Vice President of Power and Gas* Howard Smith, *Chief Financial Officer* Betsey Tuohey, *Chief People Office* Brad Guth, *Vice President of Energy Services* Brian King, *Vice President, Crude Oil and Refined Products*
Board of directors	Frank Getman, *President* and *Chief Executive Officer* Larry Robbins, Omega Advisors, Inc. Michael Latina, Elliott Associates, L.P. Ronald Andrews, Equiva Trading Co. William Kriegel, kRoad Ventures
Major investors	Equiva Trading Company, the US trading arm for Shell, Texaco, and Saudi Aramco's downstream alliances, Equilon and Motiva Conoco Inc. Williams Energy Marketing & Trading Vivendi S.A.

	Thomas H. Lee Company Sapient Corporation; Bowstreet principals from MicroArts Corporation kRoad Ventures Omega Advisors, Inc. Elliott Associates, L.P.
Strategic partners	Equiva Conoco Williams Vivendi Sithe Energies, Inc.
Major clients/members	Equiva Trading Company, the US trading arm for Shell, Texaco, and Saudi Aramco's downstream alliances, Equilon, and Motiva Conoco Inc. Williams Energy Marketing & Trading Vivendi S.A. Thomas H. Lee Company Sapient Corporation Bowstreet principals from MicroArts Corporation kRoad Ventures Omega Advisors, Inc. Elliott Associates, L.P.
Summary of recent announcements	2 August 2000 — HoustonStreet Exchange selects Optimark to enhance how energy trades on-line. HoustonStreet Exchange plans to incorporate OptiMark's patented matching engine technology into its gas, power, crude oil, and refined products exchanges. 1 August 2000 — HoustonStreet Exchange joins OASIS to drive XML standards for wholesale energy trading industry. Internationally-recognized structured information standards consortium to provide open standards development expertise. 12 July 2000 — HoustonStreet Exchange and EnronOnline link to provide greater liquidity to on-line energy markets. EnronOnline to post prices on HoustonStreet.com.

22 May 2000 — Oil industry traders buy and sell approximately US$20mn in crude oil and refined products on HoustonStreet.com's oil platform, shortly after it went live.

Latest revenue summary for 2000   HoustonStreet is a majority owned subsidiary of BayCorp Holdings and therefore has not disclosed its revenue summary.

Profile *vii*: INC2inc

Contact information	Name:	Chris Renner
	E-mail address:	chris.renner@inc2inc.com
	Phone number:	(214) 360 0061
	Mailing address:	9400 North Central Expressway Dallas, TX 75231
Name	INC2inc Technologies Corp.	
URL	http://www.INC2inc.com	
Target markets	Food and beverage manufacturing	

Summary of business goals; achievements to date

INC2inc is the premier B2B e-marketplace for the industrial food sector. We are focused on providing a total supply chain management solution between food manufacturers, and their suppliers of raw ingredients and packaging. Our services include on-line order management and transaction facilitation, reconciliation and e-payment, supply chain planning, and logistics services.

INC2inc is the only active e-marketplace transacting business for the replenishment of direct materials between existing mainline trading partners in our industry.

Date founded	March 1999
Founders	Scott Sexton and Chris Renner
Location	Headquarters: Dallas, TX
No. of employees	Over 40
Management team	Scott Sexton, *President* Chris Renner, *Chief Operating Officer* Jon Cunningham, *Chief Financial Officer* Greg Bott, *Chief Technical Officer* Jeff Makohon, *Vice President Solutions* Hill Pratt, *Vice President Business Development* Trey Hill, *Executive Director of Marketing*
Board of directors	Bo Sexton, *Chairman* Kevin Yancy, *Spyglass Equities* John Pearson, *Spyglass Equities*
Major investors	Spyglass Equities (lead VC)
Strategic partners	Ariba CSC Exodus Communications webMethods EMC^2
Major clients	HE Butt Grocery (manufacturing division) Meyers Bakeries Massey Fair/Mac Source Waucheka Cherry Burrell de Mexico
Recent announcements	INC2inc moves beyond transaction facilitation, delivering greater supply chain visibility, aggressively making the promise of collaborative commerce a reality.
Gross turnover	INC2inc has facilitated several hundred transactions, representing over US$10mn in gross volume in the first three months of live, revenue-generating transactions — May–July 2000.

Profile *viii*: Instill Corporation

Contact information	E-mail address: info@instill.com Phone number: (888) 467 8455 Mailing address: 330 Twin Dolphin Drive, Redwood City, CA 94065
Name	Instill Corporation
URL	http://www.instill.com
Target markets	Foodservice
Summary of business goals; achievements to date	Instill's business goals: Instill aims to be the leading provider of e-business services for the foodservice industry. With deep domain expertise, Instill focuses on serving the entire foodservice supply chain — from independent restaurants, small to large multi-unit operators, distributors, and manufacturers — to enhance business performance. Recent achievements: • Launch of Foodscape.com for small chains and independents on 20 May 2000.

- Partnership with National Restaurant Association and Educational Foundation to supply education and training to the foodservice industry.

- Procter & Gamble to sponsor and provide content to Foodscape.com.

- Signed strategic deals with Applebee's and Sodexho Marriott Services to use Instill Network of services.

The Instill Foodservice Network provides services to all segments of the foodservice supply chain, including operators, distributors, and manufacturers. Services within the Network include: Instill Purchase Web, an e-procurement service for enhanced control and management of foodservice purchasing; and Instill Purchase Insight, a consolidated purchase information service for monitoring contract compliance and capturing rebates. Instill Market Intelligence is an Internet-enabled service for manufacturers, providing market data across industry categories and segments. Foodscape.com, a foodservice portal specifically designed for independent restaurants and small chains, offers relevant content, analytical tools, e-commerce, and third-party services.

Date founded	1993
Founders	Mack Tilling and Ted Daley
Locations	Headquarters: Redwood City, CA. Sales offices in Atlanta, Chicago, New York, Philadelphia, southern California and Washington, DC.
No. of employees	190
Management team	Mack Tilling, *Co-founder* and *Chief Executive Officer* Anthony Wilson, *President* and *Chief Operating Officer* Ted Daley, *Vice President* and *Co-founder* John Gilmer, *Vice President, Client Services* Andy Cohen, *Vice President, Sales and Marketing* Eric Ludwig, *Vice President, Finance & Administration* Dejan Nenov, *Vice President, Engineering* Kurt Ohms, *Vice President, Operations* Dan Dorosin, *Vice President, Corporate Development* Jim Crystal, *Vice President, Sales*

Major investors	Altos Ventures
	Applebee's
	Aspen Ventures
	Charles River Ventures
	Chase Capital Partners
	Dain Rauscher Wessels
	Deutsche Bank Alex Brown
	Intel Corporation
	Mayfield Fund
	Octaine Capital
	Ohio Partners
	Piper Jaffray Ventures
	Procter & Gamble
Major clients/members	Operators:
	Applebee's Neighborhood Grill and Bar
	Brinker International;
	Delaware North
	Fine Host
	Lettuce Entertain You
	Marie Callender's
	Sodexho Marriott Services
Strategic alliances	The National Restaurant Association
	Procter & Gamble
	Technomic
	Biztro
	Hewlett-Packard Company
	Lettuce Entertain You Enterprises
	Icon LLC
	Nation's Restaurant News
	Visa USA
Summary of recent announcements	• Instill receives US$25.6mn in first closing of mezzanine round financing.
	• Instill announces key appointments. Jim Crystal, *Regional Vice President of Sales*, has been promoted to *National Vice President of Sales*. John Zimmerman, former publisher of *Food Management* magazine, has joined as *Director of Sales* for Instill Manufacturer Services, and Lloyd D. Ligier has been appointed to the position of *Vice President of Market Development*.

- Instill appoints Anthony Wilson as *President* and *Chief Operating Officer*.

- Foodscape by Instill. Foodscape by Instill is the company's newest offering, launched on 20 May 2000 at the National Restaurant Association Show. Found at www.foodscape.com, this vertical portal is specifically designed for independent restaurants and small chains, offering relevant content, analytical tools, e-commerce, and third-party services to which, historically, only large chains have had access. Strategic alliances in the venture include leaders in technology, credit services, and content, including Biztro, Hewlett-Packard Company, Lettuce Entertain You Enterprises, Icon LLC, National Restaurant Association, Nation's Restaurant News, Procter & Gamble, and Visa USA.

- The company also recently signed agreements with two of the largest foodservice operators in the US. Applebee's International Inc., the largest casual dining concept in the world, and Sodexho Marriott Services, Inc., the largest provider of outsourced food and facilities management in North America. Both companies will begin using services from the Instill Foodservice Network.

Profile *ix*:
Logistics.com, Inc.

Contact information	Name: E-mail address: Phone number: Mailing address:	George Abernathy, Vice President, Sales George_A_Abernathy@Logistics.com (781) 229 1565, ext. 205 23 Third Avenue, Burlington, MA 01803
Name	Logistics.com, Inc.	
URL	http://www.logistics.com	
Target markets	Logistics.com provides all modes of transportation procurement and management serving all industries.	
Summary of business goals; achievements to date	Logistics.com, Inc. is the only comprehensive transportation solution provider that facilitates, streamlines, and optimizes interactions between worldwide shippers, forwarders, and carriers, having transacted over US$6bn in transportation procurement services. Logistics.com's software products have enabled many of the world's largest and most respected shippers, carriers, and third parties to increase efficiencies, dramatically cut transportation expenditures, and boost profits. Building on its tradition of industry leadership, Logistics.com recently introduced the Digital Transportation Marketplace™, an independent on-line communications and trading	

environment for shippers and carriers to come together via the Internet to drive inefficiencies out of transportation planning.

Date founded	January 2000
Founder	Dr. Yossi Sheffi, Chief Executive Officer and Director of MIT's Center for Transportation Studies
Location	Burlington, Massachusetts
No. of employees	140
Management team	Dr. Yossi Sheffi, *Chief Executive Officer* Gregg Borgeson, *President* John Lanigan, *Chief Operating Officer* Carl Drisko, *Managing Director Technology and Product Strategy* Ed Simmons, *Chief Technology Officer* Bill Burke, *Chief Financial Officer* Kel Kelly, *Chief Marketing Officer*
Board of directors	N/A (privately-held company)
Major investors	Internet Capital Group (NasDAQ: ICGE), an Internet company actively engaged in business-to-business e-commerce.
Strategic partners	ICG Commerce J.D. Edwards CT Logistics Transportal Network
Major clients/members	Procter & Gamble Kraft Colgate Palmolive Ford Wal-Mart J.B. Hunt Transport Yellow Corporation MS Carriers Werner Enterprises

Summary of recent announcements

June 2000 — Strategic merger with QuoteShip.com, creating the first comprehensive transportation solutions company. The combined entity joined forces to provide on-line procurement, control systems, and optimization solutions for shippers and carriers worldwide across all modes of transportation.

May 2000 — Logistics.com launched the Digital Transportation Marketplace™, a new on-line communications and trading environment enabling real-time exchange between buyers and sellers of transportation services.

Business 2 Business

Aerospace • Agriculture • Auto • Chemicals • Electronics • Construction
Energy • Financial • Food & Beverage • Travel • Industrial Equipment
Transportation • Media • Printing • Real Estate • Food Service • Retail

Profile *x*: Neoforma.com, Inc.

Contact information	Name: E-mail address: Phone number: Mailing address:	Amanda Mogin amanda.mogin@neoforma.com (408) 468 4251 3061 Zanker Road, San Jose, CA 95134
Name		Neoforma.com, Inc.
URL		http://www.neoforma.com
Target markets		Medical supplies and equipment, new and used.
Summary of business goals; achievements to date		Goals: To retool healthcare commerce, increasing the efficiency of the healthcare supply chain and reducing administrative costs. Achievements and Awards: June 2000: *Forbes.com*, Best of the Web B2B

	April 2000: AMR Research rank #6 overall, #1 in healthcare, out of 600 B2B exchanges
	January 2000: IPO, raised approximately US$95mn
Date founded	March 1996
Founders	Jeffrey H. Kleck, Ph.D. and Wayne D. McVicker
Locations	Headquarters: 3061 Zanker Road, San Jose, CA 95134 Neoforma GAR: 3190 Kennicott Avenue, Arlington Heights, IL 60004 EquipMD: Northridge Pavilion IV, 1303 Hightower Trail, Suite 305, Atlanta, GA 30350 US Lifeline, Inc.: 25 West High Street, Carlisle, PA 17004
No. of employees	289 (as of 25 May 2000)
Management team	Robert J. Zollars, *Chairman, President* and *Chief Executive Officer* Frederick J. Ruegsegger, *Chief Financial Officer* Charles D. Brennan, *Senior Vice President, Services Delivery* Allen M. Capsuto, *Senior Vice President, Physician Business* Daniel A. Eckert, *Senior Vice President, Hospital/IDN Business* Steven E. Kane, *Senior Vice President, Human Resources and Legal* Steven J. Wigginton, *Senior Vice President, Product Development*
Board of directors	Andrew J. Filipowski, *Chairman, President* and *Chief Executive Officer*, divineinterVentures, Inc. Terence Garnett, *Managing Director*, Garnett Capital Richard D. Helppie, *Chairman* and *Chief Executive Officer*, Superior Consultant Holdings Corporation Curt Nonomaque, *Executive Vice President* and *Chief Financial Officer*, VHA Mark McKenna, *President*, Novation Madhavan Rangaswami, *Managing Director*, Sand Hill Group, LLC Robert J. Zollars, *Chairman, President* and *Chief Executive Officer* Neoforma, Inc.
Major investors	*Venture Investors:* Amerindo Investment Advisors Bowman Capital Management

Dell Computer
Delphi Ventures
divineinterVentures
Fisher Scientific
GE Equity
Owens & Minor
PSS World Medical
SAP America, Inc.
Superior Consultant
Venrock Associates
VerticalNet, Inc.

Institutional Investors:

Barclays Global Investors
Berger, LLC
Bowman Capital Management
Capital Guardian Trust Company
GE Asset Management Inc.
Mellon Bank (Private Asset Management)
Merlin BioMed Group, LLC
Northern Trust Quantititative Advisers
Portola Group, Inc.
Vanguard Group, Inc.

Strategic partners	Ariba Cisco Systems Crossworlds Dell Computer GE Medical Systems Owens & Minor Philips Medical Systems STC Superior Consultant TIBCO VerticalNet
Major clients/members	Novation, LLC HealthWorks, Inc., a for-profit affiliate of Continuum Health Partners Inc. GeriMedix

Summary of recent announcements

- Joined four group purchasing organizations and two other e-commerce companies to adopt and promote industry standards for e-commerce in healthcare.

- Created 'E-Standards Work Group'.

- Streamlined operations to focus on two key global markets — integrated delivery networks (IDNs)/hospitals and physician practices.

- Changes in executive management and the company's organizational structure.

- Reaffirmed exclusive 10-year agreement to provide e-commerce procurement services for Novation LLC, the world's largest buyer of medical supplies and the supply company of VHA Inc. and University HealthSystems Consortium (UHC).

- Modified the structure and terms of stock and warrant transactions with VHA Inc. and University HealthSystem Consortium (UHC), the national healthcare alliances that own Novation.

- Entered into strategic commercial relationship with Eclipsys Corporation and HEALTHvision, Inc.

- Completed acquisition of EquipMD, a B2B procurement company for physicians offices.

- Entered into e-commerce agreement with MEDecision Inc., a medical management software company.

- Entered into agreement with GeriMedix, a supplier of medical supplies, equipment, and services to long-term care and assisted living facilities, to move substantially all of GeriMedix's annual purchasing through Neoforma.com.

Gross turnover for 1999	US$3,627,000
Latest revenue summary for 2000	First quarter ended 31 March 2000:

- Gross value of transactions: US$4.6mn — approximately 64% increase from US$2.8mn in fourth quarter 1999.

- Net revenues: US$1.2mn — approximately 122% increase from US$540,000 in fourth quarter 1999.

- Net loss for quarter, on *pro forma* basis: US$32mn, or US$0.61 per share.

- Net loss for quarter, excluding certain non-cash charges for amortization of deferred compensation, depreciation of equipment, amortization of goodwill, and in-process research and development, on *pro forma* basis: US$17.5mn, or US$0.34 per share.

- Sale of 8,050,000 shares of common stock in initial public offering netted proceeds of approximately US$95mn.

Business 2 Business

Aerospace • Agriculture • Auto • Chemicals • Electronics • Construction
Energy • Financial • Food & Beverage • Travel • Industrial Equipment
Transportation • Media • Printing • Real Estate • Food Service • Retail

Profile *xi*: SciQuest.com, Inc.

Contact information

Name: Jenny Kobin
E-mail address: jkobin@sciquest.com
Phone number: (919) 659 2100
Mailing address: PO Box 12156
Research Triangle Park, NC 27709

Company information

Founded in 1995, SciQuest.com is an independent, open marketplace and trusted solution for buyers and suppliers of scientific products, software, services, and information. The company is dedicated to being an indispensable resource for scientific buyers and suppliers, by increasing their productivity and reducing their supply chain costs. SciQuest.com's leadership team has deep experience in science, technology, and supply chain management, enabling SciQuest.com to focus on unique challenges facing science-intensive organizations.

SciQuest.com acquired EMAX Solution Partners to create the first integrated e-business solution which can be customized and seamlessly integrated with its customers' enterprise systems, internal inventory systems, and chemical libraries. SciQuest.com maintains additional technology partnerships with IBM, Ariba, Commerce One, Intelisys, and Oracle, among others.

Among the more than 75 research organizations that have selected SciQuest.com's e-marketplace as their preferred, or exclusive on-line source for laboratory product procurement, are The Dow Chemical Company, DuPont Pharmaceuticals Company, Genzyme, Glaxo Wellcome, Merck & Co., and The Monsanto Company.

Manufacturers that have designated SciQuest.com as their exclusive North American e-marketplace, include Alltech Associates, Inc., Abion, Inc., Amersham Pharmacia Biotech, Inc., BioWhittaker, Inc., Endogen, Inc., NEN Life Science Products, Inc., PerkinElmer Instruments, Pierce Chemical Co., QIAGEN, Inc., and Shimadzu Scientific Instruments, Inc. SciQuest.com has commerce agreements with more than 760 other scientific product suppliers.

Name	SciQuest.com, Inc.
URL	http://www.sciquest.com
Target markets	Pharmaceutical, chemical, biotechnological, clinical, industrial, and educational markets
Summary of business goals	SciQuest.com is dedicated to being an indispensable resource for scientific buyers and suppliers, by reducing their supply chain costs and increasing their productivity. SciQuest.com's exclusive focus on the scientific industry and domain expertise of its senior management, makes it the best qualified to advance science through e-commerce, information systems, and supply chain solutions.

As an unbiased marketplace, SciQuest.com has won the endorsement of the industry's leading buyers and suppliers, including Merck, Glaxo Wellcome, Amersham Pharmacia Biotech, and PerkinElmer. SciQuest.com has also been recognized as a leader in the business-to-business industry. In April 2000, AMR Research Inc. rated SciQuest.com as one of the top five of 600 B2B independent trading exchanges.

SciQuest.com's e-marketplace is based on open, industry-standard e-commerce ERP/ESV standards, which offers seamless integration with legacy systems, customized implementations, and flexibility. SciQuest.com's proven technology unites science, information, and technology to maximize efficiencies and speed scientific research. In

March 2000, SciQuest.com acquired EMAX Solution Partners, Inc., the pioneer of e-research asset management and planning solutions, for the purpose of creating the first source-to-disposal on-line asset management solution. The integration of the EMAX solution into the SciQuest.com marketplace will provide research, IT, and purchasing functions with a unified view of their common resources, and will allow them to manage their purchasing and inventory more effectively; thereby, contributing positively to a company's bottom line.

Earlier this year, SciQuest.com established pilot programs with the Max Planck Institute and the Dow Chemical Company in Germany, which initiated the company's international expansion. To support its growth overseas, SciQuest.com has expanded its facilities to include offices in London, Paris, and Walldorf, Germany. In August 2000, SciQuest.com announced that John Arkebauer, a 38-year scientific industry veteran, and formerly SciQuest.com's Vice President of Sales for the Midwest, was named *President* of SciQuest.com International, the company's global division. Arkebauer will be tasked with executing SciQuest.com's business plan and customer acquisition strategy for Europe, while building management teams throughout the region.

In July 2000, SciQuest.com announced that Barrett Joyner, former President of SAS Institute North America, joined SciQuest.com as *Executive Vice President* of its newly-established e-services division. SciQuest.com's e-services division will be responsible for management of the company's million-item e-catalog, and for using SciQuest.com's vast store of transactional data to assist buyer and supplier partners in making better strategic business decisions.

Date founded	November 1995
Founders	Scott Andrews, Bobby Feigler, Peyton Anderson, and Keith Gunter
Locations	Headquarters: Research Triangle Park, NC Offices in Mountain View, CA; Philadelphia, PA; Plainview, NY European offices in London, Paris, and Walldorf, Germany
No. of employees	380

Management team	M. Scott Andrews, *Chief Executive Officer* and *Co-founder*
	W. Andrew (Andy) McKenna, *President*
	Peyton Anderson, *Vice President of Business Development*
	Lyle Brecht, *Chief Business Development Officer*
	Bobby Feigler, *Vice President of Strategic Accounts*
	Antony Francis, *Vice President of Operations*
	Rob Fusillo, *Chief Information Officer*
	Keith Gunter, *Sales Director*
	Sanjay Gupta, *Chief Marketing Officer*
	Cecil Kost, *Executive Vice President*
	Jim Scheuer, *Chief Financial Officer*
	Cliff Waits, *Vice President of National Accounts*
Board of directors	M. Scott Andrews, *Chief Executive Officer*, SciQuest.com, Inc.
	W. Andrew (Andy) McKenna, *President,* SciQuest.com, Inc.
	Bruce J. Boehm, *Special Partner*, Eno River Capital
	Noel J. Fenton, *Managing General Partner,* Trinity Ventures
	Gautam A. Prakash, *Partner*, Bessemer Venture Partners
	Lloyd Segal, *President* and *Chief Executive Officer*, Caprion Pharmaceuticals
	Timothy T. Weglicki, *Founding Partner*, ABS Capital Partners
Major investors	SciQuest.com is a publicly-held company backed by US$49.8 mn from 'angel' investors and venture capital from:
	ABS Capital Partners
	Bessemer Venture Partners
	Comdisco Ventures
	GE Equity
	Harris & Harris Group, Inc.
	Kingdon Capital
	Noro-Moseley Partners
	North Carolina Technological Development Authority
	Oxford Bioscience Partners
	Partech International Equity
	Trinity Ventures
	Vector Fund Management
	Wakefield Group.
Strategic partners	SciQuest.com has partnerships with select scientific and technology companies to execute its distinctive business model and range of solutions. Partners include:

Alltech Associates, Inc.
Ambion, Inc.
Amersham Pharmacia Biotech, Inc.
Ariba, Inc.
BioWittaker, a Cambrex Company
Endogen, Inc.
IBM, Inc.
NEN Life Science Products Inc.
PerkinElmer, Inc.
Pierce Chemical Company and QIAGEN N.V.
Shimadzu Scientific Instruments, Inc.
Yantra Corp

Strategic buyers include Dow Chemical Company, DuPont Pharmaceuticals Company, Merck & Co., and Monsanto Company.

Major clients/members   See above

Summary of recent announcements

May 2000 — EMAX Solutions launches EMAX Reagent Manager 4.0, featuring e-Commerce Channel Integration with Sigma-Aldrich.

April 2000 — AMR Research ranks SciQuest.com in the top five of 600 independent trading exchanges.

April 2000 — Strategic e-commerce agreement with Glaxo Wellcome Inc.

March 2000 — Acquisition of EMAX Solution Partners, Inc.

March 2000 — SciQuest.com becomes exclusive e-marketplace for Shimadzu Scientific Instrument.

March 2000 — Acquisition of Intralogixä, creator of first comprehensive chromatography product selection tool.

March 2000 — Intelisys and SciQuest.com team up to offer superior selection and convenience to scientific equipment buyers worldwide.

February 2000 — Monsanto Company added to list of e-commerce agreements.

January 2000 — SciQuest.com and DuPont Pharmaceuticals Company enter into strategic e-commerce agreement.

January 2000 — SciQuest.com and Merck join forces in e-commerce agreement.

January 2000 — SciQuest.com joins the Oracleâ supplier network.

December 1999 — SciQuest.com and Dow Chemical sign exclusive e-commerce agreement for purchase of laboratory products and supplies.

Gross turnover for 1999	US$3,882,441
Latest revenue summary for 2000	First quarter 2000: US$5.1mn

Contacts

Sponsor

Leigh Nixon
Director of Public Relations
RightWorks Corporation

1075 E. Brokaw Road
San Jose, CA 95131

Tel: 408 579 4060
Fax: 408 579 4010
E-mail: lnixon@rightworks.com

Authors

Key Considerations When Setting up B2B Exchanges

W. William A. Woods
CEO, Bermuda Stock Exchange

E-mail: william@b2bexchanges.com

Arthur B. Sculley
Sculley Brothers LLC

E-mail: arthur@b2bexchanges.com

Building a Winning Digital Marketplace with ICG's Gameover Scorecard

Todd Hewlin
Managing Director
Internet Capital Group
1 Market Plaza
Spear Tower, Suite 307
San Francisco, CA 94105

Tel: 415 343 3742
Fax: 415 343 3749
E-mail: thewlin@internetcapital.com

Building Brand and Community

W. William A. Woods
CEO, Bermuda Stock Exchange

E-mail: william@b2bexchanges.com

Arthur B. Sculley
Sculley Brothers LLC

E-mail: arthur@b2bexchanges.com

Supply Chain Management

Chris Renner
Founder & Executive Vice President,
INC2inc Technologies
9400 N. Central Expressway, Suite 1300
Dallas TX 75321

Tel: 214 360 0061
Fax: 214 360 0169
E-mail: Chris.Renner@inc2inc.com

Jeff Schutt,
Partner
CSC Consulting
8320 Talbot Lane
Austin, Texas 78746-4915

Tel: 440 684 3730
Fax: 512 306 8129
E-mail: jschutt@csc.com

Logistics

Christopher C. Cusick
Manager-Surface Support
23 Third Avenue
Burlington, MA 01803

Tel: 781 229 1565 ext 191
Fax: 781 229 0123
E-mail: ccusick@logistics.com

Mark W. Pluta
Alliance Manager
Logistics.com/Quoteship.com

Tel: 617 654 6263
Fax: 617 350 6320
E-mail: mpluta@quoteship.com

Business-to-Business Market Models

Blair LaCorte,
Senior VP of Strategy & E-Commerce
VerticalNet
44 Montgomery St, Suite 1420
San Francisco, CA 94104

Tel: 415 228 3630
Fax: 415 228 3640

Catalog Content Management

Trey Simonton
EVP, Business Development
ec-Content
10996 Torreyana Road
San Diego, CA 92121

Tel: 800 978 6641
Fax: 858 455 9360
E-mail: trey.simonton@ec-content.com

Selecting the Right Trading Platform

Ramesh Patil, Ph.D
Chief Technology Officer
RightWorks Corporation
1075 E. Brokaw Road
San Jose, CA 95131

Tel: 408 579 4000
Fax: 408 579 4010
Email: Ramesh.Patil@rightworks.com

Taking a Successful Exchange Public

Christopher E. Vroom, CFA
Managing Director, E-Commerce Equity Research
CSFB
201 Spear Street, 18th Floor
San Francisco, CA 94105

Tel: 415 836 6351
Fax: 415 836 7790
E-mail: chris.vroom@csfb.com

Entrepreneurs vs. Industry Consortia

W. William A. Woods
CEO, Bermuda Stock Exchange

E-mail: william@b2bexchanges.com

Arthur B. Sculley
Sculley Brothers LLC

E-mail: arthur@b2bexchanges.com

What's Next?

Bruce Temkin
Director, B2B Research and Advisory
Forrester Research, Inc
400 Technology Square
Cambridge, MA 02139

Tel: 617 613 6044
Fax: 617 613 5044
E-mail: btemkin@forrester.com

Financial Services for B2B Exchanges

Brenda Smith
Vice President
Wells Fargo Bank
Wholesale Internet Solutions

Tel: 303 293 5656
E-mail: smithbrj@wellsfargo.com